MW01068579

POLICY DRIFT

Policy Drift

Shared Powers and the Making of U.S. Law and Policy

Norma M. Riccucci

NEW YORK UNIVERSITY PRESS

New York

NEW YORK UNIVERSITY PRESS
New York
www.nyupress.org

© 2018 by New York University
All rights reserved

References to Internet websites (URLs) were accurate at the time of writing. Neither the author nor New York University Press is responsible for URLs that may have expired or changed since the manuscript was prepared.

Library of Congress Cataloging-in-Publication Data
Names: Riccucci, Norma, author.
Title: Policy drift : shared powers and the making of U.S. law and policy /
Norma M. Riccucci.
Description: New York : New York University Press, 2018. |
Includes bibliographical references and index.
Identifiers: LCCN 2017012919 | ISBN 9781479845040 (cl : alk. paper) |
ISBN 9781479839834 (pb : alk. paper)
Subjects: LCSH: Legislation—United States. | Law—Political aspects—United States.
Classification: LCC KF4945 .R53 2018 | DDC 320.60973—dc23
LC record available at https://lccn.loc.gov/2017012919

New York University Press books are printed on acid-free paper, and their binding materials are chosen for strength and durability. We strive to use environmentally responsible suppliers and materials to the greatest extent possible in publishing our books.

Manufactured in the United States of America

10 9 8 7 6 5 4 3 2 1

Also available as an ebook

Per le nonne

CONTENTS

About a month after the 9/11 attacks, a friend of mine living in New York City placed a phone call to friends in Australia to share her distress and grief about the terrorist attacks. After misdialing the number, she promptly hung up the telephone receiver. Within a matter of seconds, her phone rang and the low, deep voice on the other end asked, "Were you just trying to place a call to Afghanistan?" My friend, shaken by the intense, throaty voice and line of questioning, answered, "No, I was trying to call a friend in Australia." The line then went dead. The episode created such a fear in her that she wouldn't dial an international number for almost a year. This experience, in part, inspired me to research privacy and the Patriot Act. I began to wonder whether the government was tracking my Internet search history, and how we got to the point where this was something I would wonder.

I have long been interested in the jockeying of powers between and among the three branches of government, along with the bureaucracy, interest groups, and other stakeholders in the policy process. The strategies and methods employed by the various actors seemed provocative and in some cases enervating. I questioned, for example, how the oil and gas industries were able to flagrantly elude and violate environmental laws, and in some cases, do so in collusion with the government. How was the government allowed to repeatedly surveil the American citizenry, even with the knowledge that the activities were illegal or unconstitutional? And why were some courts willing to retreat on the progress this nation had made on civil rights?

The answers to these questions seem simple, but the complex nature of the policy process in our society precludes a simple answer. For one thing, our democratic state allows for different factions to compete with one another for power. In effect, the system is set up to produce both winners and losers and discontent in general when the policies don't work in our favor. But living in a democracy ensures that corrections and adjustments can be made to those imperfect, dissatisfying outcomes.

I have selected three significant policy areas of interest to scholars and students—surveillance and privacy rights, civil rights, and climate policy—and illustrate through a longitudinal analysis the various strategies in which policy shifts, or what Jacob Hacker calls "drifts," occur. It goes beyond the standard policy development and implementation research to study policy drift both empirically and normatively within a multilevel governance framework. Much of the research done in recent decades in public administration and policy, public management, political science, and law ignores the impact of time on public policy, especially the impact of large-scale, slow-moving, secular forces in the political, social, and economic environments.

Importantly, this book is intended for classroom use. Students of public policy, administration, and law often assume that once a law is enacted, it is implemented faithfully. In turn, those perspectives are reinforced by a media that mostly take a largely static perspective on public policy and portray efforts—such as the current effort to hinder, if not roll back, the Affordable Care Act—as unparalleled in history. In reality, such efforts are commonplace, as we have seen in the areas of Medicare and Medicaid.

I also hope that the book will frame an area of inquiry that is underdeveloped yet necessary for the attainment of a much more comprehensive understanding of public policy in all domains within the U.S. constitutional system, and provide new direction for policy studies in the United States.

It should also be noted that while this book was in press, Donald Trump was elected president of the United States. While the book seeks to add some material on his presidency, it is impossible to capture the full extent to which the Trump administration will alter the policy drifts addressed here. Nonetheless, party changes to the White House will always have consequences on policy drifts, and this speaks to the core of this book.

1

The Making of Law, Policy, and Policy Drifts

There is no finality to the public policy process. It is ongoing and continuous, and even those policies believed to be settled and stable can change or drift in unexpected directions.[1] To be sure, some policies achieve greater durability or stability, depending upon the political and legal landscapes that surround those policies. But there is no fixed formula for predicting the durability of public policy, because unanticipated levers of change such as economic, political, ideological, or social forces can modify the status quo in public policy, ultimately leading to further policy shifts or drifts. Recent history reveals this to be the case.

For example, Americans' privacy rights are guaranteed by the Fourth Amendment to the U.S. Constitution, ratified in 1791. Yet the 9/11 terrorist attacks set off what many believe to be the worst case of government-sponsored espionage since the McCarthy era.[2] Policy changes instituted by the National Security Agency under the George W. Bush administration led to a widespread warrantless surveillance program—in other words, warrantless wiretapping. This drift in public policy set off a massive number of lawsuits challenging the constitutionality of the wiretapping of the American people. Whistleblowers from Edward Snowden to Private Bradley (now Chelsea) Manning have been condemned as traitors by some, and glorified as heroes by others for leaking classified information. In May 2015 the first NSA warrantless program Snowden disclosed was ruled illegal by a federal appeals court, representing one of the first declassifications and breakdowns of the Patriot Act. However, although Congress subsequently amended surveillance policy in response to that ruling, there are renewed concerns about the government's surveillance policies and its continued efforts to spy on Americans.

Another example can be seen in the 2007 U.S. Supreme Court's decision in *Ledbetter v. Goodyear Tire and Rubber Company*, which effectively altered public policy by making it more difficult for public- and private-sector employees to file pay discrimination complaints against their employers. The Court ruled that plaintiffs charging pay discrimination under Title VII of the Civil Rights Act of 1964 must file their lawsuit within 180 days of the actual occurrence of the discriminatory practice, notwithstanding the fact that those practices cannot always be established or uncovered within that time period. The decision was a decisive blow to efforts aimed at pay equity between women and men. In response to this ruling, President Obama and the 111th Congress joined forces to pass the Lilly Ledbetter Fair Pay Act, which resets the 180 days to *after* each discriminatory act occurs and allows for recovery of back pay up to two years prior to the complaint. This act, however, can be repealed or altered at any time.

A final example can be seen in President Obama's battle against an intransigent Congress on climate policy. Republicans in particular question or deny the science surrounding global warming, and have vociferously opposed policies to curb greenhouse gas emissions. In June 2014 President Obama instructed the EPA to issue his proposed Clean Power Plan, which would cut carbon dioxide emissions and other toxic pollutants produced by power plants across the country. State governments and industry groups vowed to fight the EPA on this administrative fiat. A number of consolidated lawsuits that were filed against the EPA reached the U.S. Supreme Court in February 2016; the lawsuits charged in part that states would be severely impacted economically by the EPA's rule, causing major job losses and energy-price increases. The High Court backed industry and the states in the case, *West Virginia v. Environmental Protection Agency* (2016), temporarily blocking implementation of the Clean Power Plan, also known as the global warming rule.[3] It was a setback to the Obama administration's climate action policies and was viewed as an effort to micromanage the rulemaking authority of the EPA. With the election of Donald Trump to the U.S. presidency, climate control policy is certain to drift in directions other than those supported by the Obama administration. Hence the durability or stability of climate policy remains in question. This speaks to the essence of this book.

These three cases indicate how the three branches of government at the federal level as well as other stakeholders compete for power in an effort to alter or "fix" existing laws and policies. Changes in political, economic, and social contexts over time force modifications in policies or the interpretation of laws without fundamentally changing the existing structures of law or policy, although interpretations under the law may change. This has been referred to as "policy drift" by Jacob Hacker.[4] Policy drifts are, in effect, dependent upon changes to the social, economic, and political milieux. This conceptual framework, as Hacker points out, "illuminates and clarifies the sometimes-covert strategies that political actors adopt when trying to transform embedded policy commitments."[5] This framework, discussed more fully later in this chapter, clearly illustrates the fragmented and fluctuating nature of public policy making: law or policy can remain in a perpetual state of flux.[6] Thus, the manner in which policies or programs operate will change in significant ways over time, which may even produce adverse effects for the initial intended beneficiaries of a law or policy as originally enacted or adopted. Such was the case with the U.S. Supreme Court's *Ledbetter* decision discussed earlier. The durability of policy shifts then remains questionable.

The primary purpose of my book is to examine shared powers in the making of public policy through the framework of policy drifts. Policy drift has been underutilized as a framework for studying changes or shifts in public policy, yet it can be instrumental for sifting through the various factors that can predict or lead to the drifts. I look ultimately at the durability of the drifts based on a host of factors, including shifts in the structure or composition of stakeholders (e.g., Congress). The book offers contemporary cases to illustrate that shared powers explicate and elucidate policy drifts over time. The three areas were selected because of their ongoing complexity, relevance, and significance to the American people. The central thesis of this book is that formal levers of change, often unanticipated (e.g., U.S. Supreme Court decisions; inaction by Congress; actions by interest groups), stimulated by exogenous social, political, ideological, or economic forces, foment permutations that ultimately shape and define contemporary public policy; some segments of the population will benefit from this process, while others will not. Thus, policy drifts carry significant consequences for social and economic change. Ultimately, and most importantly, there is no finality to public policy or the policy cycle. It is ongoing and continuous. My aim reflects that of Beryl Radin and Willis Hawley in their analysis of federal reorganization. They state that the policy process is "continuous and open-ended" and "has its own functional demands" and institutional settings "where different actors have varying degrees of both authority and legitimacy."[7] Policies that were thought to be settled and stable re-open to new, often unexpected or unpredictable directions.

As this book will show, laws and public policies, whether regulatory, distributive, or redistributive, are developed and implemented in this nation in part as a result of shared powers by the executive, legislative, and judicial branches of government.[8] Each branch of government exerts power and political will in its own unique way, but a single branch does not operate at the exclusion of the others. The U.S. Constitution delineates the formal powers of the executive, legislative, and judicial branches of government. Checks and balances work to prevent the usurpation of power by any one branch. The bureaucracy also plays a vital part in policy debates to the extent that it serves as the administrative arm of the president.[9] The role of bureaucracy in its capacity as a professional administrative complex is also an important one, since bureaucratic resistance can occlude policy shifts desired by the president or Congress.[10]

But shared powers go beyond the separation of powers. Traditionally the term "shared powers" refers to relations between the federal and state governments (i.e., federalism).[11] But a broader interpretation conceptualizes shared powers as the sharing of powers between and among the three branches of the federal government, the bureaucracy, special interest groups, consumer groups, contractors, state governments, the media, and others.[12] In this sense, shared powers derive from a composite of political theories or frameworks of policy making, which will be addressed more fully later in this chapter.[13] These theories set forth the proposition that in addition to the formal powers of government, there are other stakeholders that participate in the policy-making process to promote their particular interests as well as block the interests of others. The outcome can produce fundamental changes to the policy and its initial objectives, and have an enormous impact on the interests of the stakeholders. These frameworks of policy making further hold that to the extent that competing interests exert power, democracy is better served.

The book will show that in some cases policy drifts occur as a result of the participation of and power exerted by a narrow set of policy players or stakeholders, such as the three branches of the federal government (i.e., the institutional model discussed later). In other cases, coalitions of interested parties may have greater control over the process and policy drifts (e.g., advocacy coalition framework, discussed later). The policy drifts may depend on the policy area, the stakeholders, and the specific economic, social, ideological, or political forces in operation at a particular time.[14]

Importantly, the transformations or drifts can sometimes come in large spurts or increments, as seen with the Patriot Act of 2001, discussed in chapter 2. In addition, the book does not seek to address political efforts to replace or completely eliminate an existing law or policy, such as the welfare reform bill did in 1996. There, the entitlement program Aid to Families with Dependent Children (AFDC) was completely gutted and replaced by the Temporary Assistance for Needy Families, which sought to end welfare and move recipients into jobs.

This book illustrates the impact of political processes on law and public policy over the course of time, and how each of the branches of government and other stakeholders participate in shaping the actual contours of specific laws or policies in the areas of privacy rights, civil rights, and environmental policy. This book will also help to clarify popular misconceptions, such as the idea that policy is made in a vacuum by, for example, the president or the Congress. In effect, the book shows that policy success or failure is systemic and institutional and cannot be attributed to a single branch of government, another common fallacy. The book will also address the challenges to federalism when, for example, the president uses executive orders to circumvent Congress. For instance, when the president issues an executive order on climate change, some states will inevitably file a lawsuit, claiming that it will have an adverse impact on their economies. Obviously, an executive order or action does not carry the same weight as a statute passed by the U.S. Congress, and a newly elected president can effectively vacate an executive order issued by a predecessor. While states can challenge the constitutionality of a federal statute, executive orders incur greater wrath from the states, thereby leading to lawsuits.[15]

The book will also address the implications of shared powers for the promotion of democracy, political accountability, and states' rights.[16] The shared powers model of public policy produces gains for some and losses for others. And, as noted, political actors motivated by exogenous social and economic factors may explicitly employ strategies to derail existing policies. But this was in fact envisioned by the nation's founders—a fragmented system of government, based on checks and balances, to ensure that power would not accumulate perpetually in any single body, institution, or group of individuals.

The remainder of this chapter addresses the formal (i.e., constitutional) powers of the three branches of government. Theories of policy making, including the role of various players or stakeholders in the policy process, formal or informal, including the bureaucracy, will also be discussed.

The Separation of Powers

James Madison wrote in *Federalist Paper* No. 47, "The accumulation of all powers, legislative, executive and judiciary in the same hands, whether of one, a few, or many, and whether hereditary, self-appointed, or elective, may justly be pronounced the very definition of tyranny."[17] While the English philosopher John Locke is credited with advancing the idea of separating executive and legislative powers, it was the French philosopher Montesquieu who influenced Madison and the other founders in framing a Constitution to separate the legislative, executive, and judicial powers of government in order to prevent any single branch from acquiring and accumulating complete power, the effects of which would constitute a threat to liberty, justice, and democratic rule.[18] It would, in fact, promote the form of monarchical rule that the nascent nation sought to eschew. The constitutional system of the separation of powers would have an integral structure of checks and balances, where each branch would serve as a check on the others in order to ensure a balance of power among all three branches.

The separation of powers has been seen globally as the very foundation of liberal democracy. Its historical and political significance has endured, and it has become a symbol of constancy and accountability. The separation of powers is the sine qua non of the legislative and policy-making processes in the United States. While not the only basis for public policy making, as discussed below, the U.S. Congress, the president, and the U.S. Supreme Court participate in the policy process from various perspectives.[19] The agenda setting and formulation and development of law or policy are generally executive and legislative functions, as are the implementation, evaluation, and oversight. The U.S. Supreme Court as the ultimate adjudicator also provides oversight, but its decisions can affect the implementation and outcome of law or public policy in significant ways. As this book will show, although each branch of government theoretically possesses an equal amount of power, the final outcome of a law or policy can represent a gain to one branch at the expense of the others. For example, when the U.S. Supreme Court upheld various provisions of President Obama's Affordable Care Act in *NFIB v. Sebelius* (2012) and *King v. Burwell* (2015), members of Congress, particularly the Republicans, were dealt a severe blow, and they vowed to challenge the health care plan on other grounds.[20] Not long after *Burwell*, the U.S. House of Representatives sued the Obama administration over its spending power for health care.[21]

Importantly, as scholars James Q. Wilson, John DiIulio, and Meena Bose point out, "The powers of the three branches of government are not actually separated: rather they are *shared*. The checks and balances built into the constitutional system exist because three branches of government share all the powers of that system."[22] Their point is that the "separation of powers" is a misnomer, but we continue to use the term in practice.

Policy Models and Policy Drifts

From a policy perspective, the three branches of government share powers with other stakeholders in the public policy process. There is a plethora of literature on the general aspects of the public policy-making process as well as its surrounding politics.[23] The research highlights different models or theories of policy making, including the prevalent "stages" model of policy, which sets forth the formal stages of the policy-making process. Harold Lasswell, for example, described seven stages of the policy cycle: (1) intelligence, (2) promotion, (3) prescription, (4) invocation, (5) application, (6) termination, and (7) appraisal.[24] Others have simplified and interpreted the framework as "stages heuristic," compartmentalizing the policy process into the following stages: agenda setting, policy formulation and legitimation, implementation, and evaluation.[25] There are several other models, sometimes overlapping, that political scientists and public policy scholars have advanced in order to build or improve upon existing theories. These include, for example, institutional theory, path dependency, pluralism, advocacy coalition, and punctuated equilibrium.[26] Each has its particular strengths and weaknesses.[27]

The institutional model focuses on the role of formal governmental institutions (e.g., Congress, the president) in the policy-making process. Particular emphasis is given to the legal structure of organizations. The model holds that government has a significant role in the policy process because it possesses legitimate and universal powers. As Clarke Cochran and his colleagues point out, this "model stresses the opportunities and constraints on policy that are part of the very structure of the American constitutional order: judiciary, bureaucracy, executive, legislatures, separation of powers, federalism, and so forth."[28] Major shortcomings of this approach, as many have pointed out, revolve around theoretical and empirical inconsistencies. The behavioral revolution of the 1950s questioned the veracity of institutionalism and its overemphasis on the formal, structural aspects of power and policy making. B. Guy Peters pointed to the static nature of institutions as well as difficulties in conceptualizing and measuring institutional variables; that is, there is no agreed-upon definition of institutions.[29] Many have described how "new" institutionalism seemed to replace "old" institutionalism.[30] Still, as Michael Kraft and Scott Furlong point out, "Although institutional analysis can become quite complex, institutional theory is a simple reminder that procedural rules and certain aspects of government structure can empower or obstruct political interests."[31]

The path dependency model holds that current or future policies are dependent on previous policies, and because of institutional inertia are generally resistant to change. In effect, past policies promote policy continuity.[32] However, because decisions are based on previous choices and outcomes, the process is said to benefit from positive feedback and increasing returns.[33] Paul Pierson makes this important observation regarding path dependency:

> Specific patterns of timing and sequence matter; starting from similar conditions, a wide range of social outcomes may be possible; large conse-

quences may result from relatively "small" or contingent events; particular courses of action, once introduced, can be virtually impossible to reverse; and consequently, political development is often punctuated by critical moments or junctures that shape the basic contours of social life.[34]

A major weakness of this model is posed by the entrenched policy stakeholders as well as institutions that resist positive change.

Pluralism is another prevalent model describing the public policy process.[35] Prominent political scientist Robert Dahl argued that public policy is developed as a result of the actions and behaviors of competing interests.[36] But the idea of pluralism has long been questioned by, among others, Elmer Schattschneider and, more directly, by sociologists such as C. Wright Mills, who argued that pluralism excludes those groups or classes that do not have the resources (including knowledge and material wealth) to participate in the policy process.[37] Martin Gilens and Benjamin Page directly challenge the idea of popular pluralism, arguing that the United States is characterized by a plurality of economic elites, which operate at the expense of the average citizen or the masses.[38]

Paul Sabatier advanced the advocacy coalition framework (ACF) to supplant the dominant framework at the time, stages heuristic, which he argued "has outlived its usefulness and must be replaced."[39] The ACF builds on policy frameworks where political elites are active in the policy process, particularly as they seek to respond to changing social and economic conditions in society. But it adds the dimension of participation by various advocacy coalitions, with an emphasis on how their belief systems change over time, particularly in response to negative or positive outcomes of the policy process.[40] As Christopher Weible and Paul Sabatier point out, under ACF,

> policymaking occurs in a policy subsystem, which is a policy area that is geographically bounded and encompasses policy participants from all levels of government, multiple interest groups, research institutions and the media. Within a policy subsystem, policy participants coordinate their behavior with allies in advocacy coalitions to influence policy. The policy subsystems are set within, are affected by, and sometimes affect, a broader societal context.[41]

Some argue that this framework is deficient to the degree that bureaucrats in a policy subsystem are members of advocacy coalitions, thus creating dual loyalties. In addition, it is difficult to track advocacy coalitions and determine the various factors, both internal and external, that can impact policy subsystems.[42]

Punctuated equilibrium theory (PET) holds that public policy remains stable for long periods of time, but sporadic episodes of instability foster policy change.[43] As Frank Baumgartner and Bryan Jones point out, the tenet of this model is that "the course of public policy in the United States is not gradual and incremental, but rather is disjoint[ed] and episodic. Long periods of stability are interrupted by bursts of frenetic policy activity."[44] As Thomas Birkland points out, "The balance of political power between interest groups remains relatively stable over long periods of time, punctuated by relatively sudden shifts in public understanding of problems and in the balance of power between the groups seeking to fight entrenched interests."[45] A major shortcoming of this approach is that it is difficult to determine when or how the punctuations occur, and it sometimes fails to account for those policy areas that are more stable over time, as per the path dependency model.

Nonetheless, punctuated equilibrium is an important theory for policy making and indeed may overlap with policy drifts to the extent that exogenous as well as endogenous shocks to a policy system can lead to policy change. As Gerard Boychuk points out, the two have similarities; policy drift is essentially a "more recent" model of "evolutionary change" to public policy.[46] In addition, as Juliet Carlisle and her colleagues point out, PET connotes "spurts" in policy change.[47] Drifts, too, according to Kress, Koehier, and Springer's metaphor, discussed in the next section, can be characterized by smooth sailing being suddenly interrupted by a major jolt or shock, thus leading to policy change.

In addition to the aforementioned models, there are a number of frameworks for addressing policy shifts that are not necessarily policy-making models per se, but rather explain the progression of change. Wolfgang Streeck, Kathleen Thelen, and others address such primary mechanisms of policy change as layering and conversion.[48] Layering, for example, as Thelen points out, involves "the grafting of new elements onto an otherwise stable institutional framework."[49] Incorporating private savings accounts into a traditional pay-as-you-go pension system is one example of layering.[50] But layering, similar to incrementalism, suggests adding new dimensions to existing policy.[51]

Another mechanism, according to Thelen, is conversion, which refers to adopting new goals or bringing in new actors that alter the institutional role or the core objectives of an institution.[52] But here too, conversion falls short of explaining how policy shifts in certain directions and is narrowly framed around institutions. Hacker, on the other hand, builds on the concepts of Streeck and Thelen to designate policy changes as "policy drifts."[53]

Hacker and Policy Drifts

Guenther Kress, Gustav Koehier, and J. Fred Springer first coined the term "policy drift" in their evaluation of the California Business Enterprise Program (BEP).[54] The BEP is a federally sponsored, state-administered program that places rehabilitated blind persons as shopkeepers or vendors in food facilities such as snack bars and cafeterias that are established and supported by the program. The evaluation of the BEP, according to Kress, Koehier, and Springer, led to a policy drift. That is to say, over time, there was confusion and disagreement over the purpose of the program: was it tied to vocational rehabilitation or to integrating the disabled into mainstream society? As the authors point out,

> Typically, the day-to-day process of implementing a program proceeds through a series of focused decisions in response to rather specific, and frequently unconnected, problems. . . . However, as time goes by, the consequences of these decisions may cumulatively bring changes which fundamentally alter the program and its objectives. . . . This alteration of program and policy is probably inevitable, and may be desirable, as program managers and street level bureaucrats seek to creatively and responsively implement programs in unique environments.[55]

Kress, Koehier, and Springer offer this pragmatic metaphor for the concept of policy drift: "We were drifting. We were like a boat going down the river without a motor, but we were still in relatively gentle waters—we hadn't gone over the waterfall."[56] As the metaphor suggests, policies begin to drift once they hit a precipice, the waterfall. It is easy cruising for a patch in calm, serene, stable waters. Then a sudden—sometimes volatile—incident interferes with the tranquility, and the policy is thrown into disarray. Unlike my use of the policy drift framework, however, Kress and his colleagues examine drifts that occur as a result of the complex and often turbulent process of policy *implementation* by program managers, street-level bureaucrats, and other relevant players. They illustrate how, over time, cumulative decisions by the implementers at the street level can fundamentally alter a program—the BEP—and its initial objectives.

Hacker expounds upon and refines the concept of policy drift as first advanced by Kress and his colleagues. He views policy drifts as a crucial mechanism of change that more accurately explains *transformations* in public policy. According to Hacker, "crucial policy changes" take place over time, "despite general stability in formal policies."[57] He goes on to say that policy drifts are "quite clearly mediated by politics, a result not of failures of foresight or perception, but of deliberate efforts by political actors" to change programs or policies.[58]

Hacker's use of the concept is thus very suitable for my purposes here. Moreover, unlike Kress and his colleagues, this book does not examine policy drift in the context of shifts to existing policy that result from implementation. Rather, it looks more broadly at how newer policies, in the form of laws, judicial rulings, executive actions, or interest group pressure, create turmoil that then displaces or changes the direction of earlier programs or policies. This, too, comports more with Hacker's conception of policy drift. Thus, for example, as seen at the beginning of this chapter, the book examines what happens to civil rights policy or law when the U.S. Supreme Court issues a decision that changes the fundamental direction of the policy to the point where it no longer protects those persons that the law initially intended to protect. The Court ruling sets in motion a response by other stakeholders to counteract the ruling.

Admittedly, there is no single theory or framework that completely explains the public policy process or how policy shifts or drifts over time. None of those described above are paradigmatic. Moreover, the theories are additive in a certain sense, and are thus characterized by overlapping and complementary features. As Sabatier has pointed out, all models to a certain degree capture the vital elements associated with the making of public policy: "the importance of problem perception; shifts in elite and public opinion concerning the salience of various problems; periodic struggles over the proper locus of governmental authority; incomplete attainment of legally-prescribed goals; and an iterative process of policy formulation, problematic implementation, and struggles over reformulation."[59]

Similarly, as Daniel Béland points out with respect to the use of the policy drift framework to examine social security, "Scholars have long debated the nature of institutional change in policy processes. Although there is no consensus about what the main sources of policy change are, recent scholarship by researchers . . . has provided social scientists working on public policy with useful analytical models to explore 'how institutions evolve.'"[60] As Beryl Radin has more concisely pointed out, there is no one size that fits all.[61]

The Policy Players

So who are the stakeholders in the policy process? To be sure, the three branches of government discussed earlier are key players. So, too, is the bureaucracy, operating as the administrative arm of the president or independently seeking to protect its own turf.[62] The bureaucracy consists of the departments, agencies, and commissions of the federal government. Although Congress is its funding source, the executive branch claims dominancy over the bureaucracy as its administrative arm.[63] Richard Nathan coined the term "administrative presidency" as a leadership strategy where the executive branch, by controlling bureaucrats, achieves policy gains administratively that it could not attain through legislation.[64] As Thompson points out, "the administrative presidency rests with the kinds of actions that presidents and political appointees take to reshape public programs in the absence of congressional approval."[65]

The concept of the administrative presidency, as well as "unitary executive" theory, connotes presidential unilateralism. Both are administrative strategies to control the federal branch of government in an effort to achieve public policy goals by circumventing career bureaucrats, Congress, and the courts. It is a form of executive privilege. Nathan advanced the concept of administrative presidency to describe efforts by

Presidents Nixon and Reagan to reel in a recalcitrant, uncooperative, seemingly autonomous bureaucracy to control spending and other actions of the bureaucracy; administrative presidency assumes a level of antipathy between the president and the bureaucracy. Similarly, unitary executive theory maintains that the president has exclusive control over the federal bureaucracy.[66] But it doesn't necessarily imply that the president is antagonistic toward the bureaucracy; rather, they can be working together as collaborative partners seeking mutually beneficial policy outcomes. Both strategies claim constitutional standing under Article II, Sections 2 and 3 of the U.S. Constitution. Section 2 provides that the "President shall be Commander in Chief of the Army and Navy of the United States, and of the militia of the several states, when called into the actual service of the United States." Section 3 charges the president with responsibility to "take Care that the Laws be faithfully executed." For my purposes here, these two concepts, administrative presidency and unitary executive theory, will be used interchangeably.[67]

Yet the exercise of executive authority is not always within constitutional boundaries.[68] For example, presidents have historically kept certain information hidden from Congress and have also authorized the bombing of countries without congressional authorization. As we will see in chapter 2, President Bush overrode statutes governing surveillance in the post-9/11 era. Thus, while some actions by a president may fall within constitutional limits, others may not.

On the other hand, Congress may be obliquely ceding authority to the president in an effort to avoid its own responsibilities over policy matters. That is to say, if an issue is so politically threatening that it could hurt a congressperson's bid for reelection, forsaking legislative responsibilities becomes a viable strategy. In this sense, Congress then expects the president to fill the vacuum created by its retreat.

Although the bureaucracy can serve as a tool for the executive branch, it can independently exert an enormous amount of control over the policy process through its rulemaking and regulatory powers.[69] For example, in September 2015 the EPA discovered that Volkswagen had deliberately installed software in its diesel VWs and Audis so that during yearly emissions testing these models would automatically lower emissions to legal standards, thus allowing the vehicles to spew pollutants into the atmosphere at all other times. The EPA, under its regulatory authority under the Clean Air Act, threatened to withhold approval of the company's 2016 Audi and VW diesel models until the problem had been fixed. Volkswagen agreed to make the modifications and comport with the law. In the context of federalism, bureaucracy sometimes emerges as the dominant policy player, affecting policy drifts almost unilaterally. This has been referred to as "administrative federalism," and it greatly impacts the balance of power between the federal and state governments.[70]

Thus, depending upon the circumstances, the bureaucracy has effectively assisted in executive policy actions, resisted policy shifts, maintained the status quo, or promoted its own interests or the values of the persons it serves, in defiance of the other branches or policy players.[71] Some, particularly students of public administration, view the unelected bureaucracy as the "fourth branch" of government, wielding power independently of Congress or the president.[72] In this sense, the bureaucracy competes with other players in the policy process from agenda setting to post-implementation. B. Guy Peters points out that bureaucrats "have come to be widely perceived as powerful policy-making actors within democratic regimes. . . . Both quantitative and qualitative trends in policy formation lead us to the conclusion that we must understand public bureaucracy in order to understand policy in contemporary political systems and, further, that the power of bureaucracies is increasing steadily."[73]

A number of configurations of policy participants have been advanced over the past several decades. For example, the "iron triangle" signifies the mutually beneficial policy-making relationship between Congress, the bureaucracy, and interest groups. Gordon Adams refers to iron triangles as closed systems of policy making with a high degree of expertise that "encourages a narrowing of views."[74] The relationship promotes the interests of all parties; in simple terms, it operates in this fashion: Congress provides funding for the bureaucracy, which, in the interests of the bureaucrats, ensures survival; the bureaucracy in turn apportions funding to those jurisdictions that will benefit the constituents and special interests of members of Congress; this is generally referred to as pork-barreling. Then the constituents and special interests promise to direct their voting power to the congressperson who promoted their cause. In effect, each corner of the triangle benefits.[75]

Issue or policy networks represent even broader arrangements of policy participants, including congressional staff members, bureaucrats, think tanks, special interest groups, state governments, and even the media who share interests in public policy.[76] Hugh Heclo initially challenged the concept of iron triangles as too narrow: "Looking for the few who are powerful, we tend to overlook the many whose webs of influence provoke and guide the exercise of power. These webs, or what I will call issue networks, are particularly relevant to the highly intricate and confusing welfare policies that have been undertaken in recent years."[77] In very broad terms, these webs or networks represent the shared powers of policy making. They include all groups that participate in or even challenge the process or the outcomes of the process. It is this broad conception that is adopted in this book.

Shared powers promote democratic accountability.[78] Birkland argues that without the participation of a multitude of actors in the policy process, even those not delineated or empowered by the U.S. Constitution, "our democratic system of policy formation and implementation could not function."[79] To the extent that a multitude of interests compete in the process, power will not accumulate in the hands of a few. This is the embodiment of the political culture in this nation. Certainly, elections are also a purveyor of democratic principles, but they go beyond the scope of this book. The book does recognize that some segments of the population may inevitably be marginalized in the policy-making process. For example, to the extent that certain factions of the population have no voice or organized group to express their interests, they will be devalued or disenfranchised.[80] This book will address the winners and losers of the shared powers policy framework. Importantly, however, democratic rule cannot be conflated with producing gains for all.[81] Even in the case of climate control, where human, environmental, and ecological interests seem supreme, there are those factions working against a goal that would benefit the masses. Democracy will not always produce a common good. As Eric Patashnik argues, the losers "cannot be counted on to vanish without another fight, and new actors may arrive on the scene who will seek to undo a reform to further their own agendas."[82] And, as noted, policy drifts are inevitable; as such, there is no finality to the policy process.

Policy Durability

As discussed earlier, the main contribution of this book is to apply the policy drift framework to help explain how shared powers affect public policy in three contemporary areas. It seems axiomatic that any examination of policy drift must include an assessment of policy durability or stability. The extent to which stakeholders continue to challenge public policy will affect the policy's durability. Yet, as a number of scholars have suggested, some policies will be more susceptible to drifts than others.[83] Stability in stakeholder structure or the broader policy area, for example, can help predict the durability of policy drifts. The shift in office from President George W. Bush to President Obama impinged on policy durability. So too, no doubt, will the shift from President Obama to President Trump.

The Scope of the Book

This book examines the role of shared powers in policy drifts in three areas over time: privacy rights and surveillance policy, civil rights, and climate policy. An unexpected trigger, such as a U.S. Supreme Court ruling, stimulated by social, political, ideological, or economic forces produces these drifts. And most importantly, the policy process for each one is ongoing and continuous. In effect, policies can drift over an indefinite, undetermined period of time.

Chapter 2 of this book examines privacy rights in the context of surveillance policy in the United States and abroad, and the judicial, executive, legislative, and interest group responses to those policies. The institutional model best describes the policy process in this setting. The chapter will provide a short history of U.S. government surveillance policies and then detail the experiences and practices of such policies as a result of the 9/11 attacks. Importantly, it looks at social context, which is one pivotal driver of policy drifts. So, for example, the Patriot Act enacted on October 26, 2001, was an immediate reaction to the 9/11 terrorist attacks, and it received widespread support from Congress and the American people, something the Bush administration banked on. This act represents a major drift from previous policy. Over time, however, due to concerns about privacy especially as leaked by Snowden, the American people became wary about the wholesale elimination of our privacy rights. In June 2015 Congress passed the USA Freedom Act, also known as Patriot Act II. However, there are lingering concerns about whether the civil liberties of Americans are still at risk. The politics surrounding this polemical surveillance policy and its newest iteration, as well as those who perceive benefits from it and those who do not, will be addressed in this chapter.

Chapter 3 addresses the operation of civil rights laws, legal challenges brought under those laws, and executive and legislative responses to the legal challenges. The example of pay equity, presented earlier, illustrates the permutability of Title VII of the Civil Rights Act of 1964 as amended. This chapter will also examine efforts to pass the Employment Non-Discrimination Act (ENDA), which would protect lesbian, gay, bisexual, and transgender (LGBT) employees from employment discrimination; it has repeatedly failed to pass Congress. Frustrated by the lack of progress for LGBT individuals, President Obama relied on his executive powers to extend job protections for LGBT federal employees and employees of federal contractors. This chapter will examine the politics surrounding these actions by the executive branch and the bureaucracy and more broadly the administrative presidential strategy, whereby the administration seeks to accomplish administratively through the bureaucracy that which it cannot legislatively.

Chapter 4 examines efforts to implement climate change policy as well as the judicial, executive, bureaucratic, legislative, interest group, and state government responses to those efforts. The advocacy coalition model fits here in the sense that policy is greatly affected and driven by advocacy coalitions consisting of state governments and their allies (i.e., industry groups). The politics and bureaucratic maneuvering by the EPA to finalize its Clean Power Plan, announced in August 2015, will be analyzed, along with the ensuing legal battles. Given the tensions between the states and the EPA in the area of climate control, administrative federalism seems to prevail. This chapter will also address President George W. Bush's efforts over the two terms of his presidency to gut environmental safeguards while advancing the interests of mining, coal, oil, and gas industries. The role of the EPA, the courts, Congress, and environmental groups will be addressed. The winners (e.g., industry) and losers (e.g., humans) in the shared powers model of public policy making over environmental issues will be addressed.

Chapter 5 provides a comprehensive summary and conclusions. It discusses the implications of shared powers jockeying over public policy for policy drifts and their outcomes. Do shared powers impede the ability of government to formulate coherent public policies? What are the lessons learned from the three cases presented in this book? The chapter also examines the extent to which the policy drifts discussed in the three areas may be sustainable. If policy drifts are not subject to political, social, or economic upheaval, will they remain more or less durable? When the balance of power on the U.S. Supreme Court shifts from liberal to conservative, for example, the durability of progressive policies affecting LGBT persons will be diminished. Policy drifts and their durability are inextricably linked, but certain factors can affect both drifts and durability. This issue will be fully explored in chapter 5.

2

Privacy Rights and U.S. Surveillance Policy Drifts

Those who would give up essential Liberty, to purchase a
little temporary Safety, deserve neither Liberty nor Safety.
—Benjamin Franklin[1]

Americans have become inured to a culture that thrives on security infractions. After all, we live in a big data era, where in order to gain access to the latest services or technology, we often sign over—generally inadvertently—our privacy rights when we accept "privacy policy agreements" without reading the small print. Every time we download software updates on our smartphones or computers, we all too frequently hit the "accept" key without reading the document. This leads to privacy breaches. Web cookies, for example, hide data in our computer so that websites and browsers can track our browsing sessions and save useful information, such as account names and passwords, for later retrieval. Such data can be retrieved by third parties. Private companies often maintain computerized databases on consumer buying predilections. So when we order books on Amazon, we are given recommendations for books we might like based on previous orders. Internet streaming companies such as Netflix track our movie preferences. Facebook, Twitter, Instagram, and other forms of social media readily lead to privacy infractions. We have been inculcated with the virtues that come with big data.

Importantly, however, these are actions by *private* companies or businesses, which are not subject to constitutional scrutiny. Americans are willing to accept some privacy invasions in order to keep up with technological advances. We may feel very differently when the government spies on us. Americans see this as a fundamental breach of our privacy rights guaranteed under the U.S. Constitution. It evokes an image of an Orwellian Big Brother surveilling our every move, desire, and thought; spying on individuals is a symbol for abuse of government power. But since we live in a democratic state, our expectations for privacy are much more pronounced and heightened. Thus, privacy infringements by any governmental body are viewed as an intrusion of and transgression against our fundamental rights as Americans.

Yet we have learned that when there is some cataclysmic event that provokes extreme fear, Americans are willing to "give up essential Liberty, to purchase a little temporary Safety," as Ben Franklin proclaimed in 1755 when the states were beginning to form a national framework for government. When terrorists struck American soil on September 11, 2001, forever known as the 9/11 attacks, we were willing to sacrifice our basic freedoms so that the government could protect us from further attack.

The 9/11 attacks led to significant policy drifts in surveillance policy, and hence our privacy rights. The Bush administration, whose key officials linked secrecy with security, was the primary driver of the drifts. That is, the primary concern after the attacks was to keep our borders secure, but the means to that end—secrecy—represented a major policy drift in that it resulted in widespread breaches of the privacy of the American citizenry.[2] The secret surveillance policy, as will be seen, remained relatively stable in large part because of the Bush administration's ability to convince Congress as well as incoming President Obama and other stakeholders that the policy drifts were about patriotism, in the name of national security to preserve the freedoms of the American people.

This chapter begins with a brief discussion of the historical antecedents of privacy rights. Against this backdrop, it then examines how multiple policy players or stakeholders became involved in the battle between liberty and safety. It provides a comprehensive review of congressional hearings and debates over these critical issues. The policy drift framework, with a focus on institutions, illustrates how the federal government developed a series of byzantine, convoluted laws and secret edicts in the form of policy drifts that it claimed would help win the war on terror and bring some sense of safety and security to the American people. In the end, perhaps we deserved neither liberty nor safety.

The Constitutional Right to Privacy

The legal protection of privacy rights in this nation dates back to the Bill of Rights. Although it does not expressly mention privacy, the Fourth

Amendment to the U.S. Constitution, ratified in 1791 along with the entire Bill of Rights, holds as follows:

> The right of the people to be secure in their persons, houses, papers, and effects, against unreasonable searches and seizures, shall not be violated, and no Warrants shall issue, but upon probable cause, supported by Oath or affirmation, and particularly describing the place to be searched, and the persons or things to be seized.

[handwritten margin note: these are the loopholes. what is probable cause?]

It wasn't until almost a hundred years later, with the U.S. Supreme Court's decision in *Boyd v. United States*, that the Fourth Amendment was interpreted to protect privacy rights.[3] This case involved an accusation against Boyd of falsifying documents in order to avoid paying customs fees and duties. Boyd and his importing company, E. A. Boyd & Sons, were accused of importing thirty-five cases of plate glass into New York City without paying a duty required under the 1874 amendments to the Customs Act. The question raised was whether Boyd could be compelled by the government to submit private documents and other evidence that would incriminate him, and whether submission of such documents would represent an "unreasonable search and seizure" in violation of the Fourth Amendment. The Court ruled that compelling Boyd to surrender those documents was a violation of his constitutional rights, even though an actual search did not take place. The Court held that "actual entry upon premises and search for and seizure of papers [is not necessary] to constitute an unreasonable search and seizure within the meaning of the Fourth Amendment; a compulsory production of a party's private books and papers to be used against himself or his property in a criminal or penal proceeding, or for a forfeiture, is within the spirit and meaning of the Amendment."[4]

The 1920s brought a new set of issues to Fourth Amendment privacy rights: wiretapping. Although the invention of the telegraph in 1837 and telephone in 1876 led to widespread electronic surveillance in the form of wiretapping by private detectives as well as businesses seeking to maintain their competitive edge, the Fourth Amendment applies only to actions by the government.[5] The U.S. Supreme Court first addressed the constitutionality of wiretapping by the government in the 1928 case *Olmstead v. United States*, which involved a state and federal investigation into a bootlegging operation in Seattle.[6] Olmstead was illegally smuggling alcohol into the United States from Canada in violation of not only the Eighteenth Amendment, which outlawed alcohol in the United States—thus beginning the era of Prohibition—but also the 1919 Volstead Act, which prohibited the manufacturing and importing of alcohol. It was during this era that there was a dramatic increase in the number of constitutional challenges to warrantless searches and seizures. Most of the evidence against Olmstead was obtained through eavesdropping on his phone conversations via wiretaps placed in the street outside his home.[7] Olmstead claimed that the evidence was gathered without a warrant, in violation of his privacy rights under the Fourth Amendment. The Court majority ruled against Olmstead, opining that the wiretap was not directly on Olmstead's premises, and therefore no warrant was required. The Court stated that the

> mere tapping of telephone wires off the premises of accused, over which persons accused of violating criminal laws of the United States are engaged in conversation, is not a violation of the constitutional amendment that the right of the people to be secure in their persons, houses, papers, and effects against unreasonable searches and seizures shall not be violated, and therefore evidence so obtained is not inadmissible in aid of prosecutions for the alleged offenses.[8]

The *Olmstead* Court went on to assert that "no valid search warrant could be obtained by government agents to tap the telephone lines of the defendants for the purpose of securing of the private messages and conversations relating to the possession or sale of liquor."[9]

The High Court's ruling against Olmstead is certainly indicative of the social, political, and ideological forces of the day: Prohibition. Temperance groups lobbied vigorously for adoption of the Eighteenth Amendment on moral grounds. These reformers maintained that the consumption of alcohol produced antisocial, dysfunctional, and immoral behavior, and that government had a legal responsibility to foster the social value of morality.[10] It is not surprising, then, that the High Court, under the stewardship of Chief Justice Howard Taft, did not find wiretapping to be an abridgement of Olmstead's Fourth Amendment rights. Taft, a staunch conservative who served as U.S president between

1909 and 1913, was a leader in the Progressive movement aimed at promoting morality and fighting corruption in government.

In fact, one could point to the seminal concerns of this nation's history to secure individual rights as a function of political and ideological reactions to the injustice and oppression by British monarchical rule. Indeed, the Bill of Rights was a reaction in part to the complete disregard of individual rights of citizens. The Fourth Amendment, for example, was a reaction to the egregious, arbitrary practices of the British, prior to the Revolution, to search the homes and businesses of the colonists for the smuggling of goods, or any other activity perceived to be antagonistic or hostile to the British Crown.[11]

Subsequent events around privacy rights also point to shifts or drifts, where social, political, economic, or ideological factors incite action or reaction to contemporary practices. As seen in table 2.1, which provides a cursory history of domestic and international surveillance in this country prior to the 9/11 attacks against the United States, every major event can be tied to the dominant social and political values of the day. For example, warrantless gathering of intelligence by government agencies such as the Office of Strategic Services and the Armed Forces Security Agency was justified during wartime, but at the end of World War II, it was considered illegal. Yet the onset of the Cold War, with its attendant anticommunist attitudes of distrust, suspicion, and antagonism, led the government in 1945 to continue its warrantless tracking of not only foreign governments and their citizens but also Americans in an effort to track potential subversive activities.[12]

Another example can be seen in *Katz v. United States*.[13] The zeitgeist of the 1960s was characterized by vigilant defense of civil rights and liberties. The liberal Warren Court (the U.S. Supreme Court when Earl Warren served as chief justice) used its judicial power to dramatically expand the civil rights and liberties of Americans. The FBI had been secretly recording the conversations of Charles Katz over a public pay phone, where he was transmitting illegal gambling bets across the country. In *Katz*, the Court overturned the *Olmstead* ruling, arguing that wiretapping violated Katz's privacy rights under the Fourth Amendment. The wiretap was placed not on Katz's home, but on a pay phone without a warrant. The *Katz* decision established a precedent that physical trespassing was no longer required to establish a Fourth Amend-

TABLE 2.1. Key Events Prior to 9/11 in the History of Domestic and International Surveillance

1791	Ratification of the Bill of Rights. The Fourth Amendment protects persons against unreasonable searches and seizures.
1886	*Boyd v. United States.* The Fourth Amendment protects privacy rights.
1928	*Olmstead v. United States.* Evidence submitted from wiretaps does not violate Fourth Amendment rights. (Overturned in 1967.)
1934	The Federal Communications Act is first law to legalize wiretapping, providing that information gathered by the federal government is not disclosed.
1945	The Armed Forces Security Agency (AFSA) begins project SHAMROCK, warrantless intelligence-gathering scheme that collects international telegrams coming through ITT, RCA, and Western Union to screen for espionage and Soviet spying. The program runs for 30 years.
1952	President Truman establishes the National Security Agency (NSA) to protect the nation. It absorbs the AFSA.
1967	*Katz v. United States.* The Supreme Court overturns the precedent set by *Olmstead v. United States*, opining that the Fourth Amendment does protect nontangible possessions such as phone calls and electronic transmissions as well as the "reasonable expectation of privacy" in places like home, office, hotel room, or phone booth.
1968	Omnibus Crime Control and Safe Streets Act passed, the first federal law to restrict wiretapping by requiring a court order. The law makes exception for the president to approve warrantless wiretaps if in the interest of national security.
1972	President Nixon is impeached for his part in the Watergate scandal, which included wiretapping and theft of secret documents.
1975	The Church Committee, headed by Senator Frank Church, in its investigation of intelligence gathering by the CIA, NSA, and FBI, uncovers inordinate instances of warrantless wiretappings and unauthorized use of electronic surveillance. This committee was the precursor to the U.S. Senate Select Committee on Intelligence.
1978	The Foreign Intelligence Surveillance Act (FISA), signed into law by President Carter, authorizes electronic surveillance to obtain foreign intelligence information, which may involve American citizens if suspected of espionage or terrorism. It also establishes a secret FISA court to hear requests for warrants for electronic surveillance for the purposes of obtaining foreign intelligence information.
1986	The Electronic Communications Privacy Act (ECPA) amends Title III of the Omnibus Crime Control and Safe Streets Act of 1968 to add wireless and data communications (cell phone conversations and Internet communication) to the act; designed to prevent unauthorized government access to private electronic communications. Amended in 1994 by the Communications Assistance for Law Enforcement Act and the 2001 Patriot Act.
1995	First court-ordered wiretapping leads to the arrest and conviction of Argentinian Julio Ardita, for hacking into NASA and Department of Defense computers.
2001	In the wake of 9/11, Congress passes the Patriot Act.

Source: Adopted from Catherine McNiff, "Timeline: U.S. Spying and Surveillance," www.infoplease.com, accessed September 15, 2015.

ment search and seizure case.[14] A year after *Katz*, Congress passed the Omnibus Crime Control and Safe Streets Act, representing one of the first federal laws to restrict wiretapping.

And then there was 9/11. It is this attack on American soil that produced a major drift in policy, creating significant tensions between the U.S. government and civilians, libertarians, and foreign governments. As the following sections will show, a competition for power, an effort to capitalize on the public's fear, and other political and social forces led to one of the most extensive surveillance programs in this nation's history.

The 9/11 Attacks

The attacks against America on September 11, 2001, produced an enormous sense of nationalism in this country, one perhaps not seen since the Japanese bombed Pearl Harbor. On this day, Islamic extremists of al-Qaeda hijacked four airliners and successfully carried out suicide attacks against the Twin Towers of the World Trade Center in New York City and the Pentagon in Arlington, Virginia. The fourth airliner crashed in a field in Pennsylvania, having failed to hit its presumable target of the White House or the Capitol. Close to three thousand people died in the World Trade Center and its vicinity; only six people in the Twin Towers at the time of their collapse survived. Around ten thousand others were treated for injuries. This terrorist attack triggered some of the most regressive initiatives and policies against privacy rights; at the time, most Americans supported the initiatives.

It is extremely difficult today to capture the sense of indignation and outrage that Americans experienced on September 11, 2001. Liberals and moderates alike felt violated at the most visceral level, and would possibly have supported, if asked on September 12, extreme measures to combat terrorism even if they abrogated our privacy rights; the immediate reaction stemming from not only nationalism, but fear as well, is to extend as much power as necessary to the government to protect the citizenry from further attack. Indeed, in January 2002 a Gallup poll revealed that close to 50 percent of Americans supported the government's effort to fight terrorism, even if it resulted in the abridgment of civil liberties.[15] Another Gallup poll, as seen in table 2.2, indicated Americans' support for Bush's anti-terrorism actions even in the wake of civil liberties violations.

TABLE 2.2. How Far Has the Bush Administration Gone in Fighting Terrorism, Even if Americans' Civil Liberties Are Restricted? (%)

	Too far	About right	Not far enough	No opinion
June 21–23, 2002	11	60	25	4
September 2–4, 2002	15	55	26	4
August 25–26, 2003	21	55	19	5

Source: David W. Moore, "Public Little Concerned about Patriot Act," Gallup poll, September 9, 2003, www. gallup.com, accessed September 16, 2015.

This is one of the most compelling explanations for the passage of the USA Patriot Act, signed into law by President George W. Bush on October 26, 2001 (the full title is Uniting and Strengthening America by Providing Appropriate Tools Required to Intercept and Obstruct Terrorism, a backronym for the USA Patriot Act).[16] A collective, institutional lapse in memory allowed the government to enact policy that would retard the progress made around privacy rights in this nation, catapulting us back to the 1880s and the Supreme Court's decision in *Boyd*.

The 1978 Foreign Intelligence Surveillance Act (FISA) sets the stage for the Patriot Act, which as an amendment to the FISA, represents a considerable policy drift.[17] The FISA was a reaction to the findings of the Church Committee, formally known as the Committee to Study Government Operations with Respect to Intelligence, established in 1975 and headed by Senator Frank Church (D-ID). The committee found widespread practices of illegal spying on Americans, particularly civil rights activists and Vietnam War protestors, by government agencies such as the FBI and the CIA. With respect to the FBI, the covert, illegal spy program was part of COINTELPRO (COunter INTELligence PROgram), which began in 1956 to undermine the Communist Party in the United States. Most egregious was President Nixon's use of power ostensibly under the doctrine of executive privilege to engage in warrantless wiretapping of not only presumed political adversaries but also Americans suspected of antiwar activities.[18] It may be recalled that the Watergate affair, named for the Nixon administration's illegal bugging of the Democratic headquarters in the Watergate Office Complex, led to the downfall of the Nixon presidency.

At the same time, however, the Church Committee recognized the importance of the federal government's practice of intelligence gathering when national security issues were at stake.[19] In this sense, the FISA sought to circumscribe the powers of the government by prescribing procedures for searches and surveillance, which would strike a balance between personal privacy and national security interests.[20]

The FISA established the Foreign Intelligence Surveillance Court (FISC), which consists of federal judges appointed by the chief justice of the U.S. Supreme Court. The FISC oversees requests for surveillance warrants by federal law enforcement and intelligence agencies such as the National Security Agency (NSA) and the FBI. Its decisions can be reviewed by the Foreign Intelligence Surveillance Court of Review (FISCR) and the Supreme Court. While FISC rulings and orders are highly classified, some have been released with extensive redactions. The FISC is often referred to as a "secret court," because its hearings are closed to the public.

One of the most controversial aspects of the FISA is Section 1802, which includes the following:

(1) Notwithstanding any other law, the President, through the Attorney General, may authorize electronic surveillance *without a court order* under this subchapter to acquire foreign intelligence information for periods of up to one year if the Attorney General certifies in writing under oath that—

(A) the electronic surveillance is solely directed at—

(i) the acquisition of the contents of communications transmitted by means of communications used exclusively between or among foreign powers, as defined in section 1801(a)(1), (2), or (3) of this title; or

(ii) the acquisition of technical intelligence, other than the spoken communications of individuals, from property or premises under the open and exclusive control of a foreign power, as defined in section 1801(a)(1), (2), or (3) of this title;

(B) there is no substantial likelihood that the surveillance will acquire the contents of any communication to which a United States person is a party.[21]

Surveillance, then, is allowed without a court order from the FISC, except if a U.S. citizen is involved, in which case judicial authorization is required within seventy-two hours *after* surveillance begins.[22] The USA Patriot Act, amending the FISA, vastly expanded the government's surveillance authority over U.S. citizens at the expense of accountability, privacy, and judicial oversight.[23]

The USA Patriot Act: A Significant Policy Drift

To be sure, a swift reaction to the 9/11 attacks seemed to policy makers as well as the public a prudent move. There was a shared, monumental desire to protect the nation's borders. And it was not only the Bush administration that was intent on reacting quickly to the 9/11 attacks. Many members of Congress, Democrats and Republicans alike, were also motivated by the immediacy of the attacks. A flurry of bills that sought to change anti-terrorism laws in the United States was introduced in Congress. For example, the Combating Terrorism Act of 2001 was introduced on September 13 by Senators Orrin Hatch (R-UT), Jon Kyl (R-AZ), and Dianne Feinstein (D-CA).[24] This act included measures that would allow law enforcement agencies to disclose foreign intelligence gathered through surveillance methods such as wiretaps and would allow the CIA to recruit informants against terrorist acts.[25] Similarly, the Intelligence to Prevent Terrorism Act, introduced on September 28 by Senators Bob Graham (D-FL) and Jay Rockefeller (D-WV), would require the attorney general or head of any other federal department or agency to disclose foreign intelligence acquired in the course of a criminal investigation.[26]

Interestingly, the bill that would eventually become the Patriot Act was drafted by the attorney general, John Ashcroft. Both the House and Senate essentially made modifications to this draft bill, proposed as the Anti-Terrorism Act of 2001, thus accepting much of the agenda and direction set forth by the Bush administration. On October 2, Representative F. James Sensenbrenner Jr. (R-WI), chair of the House Judiciary Committee, introduced the bill, H.R. 2975, to the Republican-controlled House. The Judiciary Committee rejected very few of the Bush administration's proposals. One proposal it rejected was a provision that would allow federal authorities to rely on evidence from foreign governments obtained by methods that would be unconstitutional in the United States.[27] In practice, we would later learn that unconstitutional methods such as waterboarding were used on foreign soil not only by foreign governments but by the United States as well to interrogate potential "terrorists" for security threats. The House Judiciary Committee voted 36–0 in favor of the bill.

There was very little deliberation on the House floor, particularly since the White House continued to place an enormous amount of pressure on members of Congress to pass the bill, even accusing potential opponents as being unpatriotic. The Bush administration suggested that any further attacks against Americans would be blamed on members who did not support the bill. Some members had not even read or seen the bill. Congressperson John Murtha (D-PA) at one point told the Speaker of the House, Dennis Hastert (R-IL),

> I have not seen a copy of the bill, and nobody on this side has been able to explain to me what is in the bill. I know in an hour that it would be very difficult to explain the intricacies of a terrorism bill which would last for some period of time.[28]

The complete lack of knowledge of the actual text of the Patriot Act was also captured by Michael Moore in his film *Fahrenheit 9/11*. Moore recorded Representative Jim McDermott (D-WA) saying that no one read the bill; Representative John Conyers Jr. (D-MI) said, "We don't read most of the bills. Do you really know what that would entail if we were to read every bill that we pass? Uh well, the good thing, it would slow down the legislative process."[29] Were most members of Congress so motivated to pass the act that they didn't find it necessary to read it?

Some members of Congress questioned, even without a document before them, the potential impact of the bill on civil liberties. For example, John Baldacci (D-ME) stated,

> The measures being enacted here have decidedly much more of an impact on individual rights and civil liberties and with no particular document in front of us with which to review and to question. When I posed questions to members of the Committee on the Judiciary just a few moments ago to ask them what was in the package and what was not in the package that we would be taking up shortly, they were unaware of it, had not been briefed on it, had not seen any actual language.[30]

Also concerned was Congressperson Peter DeFazio (D-OR), who stated shortly afterward,

> We need to give law enforcement the proper tools, yes, we do; and we need to strengthen laws where they need to be strengthened and give them more effective tools. But we also have to be careful that we do not dredge up some of the worst ideas of the past, of the fifties, of the McCarthy era, of the Hoover era.[31]

Louise Slaughter (D-NY) similarly argued,

> While all of us understand the need to give law enforcement the tools it needs to combat terrorism, the bill goes too far. In the name of protecting Americans, it eats away at some of our most cherished freedoms.[32]

Dennis Kucinich (D-OH) was one of the most outspoken critics of the act:

> "My country 'tis of thee, sweet land of liberty, of thee I sing; land where my fathers died, land of the pilgrims' pride, from every mountainside let freedom ring." Let freedom ring in the ears of those who want to still its sound. Let freedom ring even as we travel through the valley of the shadow of terrorism, for freedom is a sweeter melody. . . . Let freedom ring. If freedom is under attack from outside sources, then let us not permit an attack from within. It is an attack on freedom to let government come into the home of any American to conduct a search, to take pictures without notification. It is an attack on freedom to give the government broad wiretap authority. It is an attack on freedom to permit a secret grand jury to share information with other agencies. It is an attack on freedom to create laws which can endanger legitimate protests.[33]

Representative Ron Paul (R-TX), one of three Republicans who did not support the Patriot Act, argued that

> provisions of this bill represent a major infringement of the American people's constitutional rights. I am afraid that if these provisions are signed into law, the American people will lose large parts of their liberty—

maybe not today but over time, as agencies grow more comfortable exercising their new powers. . . . Giving the executive branch discretionary authority to seize private property without due process violates the spirit, if not the letter, of the fifth amendment to the Constitution. . . . [It] waters down the fourth amendment by expanding the federal government's ability to use wiretaps free of judicial oversight. The fourth amendment's requirement of a search warrant and probable cause strikes a balance between effective law enforcement and civil liberties. Any attempt to water down the warrant requirement threatens innocent citizens with a loss of their liberty. . . . This legislation is also objectionable because it adopts a lower standard than probable cause for receiving e-mails and Internet communications. While it is claimed that this is the same standard used to discover numbers dialed by a phone, it is also true that even the headings on e-mails or the names of web sites one visits can reveal greater amounts of personal information than can a mere telephone number.[34]

Yet the preponderance of Republican members of the House as well as hawkish Democrats seemed willing to support the act and did not see it as an infringement on civil liberties. A statement by House majority leader Dick Armey (R-TX) is illustrative of this sentiment:

The world is replete with stories of strong governments who have maintained their own security by trespassing against the rights of even their own people. Strong governments can make themselves secure. We have seen that too many times. But we have known, the committee has known, this Congress knows and the White House knows that a good government makes the people secure while preserving their freedom. And that is what this bill is. That is why we should not only vote for it, but we should thank our lucky stars we are in a democracy where we have that right.[35]

For others, the concern revolved around "safety," despite assertions of threats that were never confirmed. For example, as Ted Deutsch (D-FL) explained,

I have the same perspective that the President of the United States does and I believe the vast majority of Americans do, that we, in fact, are at war. We are at war with an enemy that has attacked this country with horrific results, 6,000 people dying in an instance at the World Trade Center, the Pentagon being attacked as well. But as we also know, these are an enemy that almost for sure has biological and chemical weapons available. It is unclear whether or not they have nuclear weapons, but it is only a matter of time before they do. And the only thing that is preventing their delivery of those biological and chemical weapons are [sic] a lack of a delivery system. So what we are faced with at this point in time is literally the potentiality of not thousands, as horrific as that is, but literally millions if not tens of millions of Americans whose lives could end in an instance.[36]

The bill was passed by the House as the Uniting and Strengthening America (USA) Act (H.R. 2975) on October 12.[37] Only sixty-six members of the House, sixty-two of whom were Democrats, voted against the Patriot Act.[38] Three Republican members of the House, Butch Otter of Idaho, Robert Ney of Ohio, and Ron Paul of Texas, voted against the act, as did the independent representative Bernie Sanders of Vermont. Key Democrats, such as Nancy Pelosi, who would later become Speaker of the House, voted to support the act. Interestingly, Pelosi responded to an October 1 briefing by NSA director Michael Hayden to the House Intelligence Committee that the NSA had, under its own authority, vastly expanded its surveillance immediately after the 9/11 attacks. Pelosi wrote to Hayden on October 11, the day before the House passed the act, inquiring whether the NSA's wiretapping program had been approved by President Bush. At the time, a clear response was not offered.[39]

At the urging of the Bush administration, the Senate version of the Patriot Act bypassed the Senate Judiciary Committee and went directly to the floor. The Senate at this time was controlled by the Democrats.[40] As in the House, there was very little debate over the bill. Senator Patrick Leahy (D-VT), then chair of the Judiciary Committee, argued that

this bill will change surveillance and intelligence procedures for all types of criminal and foreign intelligence investigations, not just for terrorism cases. . . . Yet, before final passage of this bill, the Senate should recall our nation's unfortunate experience with domestic surveillance and intelligence abuses that came to light in the mid-1970s. Until Watergate and the Vietnam War, Congress allowed the Executive branch virtually a free hand in using the FBI, the CIA, and other intelligence agencies to conduct domestic surveillance in the name of national security. It was the Cold War. Members of Congress were reluctant to take on FBI Director J. Edgar Hoover, and oversight was non-existent. . . . There would be far less controversy if these provisions were limited to information about domestic or international terrorism or espionage. Instead, they potentially authorize the disclosure throughout intelligence, military, and national security organizations of a far broader range [of] information about United States persons, including citizens, permanent resident aliens, domestic political groups, and companies incorporated in the United States.[41]

The Senate was aware, then, that the civil liberties of the American people were at stake. Nonetheless, the Senate forged ahead. Senator Leahy continued:

The bill we are passing today makes potentially sweeping changes in the relationships between the law enforcement and intelligence agencies. In the current crisis, there is justification for expanding authority specifically for counterintelligence to detect and prevent international terrorism.[42]

In the end, Leahy stressed to his colleagues that we can trust the federal government to do the right thing:

In granting these new powers, the American people but also we, their representatives in Congress, grant the administration our trust that they are not going to be misused. It is a two-way street. We are giving powers to the administration; *we will have to extend some trust that they are not going to be misused.*[43]

Only one senator, Russell Feingold (D-WI), chair of the Constitution Subcommittee, voted against the Patriot Act. He vigorously attempted to dissuade his colleagues from voting to support the act on the grounds that it violated the civil liberties of American citizens:

We must examine every item that is proposed in response to these events to be sure we are not rewarding these terrorists and weakening ourselves by giving up the cherished freedoms that they seek to destroy. . . . But we must also redouble our vigilance to preserve our values and the basic rights that make us who we are. The Founders who wrote our Constitution and Bill of Rights exercised that vigilance even though they had recently fought and won the Revolutionary War. They did not live in comfortable and easy times of hypothetical enemies. They wrote a Constitution of limited powers and an explicit Bill of Rights to protect liberty in times of war, as well as in times of peace.[44]

Most importantly, Feingold explicitly clarified for his colleagues how the Patriot Act would allow the federal government to go well beyond its surveillance powers granted under the FISA:

FISA already gives the FBI the power to get airline, train, hotel, car rental, and other records of a suspect. But this bill does much more. Under this bill, the Government can compel the disclosure of the personal records of anyone—perhaps someone who worked with, or lived next door to, or went to school with, or sat on an airplane with, or had been seen in the company of, or whose phone number was called by—the target of the investigation.[45]

On October 25, ninety-eight senators voted to support the Patriot Act; that the Senate was controlled by Democrats did not matter.[46] As noted, Senator Feingold (D-WI) voted against the bill; Senator Mary Landrieu (D-LA) did not vote. Both chambers of Congress agreed to a sunset provision to the act whereby some provisions would automatically expire on December 31, 2005.[47] It was signed into law by President Bush on October 26, 2001. The Patriot Act represents a major policy drift, amending a number of laws, particularly the FISA.[48]

Key Provisions of the Act

The Patriot Act clearly changed a key provision of the FISA. Under the FISA, warrantless surveillance and searches were allowed if the "primary purpose" was to gather foreign intelligence. The Patriot Act amended the FISA to allow surveillance when a "significant purpose" is foreign intelligence, thus leaving open the possibility of breaches to the U.S. Constitution's probable cause requirement when the main goal is ordinary law enforcement.[49] In effect, the burden would be on victims of questionable searches to appeal to the courts as to whether law enforcement agencies went beyond the scope of "foreign" intelligence in conducting a warrantless search. This provision lowers the bar for searches and the use of wiretaps.

The Patriot Act also increased the government's surveillance authority to search the records of an individual held by a third party (see table 2.3). One of the most controversial provisions is Section 215, which permits the government to collect information that is "relevant" to terrorism investigations, and allows for easier access to personal records. In effect, phone companies, Internet providers, colleges, and even doctors

TABLE 2.3. Patriot Act, Title II: Enhanced Surveillance Procedures (Key Provisions)

Section	Provision
201	Authorizes interception of wire, oral, and electronic communications relating to terrorism.
202	Authorizes interception of wire, oral, and electronic communications relating to computer fraud and abuse offenses.
203	Allows government agencies to share criminal investigative information.
204	Clarifies intelligence exceptions from limitations on interception and disclosure of wire, oral, and electronic communications.
206	Allows for roving wiretaps or surveillance authority under the FISA of 1978.
209	Allows for seizure of voicemail messages pursuant to warrants.
210	Allows law enforcement to subpoena additional subscriber records of electronic communications from service providers.
213	Allows for "sneak and peak" search warrants, allowing for a delay in notice of the execution of a warrant.
214	Allows the FBI to install pen register and trap and trace devices more easily.
215	Allows easier access to personal records and other items under the FISA.
216	Expands reach of pen registers and trap and trace devices to email and Internet, as well as telephone communications.
218	Lowers the bar for conducting foreign intelligence searches and wiretaps.
219	Allows for single-jurisdiction search warrants for terrorism.
220	Allows for nationwide service of search warrants for electronic evidence.
224	Authorizes sunset of certain amendments on December 31, 2005.
225	Provides immunity for compliance with FISA wiretap.

Source: Adapted from USA Patriot Act, Public Law 107–56, www.gpo.gov, accessed September 24, 2015.

could be compelled to provide records on their clients to the NSA or FBI. For Internet providers, this could include logs of the websites a person visits as well as the addresses of emails coming to and from the person's computer. The act made it easier for federal authorities to obtain pen registers, which are automatic mechanisms that trace all phone numbers from a designated telephone line. The act included a number of other drifts from the FISA, but much of the fallout would not be known until much later, especially after the *New York Times* revealed in December 2005 that President Bush had authorized warrantless wiretapping of U.S. citizens prior to passage of the Patriot Act.[50]

The Executive Branch's Dominance over Public Policy

President Bush maintained that his actions after 9/11 were permissible and justifiable; he claimed that such authorization was "fully consistent" with his "constitutional responsibilities and authorities."[51] By framing the issue in this fashion, he was successful in convincing other stakeholders, including Congress, that his actions were crucial to national security, thus enabling the nation to detect and prevent terrorist attacks for the ultimate goal of protecting the American people. This in large part ensured the durability and stability of the surveillance programs.

The Bush administration believed that it had the authority to override the constitutional rights of American citizens for the sake of combating terrorism.[52] A unitary executive branch construed its powers as such under the Patriot Act, along with (1) secret executive orders issued by President Bush, which authorized the NSA to conduct warrantless wiretaps on phone calls made by U.S. citizens and others living in the United States;[53] (2) an order issued by Attorney General John Ashcroft that expanded the government's search and surveillance powers;[54] and (3) a special appeals court order that upheld the Justice Department's expansive powers.[55] The bureaucracy, particularly the NSA, provided the president with the necessary tools and infrastructure. The Bush administration's surveillance and data collection programs did not obey statutory limits on government spying, and the administration justified its actions on the grounds that it was hunting for terrorist cells.[56]

But, as noted, perhaps most American citizens at the time seemed willing to support this position. Immediately after the 9/11 attacks,

Americans lived in a state of panic, wondering whether and when the terrorists might strike again. Certainly, this fear and sense of danger were reinforced, perpetuated, and inflated by the government in many ways. Recall, for example, the Bush administration's Terror/Emergency Alert System. Created on March 11, 2002, by a presidential directive to the Office of Homeland Security, then in the White House, it was intended to provide information on the risk of potential terrorist attacks.[57] The system identified four color-coded threat levels:

- Red—severe risk
- Orange—high risk
- Yellow—elevated or significant risk
- Green—low risk

But the exclusive use of power by the executive branch goes even further. For example, although the Bush administration cited the September 11 attacks as the main impetus for the government's warrantless surveillance efforts, there was some advance knowledge that the NSA had been surveilling Americans well before 9/11 for the purpose, at least officially, of uncovering potential computer hackers, which may or may not include foreign government agents seeking to hack into any of the government's computer systems, particularly those of the Defense Department. As early as February 2001, the NSA made an appeal to Qwest, a U.S. telecommunications company that provides wireless and Internet connectivity, to reveal information about its customers and their phone calls for potential terrorist activities. Qwest's CEO, Joe Nacchio, refused unless the NSA could provide a court order from the FISA Court (FISC).[58]

In addition, the CIA, the FBI, and the executive branch were aware of potential terrorist attacks, particularly in light of the failed Bojinka plot, the 1995 al-Qaeda terrorist plot to blow up several airliners and their passengers as they flew from Asia to America. For example, the *Washington Post* reported on September 27, 2001,

The FBI had advance indications of plans to hijack U.S. airliners and use them as weapons, but neither acted on them nor distributed the intelligence to local police agencies. From the moment of the September 11 attacks, all high-ranking federal officials insisted that the terrorists' method of operation surprised them. Many continue to stick to that story. Actually, elements of the suicide hijacking plan were known to the FBI as early as 1995 and, if coupled with current information, might have uncovered the plot.[59]

Shane Harris in his 2010 book *The Watchers* writes that the

government had failed to "connect the dots" about terrorism, specifically the Al Qaeda network. It wasn't widely known that some of the 9/11 hijackers were already on terrorist watch lists when they entered the United States. Mysterious phone calls intercepted on September 10, which hinted at the next day's calamity, weren't translated in time to be of any use. No one—no *system*—had gathered all the pieces of the puzzle and put them together.[60]

Amy Zegart's *Spying Blind* (2007) also describes the intelligence community as being "asleep at the switch" on 9/11.[61] She notes that CIA director George Tenet failed in his efforts to expand the Counterterrorism Center, leaving only a handful of analysts assigned to surveilling Osama bin Laden. Similarly, the FBI had declared terrorism its number one priority in 1998, but on 9/11 only 6 percent of FBI personnel were working on counterterrorism. Zegart ascribes these organizational pathologies to "(1) [cultural deficiencies] that led intelligence agencies to resist new technologies, ideas, and tasks; (2) perverse promotion incentives that rewarded intelligence officials for all the wrong things; and (3) structural weaknesses dating back decades that hindered the operation of the CIA and FBI and prevented the U.S. Intelligence Community from working as a coherent whole. It was these core weaknesses that caused U.S. intelligence agencies to blow key operational opportunities. . . . that might have disrupted the September 11 plot."[62]

In short, the executive branch justified its broad scope of powers as necessary to combat terrorism even before the 9/11 attacks. It thus had gained the upper hand in the policy movement around the 9/11 attacks, in large part by capitalizing on the public's fear. Perhaps this partly explains why Congress was very willing to accede to the Bush administration's directives, even though they would compromise the privacy rights of Americans. It took several years and various social and ideological forces before shifts in public opinion on surveillance policy in the United States would ensue. Only then would there be some movement in and jockeying around the political landscape on the issue of privacy rights.

Challenging President Bush and the Patriot Act

A number of factors gradually led to the nation's questioning of the government's surveillance policy. One was certainly the exposure of faulty intelligence around Saddam Hussein's accumulation of weapons of mass destruction (WMD) in Iraq. Not long after the 9/11 attacks, President Bush, along with Vice President Dick Cheney, Secretary of Defense Donald Rumsfeld, and National Security Advisor Condoleezza Rice, insisted that Hussein had been stockpiling nuclear arsenals since the Gulf War in 1991 in defiance of international law; and that, given Hussein's record as constructed by Western nations of being a brutal dictator, he would use the WMD to obliterate America.[63] The *New York Times* published a number of stories with sources purporting to verify this information.[64] To the extent the American people trusted this information (and we were urged to by some members of Congress, as noted earlier), we lent support to the Bush administration's invasion of Iraq. In fact, a Gallup poll indicated at the time that 72 percent of Americans supported the invasion.[65] Not only were Americans concerned for the nation's security, but perhaps more broadly, they bought in to the administration's desire to spread its version of democracy across the Middle East. Sacrificing privacy rights seemed a small price to pay.

But slowly the claim about WMD in Iraq began to unravel, as did the concomitant need for extensive surveillance practices. Joseph Wilson, a former diplomat, was sent by the CIA in 2002 on a mission to investigate whether Iraq was purchasing and importing yellowcake uranium from Niger. He reported back to the Bush administration and later wrote an op-ed piece in the *New York Times* that no such transactions were taking place.[66] With this knowledge, the American people felt that they had been lied to about the reason for invading Iraq and felt completely misled by the government's efforts to secure the nation's borders. In an apparent retaliation for the public revelation of this finding, Deputy Secretary of State Richard Armitage exposed the identity of Wilson's wife,

Valerie Plame, a covert CIA officer, who had recommended Wilson for the reconnaissance mission. With her identity exposed, Plame's career with the CIA was over.[67]

In addition, it was learned that a reporter for the *New York Times*, Judith Miller, whose articles claiming there were WMD in Iraq had helped bolster the Bush administration's case for war as well as secrecy, had been basing her contributions to various stories on fallacious information.[68] The media also published stories about military analysts who criticized the war. For example, Gregory Hooker, an intelligence analyst for the U.S. military's Central Command, went public with a report he wrote in 2005 claiming that the Bush administration's invasion plans had been developed without consideration of the aftermath; he argued that "civilians" in the Bush administration had "injected numerous ideas into the dialogue, many of which were amateurish and unrealistic."[69]

The American Civil Liberties Union (ACLU) was one of the organizations that waged a consistent battle against the federal government for its violations of individual civil liberties under the Patriot Act. In 2003, for example, the ACLU filed the first constitutional challenge to Section 215, a contentious provision of the Patriot Act that gives the government easier access to personal records under the FISA, in *Muslim Community Association of Ann Arbor v. Ashcroft*.[70] It was filed on behalf of six Islamic nonprofit groups that provide a range of services to local communities in Michigan and across the country. The plaintiffs charged that the Patriot Act violated (1) the Fourth Amendment by authorizing the FBI to execute searches without probable cause and without providing targeted individuals with notice; (2) the First Amendment by prohibiting a person from disclosing the fact that the FBI sought personal records; (3) the First Amendment by authorizing the FBI to investigate persons based on the exercise of their rights to freedom of expression, association, and religion; and (4) the Fifth Amendment by authorizing the FBI to deprive persons of property without due process. Not surprisingly, the federal government sought to dismiss the case on the grounds that the plaintiffs lacked standing to challenge Section 215. Although district court judge Denise Hood, a Clinton appointee, heard arguments on both sides in 2003, it wasn't until 2006 that she issued a decision rejecting the government's arguments to dismiss the case. But in an odd twist, before the court issued a substantive ruling on the case, the ACLU dropped the lawsuit, stating that it believed that some improvements had been made to the Patriot Act with its reauthorization in 2006, such as allowing a person receiving requests for documents from the government to retain an attorney. Nevertheless, this legal challenge was indicative of a larger public backlash against the policy.

In another lawsuit filed in 2003, the ACLU, along with the Electronic Privacy Information Center (EPIC) and other organizations, brought a civil action against the Department of Justice seeking information about the records it was seizing and collecting under Section 215 of the Patriot Act. The lawsuit was prompted by the DOJ's refusal to fill a Freedom of Information Act (FOIA) request for such information. In May 2004 federal district court judge Ellen Huvelle, a Clinton appointee, ordered the Justice Department to "process plaintiffs' request for all records relating to [the Patriot Act] . . . as soon as practicable."[71]

In addition, the ACLU and an Internet access corporation filed a lawsuit in 2004 challenging the constitutionality of the FBI's authority to obtain sensitive customer records from that corporation. The Internet company had been subject to a gag order from the FBI, which ordered it not to disclose the fact that it was seeking records from its clients. In *Doe v. Ashcroft*, district court judge Victor Marrero, a Clinton appointee, ruled that the FBI had abridged the Fourth Amendment rights of the plaintiff in its efforts to seize customer records, and also violated the plaintiff's First Amendment rights in issuing the gag order.[72]

The ACLU was also successful in lobbying city governments to pass resolutions criticizing the Patriot Act. By January 2003, some twenty-two cities and towns representing almost 3.5 million residents passed such resolutions, with a number of others following.[73] While the resolutions did not affect the implementation of the act, they symbolized efforts to combat the act's erosion of civil liberties.

Another case that addressed privacy rights under the Patriot Act involved Brandon Mayfield, a Portland attorney who was wrongly suspected of involvement in the Madrid train bombing case in 2004. Mayfield was never formally charged, and the FBI later acknowledged serious errors in its investigation. Mayfield's home and law office were placed under secret government surveillance; he filed suit arguing that his constitutional rights to privacy under the Fourth Amendment had been violated. In 2007 district court judge Ann Aiken, a Clinton appointee, in

Mayfield v. United States, ruled in favor of Mayfield.[74] In 2009 the three-member panel of the Appeals Court for the Ninth Circuit, all Clinton appointees, reversed, stating that Mayfield had no standing to pursue his Fourth Amendment case under portions of the Patriot Act. In 2010 the U.S. Supreme Court denied Mayfield's request to review the case.[75]

There were additional constitutional challenges to the Patriot Act that the nation eventually became aware of. In 2005 district court judge Audrey Collins, a Clinton appointee, ruled, in *Humanitarian Law Project v. Gonzales,* in favor of several U.S. groups and individuals who sought clearance to provide aid and assistance to political organizations in Turkey and Sri Lanka that engage in some form of lawful as well as unlawful activities.[76] They challenged those portions of the Patriot Act that ban advice or assistance to designated "terrorist" organizations as a violation of the First Amendment's guarantee of free speech. The district court struck down that portion of the act, claiming that the relevant language of the act was too broad and vague, thus ruling for the plaintiffs. In 2007 a three-member panel of the U.S. Court of Appeals for the Ninth Circuit, all appointed by Democratic presidents, agreed in part, opining that the language of the act is too vague to be understood by individuals of "ordinary" intelligence.[77] To survive a vagueness challenge, the appeals court asserts, a statute "must be sufficiently clear to put a person of ordinary intelligence on notice that his or her contemplated conduct is unlawful."[78] The appeals court ruled that the Patriot Act's bans on training, service, and some kinds of expert advice were too vague to be supported, but it upheld the bans on personnel and expert advice derived from scientific or technical knowledge. That portion of the appellate court's ruling on training, service, and some types of expert advice was overturned in 2010 by a 6–3 U.S. Supreme Court ruling in *Holder v. Humanitarian Law Project.*[79] Thus, the Patriot Act can ban groups from providing *any* type of support to foreign terrorist organizations, even if the assistance takes the form of training for peacefully resolving conflicts.

In these early cases, at least the lower courts, with judges appointed by Democratic presidents, seemed inclined to support privacy rights. But the Bush administration continued with its mass surveillance policies. In effect, the executive branch disregarded judicial proceedings and decisions that sought to curb the reach of the Patriot Act.

Others, particularly major media outlets that were initially supportive of the Bush administration, began to rally against the administration's war on terror as a major threat to the basic values of all Americans; some went so far as to argue that even potential terrorists should not be exempt from America's system of laws.[80] An opinion piece by the editors of the *New York Times*, for example, published on November 16, 2001, stated that in an

> effort to defend America from terrorists, Mr. Bush is eroding the very values and principles he seeks to protect, including the rule of law. . . . The administration's action is the latest in a troubling series of attempts since Sept. 11 to do an end run around the Constitution. . . . By ruling that terrorists fall outside the norms of civilian and military justice, Mr. Bush has taken it upon himself to establish a prosecutorial channel that answers only to him. The decision is an insult to the exquisite balancing of executive, legislative and judicial powers that the framers incorporated into the Constitution. With the flick of a pen, in this case, Mr. Bush has essentially discarded the rulebook of American justice painstakingly assembled over the course of more than two centuries.[81]

In addition, members of the House who were wary of the Patriot Act and voted against it continued their opposition. Dennis Kucinich (D-OH), for example, continued to voice his disapproval of the act because of its wholesale dismissal of our Fourth Amendment rights. He made repealing the act one of his campaign promises when he joined the presidential race in 2003.[82] Even John Kerry, who as a senator at the time voted to support the Patriot Act of 2001, reversed his position when he was running for president in 2004. Kerry advocated "replacing the Patriot Act with a new law that protects our people and our liberties at the same time."[83]

Despite the aforementioned forces that could have turned the tide against the Patriot Act and continued violation of our privacy rights, Congress in 2006 once again voted overwhelmingly to renew the Patriot Act. John Kerry, despite his position on the act when he ran for president, was among those who voted to renew the policy. This turn of events begs the questions: Did members of Congress genuinely support the Patriot Act, or was it a symbolic gesture to demonstrate to their constituents that they were patriotic and would do whatever necessary to keep them safe and free from harm? Or did they genuinely believe that sacrificing our constitutional rights to privacy was an absolute necessity when national security issues were at stake? In either case, Congress continued to support or acquiesce to the Bush administration's efforts to combat terrorism via a secret spying program.

The Bush Administration Fires Back with Another Round

When several provisions of the Patriot Act expired in December 2005, President Bush, reelected to a second term, once again moved quickly to renew the act. The United States was still at war with Iraq as well as with Afghanistan, which it had begun bombing in October 2001 in its efforts to hunt down the 9/11 architect, Osama bin Laden, and his al-Qaeda fighters. Bush again relied on the threat of attack to mobilize support for reauthorization of the act. He maintained that "America remains a nation at war. . . . In the face of this ruthless threat, our nation has made a clear choice. . . . We are not going to be attacked again."[84] The U.S. Congress responded favorably after temporarily extending the expiration date of the act on two occasions so that members could debate the issue of civil liberties.

In July 2005 the Senate passed a reauthorization bill that called for some changes to the initial act. The Republican-controlled House's version retained most of the act's original language.[85] One revision would allow individuals who received requests for personal documents to engage an attorney. The Republican-controlled Senate's version was initially seen as a rebuke to the Bush administration, which lobbied heavily for full reauthorization of the Patriot Act as passed in 2001. Bush made a series of calls to members of Congress seeking their support for reauthorization. In the swearing-in ceremony for Attorney General Ashcroft's successor, Alberto Gonzales, Bush insisted that Gonzales must be provided with the tools he would need to fight the war of terror:

> Attorney General Gonzales now joins every employee at the Department of Justice in an urgent mission to protect the United States from another terrorist attack. . . . We must provide you all the tools you need to do your job. And one of those tools is the Patriot Act, which has been vital to our

success in tracking terrorists and disrupting their plans. Many key elements of the Patriot Act are now set to expire at the end of this year. We must not allow the passage of time or the illusion of safety to weaken our resolve in this new war. To protect the American people, Congress must promptly renew all provisions of the Patriot Act this year.[86]

The Senate bill, sponsored by Senators Arlen Specter (R-PA) and Dianne Feinstein (D-CA), placed restrictions on the FBI's power to seize business records and financial documents; it also placed a four-year limit on the act's two most controversial provisions, Sections 206 and 215, roving wiretap authority and secret searches of personal records, respectively (see table 2.3). Some senators sought to renew the Patriot Act by a simple majority. But the Senate required sixty votes to override a filibuster and end debate (referred to as "invoking cloture"). Cloture would have brought the Patriot Act to a final vote. But only fifty-two senators voted to end the debate; forty-seven voted against cloture.

The debate on the Senate floor revolved in part around Americans' privacy rights. Some senators argued, for example, that very few changes to the protection of civil liberties were being written into the bill. Senator Feingold (D-WI), for example, the lone detractor from the first Patriot Act, argued, "This bill does not address all of the problems with the PATRIOT Act. . . . I want to be clear that this will not be the end of my efforts to further fix the PATRIOT Act."[87] He later argued that the bill had not gone far enough:

> I have been to the floor several times in the past few days to try to convince my colleagues that we should not be reauthorizing the PATRIOT Act without addressing the legitimate concerns of law-abiding Americans across the country. I am under no illusions that I will have more success making that argument now than I had yesterday, or the week before the recess. And I know that some of my colleagues may be wishing I would sit down and stop badgering them about this. But the stakes are too high to sit idly by while the Senate prepares to disappoint the millions of Americans who have been hoping, asking, advocating for years that we fix the PATRIOT Act. Some may see the vote we are about to have as relatively trivial. They are mistaken. While the bill we are voting on makes only

minor and, to quote the senior Senator from Pennsylvania, cosmetic changes to the PATRIOT Act, its significance is far greater.[88]

Senator Leahy (D-VT), who so vehemently urged his colleagues to pass the act in 2001, argued that the revised bill retained most of the "police state" provisions from the first Patriot Act: "Because the Republican leadership obstructed efforts to improve the bill, the 'police state' provisions . . . remain uncorrected."[89]

On March 2, 2006, eighty-nine Senators voted to support the 2006 act (provisions discussed shortly). Only ten senators opposed: Akaka (D-HI), Bingaman (D-NM), Byrd (D-WV), Feingold (D-WI), Harkin (D-IA), Jeffords (I-VT), Leahy (D-VT), Levin (D-MI), Murray (D-WA), and Wyden (D-OR). Inouye (D-HI) did not participate in the vote on the 2006 Patriot Act Renewal. Senator Barack Obama (D-IL) voted to support renewal of the act. So, too, did Senators Ted Kennedy (D-MA), Hillary Clinton (D-NY), and John Kerry (D-MA).[90]

Although the House bill mirrored the initial act, there was, once again, debate on the House floor revolving primarily around Sections 206 and 215, roving wiretaps and secret searches of personal records.[91] John Gingrey (R-GA) argued that Congress has a responsibility to protect Americans' constitutional rights. But, basing his assertions on Justice Department reports, he went on to emphasize,

since its enactment, there have been zero, and let me repeat zero, verified instances of civil liberty abuses under the USA PATRIOT Act found by the Inspector General of the Justice Department. And I firmly hope as we move forward with [this bill] and we continue to operate under the PATRIOT Act that that statistic will remain intact.[92]

An incensed Louise Slaughter (D-NY) countered with the following:

We have evidence which suggests, in contrast to information coming out of the Justice Department, that many of these measures have resulted in the violation of the civil liberties of American citizens. In addition, we understand that some of the extended search and seizure powers used by the law enforcement are apparently not being used for their intended purpose, which is strictly to fight terrorism, and that is unacceptable.[93]

Not surprisingly, Representative Dennis Kucinich (D-OH) continued to oppose the Patriot Act, arguing that the law violates Americans' civil liberties. He urged his colleagues to consider this issue:

> It has become crystal clear that this administration is currently and will continue to abuse, attack and outright deny the civil liberties of the people of this country in defiance of our constitution. . . . The administration is illegally wiretapping American citizens, illegally collecting information on peace groups and illegally signing statements to ignore the torture ban recently enacted by this Congress. . . . The administration is violating the laws Congress has passed, and they are violating the U.S. Constitution. I will not vote to give this administration any police powers until I am assured that their attack on our democracy is reined in. This Congress is walking away from the checks and balances of our democracy.[94]

Notwithstanding some opposition to reauthorization, the Patriot Act passed the House on March 2, 2006. There were 280 members of the House who voted in favor of reauthorizing the Patriot Act, 66 of whom were Democrats; 138 opposed, of which 13 were Republican and one independent.[95] The Patriot Improvement and Reauthorization Act was signed into law by President Bush on March 9, 2006; most of its powers as prescribed by the 2001 Patriot Act were retained, as will be discussed below.

Not surprisingly, a number of groups and organizations lobbied Congress to repeal the Patriot Act. A large contingent consisted of cyberspace advocacy groups, such as the Electronic Frontier Foundation, the Electronic Privacy Information Center, and the Center for Democracy and Technology. Because of concerns around disclosure of personal library records to the FBI, the American Library Association and the American Booksellers Foundation for Freedom of Expression also worked to abolish the Patriot Act. Even National Public Radio (NPR) sought to make more transparent the controversial nature of the revisions or lack thereof. NPR provided a clear presentation of the pros and cons of the controversial provisions of the act with regard to access to records and roving wiretaps.[96] Notwithstanding the opposition mounted from many other groups and organizations, revisions to the Patriot Act were passed.

Minor Drifts from the 2001 Patriot Act

The sixteen provisions of the 2001 act scheduled to expire in December 2005 were reauthorized by the 2006 Patriot Act. It extended fourteen provisions permanently, but subjected two provisions—Sections 206 and 215—to a sunset of December 31, 2009. The former allowed the government to obtain roving wiretaps and the latter made it easier for the government to conduct secret searches of personal records. Another controversial provision, Section 6001, which was extended, was aimed at thwarting the so-called lone wolf terrorist, an individual terrorist not affiliated with any specific organization or group.[97] This provision was also subject to sunset in 2009. It was intended to prevent the lone wolf or "independent" terrorist from slipping through the cracks of government surveillance in that it would allow the government to spy on any "non-U.S. person" who might be involved in terrorism but is not part of a terrorist group or is not an agent of a foreign power. It in effect widens the surveillance net.

There were some amendments in the 2006 act aimed at increasing the procedural safeguards that had fallen by the wayside in the 2001 act. These included, for example, (1) greater congressional oversight, (2) enhanced procedural protections, (3) a judicial review process for perceived Section 215 abuses, (4) nondisclosure requirements for Section 215, and (5) National Security Letters (NSLs) restrictions. More specifically, the amendments included the following:

Congressional Oversight. Section 106(h) of the act requires the attorney general to submit to Congress an annual report regarding the use of section 215 authority. The report must include (1) the total number of applications or orders made for section 215; and (2) the total number of such applications for library circulation records and patron lists; firearms sales records; tax return records; educational and medical records.

Enhanced Procedural Protections. Section 106(a)(2) of the act requires that application for a 215 order must be personally approved by one of the following three high-level officials: the FBI director, the FBI deputy director, or the executive assistant director for national security. The 2006 act also stipulates that FISA orders for roving wiretaps must include information about the "specific target of the electronic surveillance identified or described in the application." Also, FBI agents must notify the court every ten days after the device or wiretap location changes. Agents must also explain the facts and circumstances that justify the new surveillance.

Judicial Review Process. Section 106(f) of the act establishes a judicial review process for recipients of 215 orders to challenge their legality before a judge selected from a pool of FISA court judges.

Nondisclosure Requirements. Permits a recipient of a 215 order to disclose its existence to an attorney to obtain legal advice, as well as to other persons approved by the FBI.

NSL Restrictions. NSLs are a tool similar to a subpoena. They are generally used by the FBI to obtain information from companies as part of national security-related investigations. Unlike a Section 215 order for tangible items, an NSL does not need prior approval from a judge.[98] The use of NSLs increased dramatically after the Patriot Act was passed in 2001. Section 115 of the 2006 Act authorizes judicial review of a NSL.[99]

These amendments did not go very far to protect the civil liberties of Americans, particularly our privacy rights, and it is questionable as to whether any of these provisions were followed. For example, the U.S. Justice Department, as of March 2005, reported that only thirty-five FISC orders had been issued under Section 215 authority, none of which involved libraries or bookstores or medical or gun sale records.[100] In actuality, it was never clear as to how many orders were actually issued. As seen in the House debates presented above, data and other communications coming from the Justice Department as well as the FISC were generally disputed. And certainly, as will be discussed later, there were continual revelations of warrantless surveillance by the federal government.[101] The question is, Were the American people once again being lied to, and if so, had their trust and faith in the government begun to erode?

What makes the swift actions by the president and Congress even more curious is that prior to passage of the 2006 act, an investigative report by the *New York Times* dated December 16, 2005, exposed the secret, unconstitutional spying or surveillance activities of the government. Even more disconcerting is that this report, at the urging of the White House, had been suppressed for a year. A major media outlet had knowledge of the government's illegal activities since December 2004, but to comply with the executive branch's demands, concealed its findings until a year later. The report begins,

Months after the Sept. 11 attacks, President Bush secretly authorized the NSA to eavesdrop on Americans and others inside the United States to search for evidence of terrorist activity without the court-approved warrants ordinarily required for domestic spying, according to government officials. . . . Under a presidential order signed in 2002, the intelligence agency has monitored the international telephone calls and international e-mail messages of hundreds, perhaps thousands, of people inside the United States without warrants over the past three years in an effort to track possible "dirty numbers" linked to Al Qaeda, the officials said. The agency, they said, still seeks warrants to monitor entirely domestic communications.[102]

Thus, it was revealed that since 2001 the U.S. government was eavesdropping with the cooperation of major telecommunications companies and Silicon Valley on phone conversations, computer searches, and emails, inside the country without court approval, completely crossing the boundaries of legal and constitutional searches.[103] Americans' records were accessed by the NSA on an ongoing basis, twenty-four hours a day, on the remote possibility of some connection to terrorism. Billions of records were released not only by phone companies and Silicon Valley firms but also by hotels, banks, airlines, and car-rental companies.

The *New York Times* report notes that several current and former officials of the NSA were willing to disclose, under anonymity, their concerns about the NSA's unconstitutional actions.[104] These officials stated that the Bush administration had briefed congressional leaders about the program.

Congressional leaders from both political parties were brought to Vice President Dick Cheney's office in the White House. The leaders, who included the chairmen [*sic*] and ranking members of the Senate and House intelligence committees, learned of the NSA operation from Mr. Cheney, Lt. Gen. Michael V. Hayden of the Air Force, . . . and George J. Tenet, then the director of the CIA.[105]

Members of Congress also knew that a number of details about the spying program would remain secret. Interestingly, even Senator John D. Rockefeller IV (D-WV) expressed his reservations about the administration's eavesdropping activities. Rockefeller, who was vice chair of the Senate Intelligence Committee at the time, was also a judge presiding over one of the secret FISCs that oversaw and approved intelligence matters such as eavesdropping. Rockefeller voted in favor of the 2006 Patriot Act.

Conflict of interest.

The administration continued to justify the program as a necessary feature of its war on terror. President Bush maintained that he had "broad powers to order such searches, derived in part from the September 2001 Congressional resolution authorizing him to wage war on Al Qaeda and other terrorist groups."[106] The president also claimed that his authority under Article II of the Constitution to conduct foreign surveillance superseded statutory requirements under the FISA or the Patriot Act.

President Bush was exerting unitary power over the executive branch. As noted in chapter 1, much has been written about "unitary executive" theory, which holds that the president holds exclusive constitutional powers to control the entire federal civilian administrative apparatus.[107] Article II, Section 3 of the U.S. Constitution charges the president with responsibility to "take Care that the Laws be faithfully executed." This is an administrative presidency strategy claimed by the president to influence or even control public policy, in particular the war on terrorism, by circumventing Congress. But President Bush may have overstepped constitutional boundaries here by ignoring existing statutes governing surveillance as well as by justifying illegal interrogation methods of suspected terrorists, allowing for indefinite detention of those suspected and the use of military tribunals to prosecute them, all without congressional approval or judicial review.[108] This was a direct assault on conventional methods of power sharing in creating U.S. law and policy.

Vice President Dick Cheney also justified the administration's actions to bypass court review and authorize warrantless domestic eavesdropping, which, he argued, were

> part of a concerted effort to rebuild presidential powers weakened in the 1970s as a result of the Watergate scandal and the Vietnam War. . . . Watergate and a lot of the things around Watergate and Vietnam, both dur-

ing the 1970s, served, I think, to erode the authority. . . . The president needs to be effective, especially in the national-security area.[109]

This suggests that a hidden agenda of the Patriot Act was to strengthen the powers of the executive branch.

The *New York Times* report, along with other media outlets' accounts of the administration's secret activities, certainly pointed to an utter lack of transparency around the executive and legislative branches' actions to pass not only the 2001 Patriot Act but its 2006 revisions as well. These reports further indicate the unequivocal willingness of both branches of government to undermine our constitutional rights to privacy for the sake of what they maintained was national security.[110] This can be summed up by Justice Department attorney John Yoo, who argued that "while such actions could raise constitutional issues, in the face of devastating terrorist attacks 'the government may be justified in taking measures which in less troubled conditions could be seen as infringements of individual liberties.'"[111] With both the executive and congressional branches of government supporting the secret surveillance program, the policy drifts were certain to endure. From an institutional standpoint, two of the most powerful government organizations teamed up to create public policy that compromised Americans' privacy. Even the courts were unwilling to explicitly end the surveillance policies.

Amendments to the FISA

In 2007 Congress hastily passed and President Bush signed the Protect America Act of 2007, a temporary measure that further amended the FISA.[112] It formally removed the warrant requirement for government surveillance of foreign intelligence targets "reasonably believed" to be outside the United States. President Bush argued that the FISA was out of date because it did not apply to new technologies such as disposable cell phones and Internet-based communications. The act was thus intended to close a loophole created by new technology. According to Bush,

> To fix this problem, my administration has proposed a bill that would modernize the FISA statute. This legislation is the product of months of discussion with members of both parties in the House and the Senate. . . .

It seeks to restore the FISA to its original focus on protecting the privacy interest of people inside the United States, so we don't have to obtain court orders to effectively collect foreign intelligence about foreign targets located in foreign locations.[113]

The Bush administration, along with Republican congressional leaders, particularly Senator Mitch McConnell (R-KY), continued to argue that the nation was at risk of further terrorist attacks, thus justifying this legislation. Those Democrats facing reelection in relatively conservative districts the following year also helped to secure passage of the bill. It passed both houses of Congress, each of which was controlled by the Democrats, on August 3, 2007. The House vote was 227–183; 41 Democrats supported the Protect America Act, while only two Republicans opposed it: Timothy Johnson of Illinois and Walter Jones of North Carolina.[114] Key Democrats who opposed the bill included House Speaker Nancy Pelosi of California and, not surprisingly, liberal senators Dennis Kucinich and Louise Slaughter.

The Senate vote was 60–28. Republican senators voted overwhelming to pass the act; 16 Democrats and one independent (Joe Lieberman of Connecticut) voted for the bill. Key senators who opposed the bill included Obama, Clinton, Kennedy, Feingold, Leahy, and Senate majority leader Harry Reid (D-NV).[115] Senator John Kerry, along with eleven other senators, did not cast a vote.[116] President Bush signed the bill into law on August 5, 2007. The only concession congressional Democrats were able to secure was that the act would expire, or sunset, in six months. The purpose of sunset clauses is putatively to give Congress further opportunity to examine the efficacy and exigencies of specific policies at a later date. Importantly, as Liu points out, "Although . . . provisions are set to sunset, grandfather clauses permit them to remain effective with respect to investigations that began, or potential offenses that took place, before the sunset date."[117]

The Protect America Act included several controversial provisions, including one that replaced the FISA's requirement of a warrant to conduct surveillance with a system of NSA internal controls; and one that authorized the monitoring of all electronic communications between Americans "reasonably believed to be outside the United States" without a warrant or court order.[118]

Implications?

Civil liberties groups and humanitarian organizations criticized the Protect America Act, claiming that it authorized massive intelligence gathering without any oversight. The ACLU referred to it as the "Police America Act." These groups argued that the act reinforced the secret powers of the federal government under the Patriot Act. But again, both the executive and legislative branches were still able to capitalize on the "war on terror" and the fear that the nation would once again be attacked by terrorists.

When the Protect America Act expired after six months, in February 2008, the executive and legislative branches again moved quickly to pass the FISA Amendments Act of 2008, which reauthorized many provisions of the Protect America Act in Title VII of the FISA, including the granting of immunity for telecommunications companies that cooperate with government in intelligence gathering and surveillance. Under the 2008 amendments, the federal government is able to obtain a one-year FISC order, without probable cause, for general bulk collection of Americans' international communications without specifying who will be surveilled. The administration could make this decision exclusively, without any judicial review.[119] As Liu notes, "some provisions of Title VII could be characterized as relaxing FISA's traditional standards for electronic surveillance and access to stored communications."[120]

The FISA Amendments Act passed the House overwhelmingly by a 293–129 vote.[121] It passed the Senate, after a filibuster led by Senators Russ Feingold and Chris Dodd (D-CT), by 69–28. Senator Obama voted to support the amendments; Senators Clinton, Kerry, Feingold, and Leahy voted against.[122] The bill was signed into law by President Bush on July 10, 2008. The act would sunset at the end of 2012.[123] It was this amendment, as will be discussed later, that served as the legal basis for the mass surveillance that Edward Snowden disclosed in 2013.

The ACLU immediately filed a lawsuit challenging the eavesdropping provisions of the FISA Amendments Act of 2008 as a violation of free speech and privacy rights under the First and Fourth Amendments. The case, *Amnesty et al. v. McConnell*, was dismissed by federal district court judge John G. Koeltl, a Clinton appointee, on the grounds that the plaintiffs could not prove their claims.[124] The decision was overturned by the U.S. Court of Appeals for the Second Circuit in 2011.[125] The three-member panel, all Clinton appointees, argued that the government's eavesdropping violated the Fourth Amendment. However, on appeal to the U.S. Supreme Court, the lawsuit, now titled *Amnesty v. Clapper*, was dismissed. In a 5–4 decision, the High Court ruled that the plaintiffs did not have standing to sue because they "failed to show any threat of imminent harm or any concrete injury traceable to the statute."[126] The decision was reached along ideological lines, with the conservative bloc (Justices Alito, Scalia, Kennedy, Thomas, and Roberts) in the majority and the liberal bloc (Justices Sotomayor, Ginsburg, Breyer, and Kagan) in the minority. To the extent that the judicial branch of the federal government is controlled by a conservative majority, the surveillance policy drifts remain durable or stable. Again, from an institutional standpoint, all three branches of the federal government worked to support and maintain the policy drifts.

Obama Becomes President

In 2008 Barack Obama was elected president of the United States. One of his campaign promises was to end the war in Iraq when he took office; the war didn't officially end until 2011. Although the United States withdrew military operations from Iraq in 2011, it became involved again in 2014 as part of a coalition to respond to offensives carried out by the Islamic State of Iraq and Syria (ISIS or ISIL).[127] In addition, the war in Afghanistan was raging on and in fact was escalated by President Obama with his deployment of an additional thirty thousand U.S. troops.[128] Osama bin Laden was still being sought by the United States. Recall that then Senator Obama voted to support reauthorization of the Patriot Act in 2006, voted against the Protect America Act of 2007, but voted in favor of the FISA Amendments Act of 2008.

Another one of President Obama's campaign promises was to end warrantless wiretapping. He vowed to "repeal the U.S. Patriot Act . . . and consider replacing that shoddy and dangerous law with a new, carefully crafted proposal that addressed in a much more limited fashion the legitimate needs of law enforcement in combating terrorism."[129] But within three months of Obama's assuming office, the *New York Times* once again revealed that the U.S. government had overstepped its wiretapping authority, this time under the FISA Amendments Act of 2008. It reported that the NSA had

intercepted private e-mail messages and phone calls of Americans in recent months on a scale that went beyond the broad legal limits established by Congress [in the 2008 Act]. . . . Several intelligence officials, as
well as lawyers briefed about the matter, said the NSA had been engaged
in "overcollection" of domestic communications of Americans. They described the practice as significant and systemic, although one official said
it was believed to have been unintentional.[130]

Even more troubling was Obama's decision in February 2010 to sign
a one-year extension of those provisions of the Patriot Act set to expire
on December 31, 2009. The provisions included

- court-approved roving wiretaps that permit surveillance on multiple
  phones;
- court-approved seizure of records and property in anti-terrorism operations;
- surveillance against a "lone wolf," a non-U.S. citizen engaged in terrorism
  who may not be part of a recognized terrorist group.[131]

Democratic leaders in Congress yet again endorsed the Patriot Act,
even though its transgressions against Americans' privacy rights had been
exposed. Were Americans still living in fear or simply apathetic to these issues? Were they not lobbying their legislators to repeal the act? One explanation for our reticence is that we knew very little about the Patriot Act's
extension: Congress embedded (in other words, hid) the vote to renew the
Patriot Act in an amendment to the Medicare Physician Payment Reform
Act of 2010. The House roll call for that amendment, which included the
concealed agenda item of extending provisions of the Patriot Act, was 315–
97. Democrats who voted in favor outnumbered Republicans: 162 Democrats and 153 Republicans voted to extend the Patriot Act.[132] Although a
number of senators publicly denounced the measure, the Senate passed it
unanimously by voice vote without debate.[133]

More Chinks in the Armor

In November 2009 Private Bradley (now Chelsea) Manning, an
intelligence analyst for the Army, who had extensive access to

classified databases, began communicating with Julian Assange, head of WikiLeaks, to determine whether Assange could be trusted with secret military documents that Manning was about to disclose.[134] WikiLeaks is an international, nonprofit organization that publishes news leaks and secret or classified information from anonymous sources. In January 2010 Manning began to download close to 500,000 documents that would become known as the "Iraq War logs" and the "Afghanistan War logs." Shortly afterward, he sent these documents to WikiLeaks.[135] On February 18, 2010, WikiLeaks posted the first of the material from Manning.[136] Many of the documents were classified diplomatic cables between American and foreign embassies, which could potentially expose the behavior and actions of the U.S. military.

One of the most disturbing actions involved Manning's leaking of a video of an American helicopter attack in Baghdad in 2007. The attack killed twelve people, including a reporter and a driver for Reuters.[137] Although these revelations are not directly related to the Patriot Act, Manning is considered one of the national security whistleblowers, seeking to expose the nature of the wars in Afghanistan and Iraq, particularly the collateral damage (i.e., the killing of innocent civilians). The concerns around the leaks revolve more around military and diplomatic communications rather than privacy rights. Manning claimed that he was motivated to promote more transparency over U.S. foreign policy. Others claimed that Manning's motivation stemmed from his efforts to retaliate against the military for its negative and regressive policies toward gay and lesbian personnel. Manning would later transition from male to female.[138] In any case, it was yet another event that revealed the government's secret activities to the American people.

In May 2010 Manning was arrested and charged on a number of counts, including "aiding the enemy." In July 2013 an Army judge acquitted Manning of aiding the enemy, which could have resulted in a death sentence, but Manning was found guilty of espionage under the 1917 Espionage Act. Manning was sentenced to thirty-five years in prison, but in January 2017 President Obama commuted her sentence. After serving seven years of her sentence, she was released in May 2017.[139] Manning's actions, however legal they may or may not be, created further public outcry regarding U.S. military action in the Middle East, eroding the popular support for fighting terrorism that previously fueled support for the Patriot Act. It certainly brought greater transparency to U.S. government operations in Iraq, which the public would eventually demand regarding the government's secret surveillance program.

Democracy's "Snooze Button"

At this point, one might again ask why there have been so many sunsets and subsequent extensions of the FISA or Patriot Act. As noted earlier, the purpose of a sunset clause is to force Congress to reconsider a law or portions of a law before they expire. Sofia Ranchordá suggests that "sunset clauses have been used to guarantee a renewed legislative oversight on a particular legislative topic and respective laws. Sunset clauses can be employed to . . . terminate laws that are no longer necessary or effective."[140] She goes on to note that, with respect to the Patriot Act, "sunset provisions were included in order to limit the duration of measures constraining fundamental rights."[141] But by continually extending the act with virtually no discernible changes, Congress in effect placed no limit on the duration of measures that compromised Americans' privacy rights.

Because Sections 206 and 215—roving wiretap authority and secret searches of personal records—are two of the most controversial aspects of the Patriot Act, Congress has repeatedly voted to push back the expiration date of these two provisions. Perhaps these were symbolic gestures on the part of members of Congress to appease their constituents or cajole them into thinking that their best interests were being carefully guarded and protected; or perhaps it has more to do with promoting democratic governance through smoke and mirrors. David Fahrenthold aptly refers to sunset provisions as "democracy's snooze button."[142]

In May 2011 extensions were again made to the Patriot Act in an effort to prevent significant sections from expiring. Interestingly, the bill would formally be known as the Patriot Sunsets Extension Act. Sections 206 and 215 would once again be extended, as would the lone-wolf provisions, applying to individual terrorists not affiliated with specific organizations. These amendments were extended until June 1, 2015.

By now, it seemed like déjà vu: the extensions of the controversial provisions once again provoked some debate in Congress, but they passed both houses. In the House, Kucinich strongly opposed the bill as "another abdication of our constitutional duty to conduct oversight and protect our most basic civil liberties."[143] In the Senate, Patrick Leahy (D-VT) and Rand Paul (R-KY) led a bipartisan effort against the bill. Senator Paul is the son of the former representative Ron Paul (R-TX), who it may be recalled was one of three Republicans in the House who voted against the first Patriot Act, passed in 2001. A supporter of the Tea Party movement and a staunch libertarian, Rand Paul would go on to join an advocacy group, FreedomWorks, in filing a Fourth Amendment class-action lawsuit against the government for its bulk collection of Americans' phone records, as will be further discussed later in this chapter.

Senator Paul argued that

> there has been a lot of discussion of the PATRIOT Act, and we are told basically that we wouldn't be able to capture these terrorists if we didn't give up some of our liberties, if we didn't give up some of the fourth amendment and allow it to be easier for the police to come into our homes. We were so frightened after 9/11 that we readily gave up these freedoms. We said: Well, the fourth amendment is not that important. We will just let the government look at all of our records, and we will make it easier for the government to look at our records. The question we have to ask, though, is whether we would still be able to catch terrorists by using the fourth amendment as it was intended and having the protections of the fourth amendment.[144]

He goes on to point to the wide net cast by government surveillance, and exposes the fact that it has absolutely nothing to do with terrorist activities:

> Right now, if someone has a Visa bill that is over $5,000 and chooses to pay for it over the phone, which is a wire transfer, the government is probably looking at their Visa bill. They don't have to show probable cause, and they don't have to have a judge's warrant. This does apply to U.S. citizens. . . . With regard to these suspicious activity reports, we have done over 4 million of them in the last 10 years. We are now doing over 1 million a year. These suspicious activity reports, all the trigger is—it doesn't have to have anything to do with terrorism. The trigger is just that someone has over $5,000 that they have transferred by bank account.[145]

The Republican-controlled House passed the bill 250–153; 54 Democrats voted to approve the bill, and 31 Republicans voted against it. John Boehner (R-OH), Speaker of the House, did not vote; Democrats who opposed the bill included House Speaker Nancy Pelosi of California, Kucinich, and Slaughter.[146] The Democratic-controlled Senate passed the bill 74–23; 30 Democrats supported the bill. Four Republicans opposed the bill: Dean Heller (NV), Mike Lee (UT), Lisa Murkowski (AK), and Rand Paul (KY). Senate minority leader Mitch McConnell (R-KY) obviously voted to support it, as did the bill's sponsor, Mary Landrieu (D-LA).[147] Other Democrats voting to support the bill included John Kerry (MA), who has flip-flopped on his Patriot Act votes, Senate majority leader Harry Reid (NV), Dianne Feinstein (CA), and Kirsten Gillibrand (NY).

On May 26, 2011, President Obama signed the bill while out of the country; he authorized the use of an "autopen," which is a signature reproduction device. A year later, he signed the FISA Amendments Act Reauthorization Act of 2012, which extends Title VII of the FISA until December 31, 2017. Recall that the FISA Amendments Act of 2008, which was the legal basis for mass surveillance programs conducted without probable cause, expired at the end of 2012.[148] Despite President Obama's campaign promises, he pushed for and maintained the policies of the Bush administration. He justified his continued support for aggressive surveillance by the NSA because it aided in the hunt for Osama bin Laden, who was finally killed by Navy SEALS on May 1, 2011, weeks before he signed the bill extending the Patriot Act. President Obama announced that the United States had conducted an operation that killed bin Laden. He went on to say that the "death of bin Laden marks the most significant achievement to date in our nation's effort to defeat Al Qaeda. But his death does not mark the end of our effort. There's no doubt that Al Qaeda will continue to pursue attacks against us. We must and we will remain vigilant at home and abroad."[149] Obama, like Bush before him, continued to stoke the fears of the American people. Obama also needed to show his prowess in the war on terror as a platform in his 2012 reelection bid. The federal government seemed to be running on autopilot, and the concern for privacy rights was perhaps no longer on Americans' radar screens.

Edward Snowden Blows the Whistle

On June 6, 2013, the *Guardian* ran an article that exposed the extent to which the NSA was spying on Americans. The article began by stating that the "National Security Agency is currently collecting the telephone records of millions of U.S. customers of Verizon, one of America's largest telecoms providers, under a top secret court order issued in April."[150] It goes on to say that the FISC order

> shows for the first time that under the Obama administration the communication records of millions of U.S. citizens are being collected indiscriminately and in bulk—regardless of whether they are suspected of any wrongdoing. The secret Foreign Intelligence Surveillance Court . . . granted the order to the FBI on April 25, giving the government unlimited authority to obtain the data for a specified three-month period ending on July 19. Under the terms of the blanket order, the numbers of both parties on a call are handed over, as is location data, call duration, unique identifiers, and the time and duration of all calls. . . . The court order expressly bars Verizon from disclosing to the public either the existence of the FBI's request for its customers' records, or the court order itself. . . . The information is classed as "metadata," or transactional information, rather than communications, and so does not require individual warrants to access.[151]

playing the system.

Although data breaches under the Bush administration had been widely exposed, as discussed earlier, the revelation of this top-secret document indicated for the first time that the Obama administration had continued the government's surveillance of the American people on a massive scale. The NSA, even under his administration, had hacked into fiber-optic cables that linked datacenters of Yahoo and Google outside the United States. Interestingly, Senators Ron Wyden (D-OR) and Mark Udall (D-CO) had made public statements over a period of two years denouncing the Obama administration's secret surveillance activities. But they were largely ignored.

It wasn't until several weeks later that we learned that the disclosure of the information had been made by Edward Snowden, a contract employee for the NSA.[152] Snowden said that much of what he was witnessing "really disillusioned me about how my government functions and what its impact is in the world. I realized that I was part of something that was doing far more harm than good."[153] He went on to say that

> Obama's campaign promises and election gave me faith that he would lead us toward fixing the problems he outlined in his quest for votes. Many Americans felt similarly. Unfortunately, shortly after assuming power, he closed the door on investigating systematic violations of law, deepened and expanded several abusive programmes, and refused to spend political capital to end the kind of human rights violations we see in Guantanamo, where men still sit without charge.[154]

Snowden believed that surveillance by the government had spiraled out of control at the expense of Americans' privacy rights. He maintained that the American people had been betrayed.

> Billions of U.S. communications are being intercepted. In gathering evidence of wrongdoing I focused on the wronging of the American people, but believe me when I say that the surveillance we live under is the highest privilege compared to how we treat the rest of the world. [The program is] indiscriminate and it's sweeping. It's a government program designed to collect information about all Americans, not just people where they believe there's reason to think they've done anything wrong.[155]

Upon Snowden's disclosures, the editors of the *New York Times* lambasted President Obama:

> Within hours of the disclosure that federal authorities routinely collect data on phone calls Americans make, regardless of whether they have any bearing on a counterterrorism investigation, the Obama administration issued the same platitude it has offered every time President Obama has been caught overreaching in the use of his powers: Terrorists are a real menace and you should just trust us to deal with them because we have internal mechanisms (that we are not going to tell you about) to make sure we do not violate your rights. Those reassurances have never been persuasive—whether on secret warrants to scoop up a news agency's phone records or secret orders to kill an American

suspected of terrorism—especially coming from a president who once promised transparency and accountability. The administration has now lost all credibility on this issue. Mr. Obama is proving the truism that the executive branch will use any power it is given and very likely abuse it.[156]

In addition, members of Congress scrambled around to introduce various bills to address concerns regarding privacy and civil liberties (e.g., the Intelligence Oversight and Surveillance Reform Act, the Ending Secret Law Act, the FISA Court in the Sunshine Act, and the USA Freedom Act, which was introduced in 2013 and passed only in the House). Had Congress just now realized the extent to which our privacy rights were being violated? Well, yes, according to some members of Congress. Representative Jim Sensenbrenner (R-WI), for example, a staunch opponent of the Patriot Act, argued that the attorneys for the Bush and Obama administrations "intentionally misinterpreted Section 215 and kept lawmakers in the dark about the bulk collection." Many, he said, including himself, "had little knowledge of the breadth of the data collection until the 2013 leaks from whistleblower Edward Snowden. . . . Congress never intended Section 215 to allow bulk collection. This program is illegal and based on a blatant misinterpretation of the law."[157] Yet it seems incredible that Congress was completely in the dark about the degree to which our constitutional right to privacy had been abrogated.

The Courts Weigh In Again

Several lawsuits were filed upon disclosure that the NSA was collecting phone data from millions of Americans. The sense of urgency around these cases seemed much greater than that of the cases filed before the Snowden revelations, perhaps because of the publicity surrounding the leaks. Larry Klayman, a conservative activist and founder of Judicial Watch and Freedom Watch, filed his first federal lawsuit the day after the *Guardian* published Snowden's revelations. Klayman charged that the U.S. government was conducting "a secret and illegal government scheme to intercept and analyze vast quantities of domestic telephonic communications" in violation of the First, Fourth, and Fifth

Amendments.[158] Judge Richard J. Leon of the U.S. District Court for the District of Columbia, appointed by President George W. Bush, ruled that the bulk collection of American telephone metadata violated the plaintiffs' privacy rights under the Fourth Amendment.[159] In *Klayman v. Obama*, Judge Leon stated,

> I cannot imagine a more "indiscriminate" and "arbitrary invasion" than this systematic and high-tech collection and retention of personal data on virtually every single citizen for purposes of querying and analyzing it without prior judicial approval. Surely, such a program infringes on "that degree of privacy" that the Founders enshrined in the Fourth Amendment. Indeed, I have little doubt that the author of our Constitution, James Madison, who cautioned us to beware "the abridgement of freedom of the people by gradual and silent encroachments by those in power," would be aghast.[160]

Responding to the government's claim that the collection of metadata—which reveals who is talking with whom—was necessary for protecting the nation's borders, the court went on to say that there had not been "a single instance in which analysis of the NSA's bulk metadata collection actually stopped an imminent attack, or otherwise aided the Government in achieving any objective that was time-sensitive in nature."[161] Interestingly, in rendering its ruling, the district court drew heavily on the 1979 U.S. Supreme Court decision in *Smith v. Maryland*.[162]

Briefly, *Smith v. Maryland* involved a local government's temporary use of a pen register on Michael Lee Smith, suspected of robbing a woman and, after learning that she identified him to the police, making threatening phone calls to her home. Recall that a pen register is an automatic mechanism that can trace all phone numbers from a designated telephone line. The lower courts ruled against Smith, who appealed the case to the U.S. Supreme Court. In a 5–3 decision, the Court ruled against Smith, arguing that a pen register is not a search because the petitioner, by dialing his phone, "voluntarily conveyed numerical information to the phone company."[163] And because the telephone conversations were not recorded, Smith did not have a reasonable expectation of privacy in the numbers he dialed. The *Smith* decision thus left pen registers completely outside constitutional protection under the Fourth Amendment.

The *Klayman* court, while not overturning *Smith v. Maryland*, found the Court's analysis somewhat outdated:

> When do present-day circumstances—the evolutions in the Government's surveillance capabilities, citizens' phone habits, and the relationship between the NSA and telecom companies—become so thoroughly unlike those considered by the Supreme Court thirty-four years ago that a precedent like *Smith* simply does not apply? The answer, unfortunately for the Government, is now.[164]

The *Klayman* court reasoned that in *Smith v. Maryland*, the pen register was operational for only about two weeks. In addition, according to the court, the "relationship between the police and the phone company in *Smith* is nothing compared to the relationship that has apparently evolved over the last seven years between the Government and telecom companies."[165] In his last, most fervent point, Judge Leon ruled that

> the almost-Orwellian technology that enables the Government to store and analyze the phone metadata of every telephone user in the United States is unlike anything that could have been conceived in 1979. In *Smith*, the Supreme Court was actually considering whether local police could collect one person's phone records for calls made after the pen register was installed and for the limited purpose of a small-scale investigation of harassing phone calls. . . . The notion that the Government could collect similar data on hundreds of millions of people and retain that data for a five-year period, updating it with new data every day in perpetuity, was at best, in 1979, the stuff of science fiction.[166]

Notwithstanding the district court's impassioned ruling in *Klayman*, it issued a preliminary injunction barring the government from collecting plaintiffs' call records, but most surprisingly stayed the order pending appeal by the U.S. government.

In 2015 the U.S. Court of Appeals for the D.C. Circuit, in a very convoluted ruling, reversed the district court's decision in *Klayman* and remanded the case for further proceedings.[167] The appeals court argued in part that the case could go forward but the plaintiffs had not met a threshold requirement of showing that *their own* records were being collected; it thus questioned whether they had standing to sue. The three-member panel, all Republican appointees, stated that the

> record, as it stands in the very early stages of this litigation, leaves some doubt about whether plaintiffs' own metadata was ever collected. . . . Plaintiffs must establish a "substantial likelihood of success on the merits." Although one could reasonably infer from the evidence presented the government collected plaintiffs' own metadata, one could also conclude the opposite. Having barely fulfilled the requirements for standing at this threshold stage, Plaintiffs fall short of meeting the higher burden of proof required for a preliminary injunction.[168]

The procedural ruling here does not address the constitutionality or legality of the NSA program. As such, the ruling provided the NSA with a green light to continue collecting the phone records of millions of Americans, at least until, as the court argued, a new law banning the practice was passed.

In another high-profile case spurred by Snowden's revelations, Senator Rand Paul (R-KY) along with FreedomWorks also sued the government in 2014 over its collection of bulk telephone metadata. In *Paul v. Obama*, Senator Paul alleged that the phone metadata program violated the Fourth Amendment. But in light of the *Klayman* decision, the case was ultimately dismissed in May 2015.[169]

In 2013 the ACLU, also in response to the disclosures by Snowden, challenged the legality of the NSA's bulk phone metadata collection program. In *ACLU v. Clapper*, the U.S. district court dismissed the case, arguing that the metadata collection did not violate the Fourth Amendment.[170] District court judge William H. Pauley III, appointed by President Clinton, justified the program on the grounds that the war against terror sometimes requires the collection of large amounts of information and that Section 215 of the Patriot Act impliedly precludes judicial review. The court argued that "there is no way for the Government to know which particle of telephony metadata will lead to useful counterterrorism information. When that is the case, courts routinely authorize large-scale collections of information, even if most of it will not directly bear on the investigation."[171]

On appeal, the U.S. Court of Appeals for the Second Circuit reversed. The three-member panel, all Democratic appointees, unanimously ruled that provisions of the Patriot Act never legitimately authorized the bulk collection of domestic calling records.[172] The court ruled that the law has

> never been interpreted to authorize anything approaching the breadth of the sweeping surveillance at issue. . . . The sheer volume of information sought is staggering; while search warrants and subpoenas for business records may encompass large volumes of paper documents or electronic data, the most expansive of such evidentiary demands are dwarfed by the volume of records obtained pursuant to the orders in question here.[173]

Interestingly, the court seemed to question Congress's failure to fully grasp privacy breaches insofar as it continued to renew the Patriot Act. The court argued that if it acceded to the government's practices,

> it could use § 215 to collect and store in bulk any other existing metadata available anywhere in the private sector, including metadata associated with financial records, medical records, and electronic communications (including e-mail and social media information) relating to all Americans. Such expansive development of government repositories of formerly private records would be an unprecedented contraction of the privacy expectations of all Americans. Perhaps such a contraction is required by national security needs in the face of the dangers of contemporary domestic and international terrorism. But we would expect such a momentous decision to be preceded by substantial debate, and expressed in unmistakable language. *There is no evidence of such a debate in the legislative history of § 215.*[174]

Although the court ruled that the telephone metadata program was illegal (i.e., in violation of Section 215 of the law), it did not rule that the program violated the First or Fourth Amendments.[175] The court in part yielded to the executive branch in that it did not issue an injunction. The appeals court remanded the case to the federal district court for further proceedings. The district court has not issued another ruling, and given the passage of the USA Freedom Act in 2015 as discussed below, it is unlikely that it will.[176]

One additional high-profile case was *Smith v. Obama*.[177] In this case, Anna Smith, an emergency neonatal nurse from Idaho, along with the Electronic Frontier Foundation (EFF), the ACLU, and the ACLU of Idaho, filed suit against the government on the grounds that Smith's privacy rights had been violated by the NSA's routine collection of her metadata through Verizon. Although the federal district court raised concerns about the constitutionality of the NSA's actions, it dismissed the case, claiming that Smith "has no expectation of privacy in the telephone numbers that she dials."[178] The district court judge, B. Lynn Winmill, appointed by President Clinton, cited the Supreme Court's 1979 decision in *Smith v. Maryland* to justify the ruling, arguing that the High Court's ruling in 1979 had never been overturned and thus "continues to bind this Court."[179] Unlike the district court's ruling in *Klayman*, which interpreted the *Smith v. Maryland* ruling very narrowly, the *Smith* court followed the reasoning of the 1979 High Court case.

Anna Smith appealed the decision to the Ninth Circuit Court of Appeals, which heard arguments on December 8, 2014.[180] In March 2016 the appeals court ruled that Smith's claims of ongoing collection of metadata were moot in light of passage of the USA Freedom Act, discussed below, which ended the government's bulk collection of domestic phone records. The court vacated and remanded the case for dismissal.[181]

These judicial rulings, whether issued by judges appointed by Democratic or Republican presidents, seemed to provide a nod to the executive as well as the legislative branches. The lower courts in some cases clearly do not agree with the government's mass surveillance programs, and in one case found them illegal; but they fall short of halting the programs or ruling that they are in violation of the Fourth Amendment. Perhaps they are playing politics, as seen in the U.S. Court of Appeals for the Second Circuit ruling in *ACLU v. Clapper* discussed above; in that case, the court clearly expects Congress, not the courts, to properly legislate the issues, and even questions why it has allowed the privacy abuses to continue with each iteration of the Patriot Act.

Patriot Act Redux

At least since the passage of the Patriot Act in October 2001, the executive branch has been secretly surveilling the American people. And with each subsequent amendment, Congress has provided a legal basis for the spying programs. The courts have weighed in and in some cases have attacked the surveillance programs, but have still allowed them to continue. With expiration of these programs on June 1, 2015, the executive and legislative branches again set in motion another round of activity to, for at least some members of Congress, protect this nation's borders. In light of Snowden's revelations, however, others wanted a new law that would end the NSA's bulk collection of Americans' metadata and stop the FISC from issuing secret orders enabling the NSA's secret activities.

Several members of the House as well as Senators Leahy (D-VT) and Mike Lee (R-UT) immediately seized on the appeals court ruling in *ACLU v. Clapper* as justification for scaling back the Patriot Act.[182] They issued a statement holding that "Congress should not reauthorize a bulk collection program that the court has found to violate the law. We will not consent to any extension of this program."[183] President Obama was also supportive of ending the NSA's metadata program.

On April, 28, 2015, Representative Sensenbrenner (R-WI) introduced to the House the USA Freedom Act, sometimes referred to as the Patriot Act II.[184] While some Republican leaders supported extending the controversial aspects of the government's surveillance program through December 31, 2017, many in the House, particularly the Democrats, supported ending them. Remarks by Sensenbrenner in an earlier debate reflect the concerns of Democrats and some Republicans:

> I believe the PATRIOT Act made America safer by enhancing the government's ability to find and stop terrorist attacks. We were careful to maintain the civil liberties that distinguish us from our enemies. We are here today because the government misapplied the law and upset the balance between privacy and security that we had fought to preserve 13 years ago. In a feat of legal gymnastics, the administration convinced the FISA Court that, because some records in the universe of every phone call Americans made might be relevant to counterterrorism, the entire universe of calls must be relevant. That decision opened the floodgates

to a practice of bulk collection that Congress never intended when the PATRIOT Act was passed. Senator Leahy and I introduced the USA FREEDOM Act to end bulk collection, increase transparency, and to re-establish a proper balance between privacy and security.[185]

He continued,

The FREEDOM Act gives private companies greater discretion to disclose their cooperation with the government. These disclosures give the companies increased autonomy and will alert the public to the extent of data collection. The bill also requires public notification of any FISC decision that contains a significant construction of law—expressly including interpretations of the "specific selection term." This is the end of secret laws. If the administration abuses the intent of the bill, everyone will know.[186]

This statement captures the essence of the act that eventually passed: the government would no longer expressly collect bulk metadata, but because private telecommunications companies retain such data, they would be available for government searches in cases when the FISC approves. So the government could continue to spy on Americans via private companies' data banks. Companies such as AT&T, Verizon, and Sprint would hold on to phone records for eighteen months to five years.

There was an extraordinary degree of bipartisan support for this bill, passing the House 338–88.[187] There were 196 Republicans who voted for the bill, and 142 Democrats. Key Democrats who voted to support included Pelosi and Slaughter, who had been one of the major opponents of all iterations of the Patriot Act (Kucinich, also a major opponent, was no longer serving in Congress). House Speaker John Boehner (R-OH), who would not permit amendments to the bill on the House floor, supported the bill. Many of the House members who opposed the bill supported a stronger bill that would renew the existing version of the act calling for bulk data collection.

Senate majority leader Mitch McConnell (R-KY) was intent on maintaining the NSA's existing programs, and promised to gain bipartisan support to undercut the House's version of the bill, which he criticized as "'an untested, untried and more cumbersome system' that would neither 'keep us safe or protect our privacy. Section 215 helps us find a needle in the haystack. But under the USA Freedom Act, there might not be a haystack at all.'"[188]

Senator Rand Paul, McConnell's junior home-state colleague, disagreed. Paul wanted the law to be directed explicitly to terrorists, not Americans. He argued that

> one of the promises that was given when the PATRIOT Act was originally passed was that, in exchange for allowing a less than constitutional standard, we would only use the actions against . . . terrorists and against foreigners. We found that 99 percent of the time, section 213 is used for domestic crime. I believe that no section of the PATRIOT Act should be passed unless our targets are terrorists—not Americans.[189]

Senator Leahy, who co-sponsored the Senate's version of the bill with Senator Lee, supported the House's version of the bill:

> Section 215 of the USA PATRIOT Act expires in a matter of weeks. Senator Lee and I have a bipartisan bill, the USA FREEDOM Act, that would end the use of section 215 to authorize the bulk collection of Americans' phone records and replace it with a more targeted program. It also would enact other important reforms to bring more accountability and transparency to government surveillance. . . . Last week, some opponents came to the floor to voice their opposition. They claimed that ending this bulk collection program would somehow put our national security at risk and that a bulk collection program like this could somehow have prevented the September 11 attacks. . . . But numerous national security experts also have concluded that the NSA's bulk collection program is not essential to national security. . . . We can end the dragnet collection of innocent Americans' phone records and keep our country safe.[190]

Senator Harry Reid (D-NV) also supported the House's version and criticized Senator McConnell for his recalcitrance and negligence:

> 2 years ago the American people first became aware that the National Security Agency was collecting private information about their phone calls. This is called the Snowden revelation. Under the banner of national security, the National Security Agency was mining information about

[handwritten margin notes: I'm on the fence... I see the issue but at the same time I'm not calling anyone that I can y they know about. It's simple. The principle they are upset about. Yet they don't get upset about the violations police make to Americans visually!]

home phone calls and how long they lasted. They found out whom they were calling—and not only that. They found out whom the call was between. They also determined how long that call lasted. NSA essentially was conducting a dragnet, without first attempting to determine whether that information was relevant to a national security problem. NSA ran this program under the authorities granted to them by section 215 of the PATRIOT Act, which expires on June 1 of this year. . . . There have been bipartisan and bicameral calls for the Senate to take up that legislation. Yet again, instead of committing to bringing up this bipartisan bill, last month the senior Senator from Kentucky [McConnell] introduced a bill that would extend the authorities for the National Security Agency's bulk collection program for 5 1/2 years. . . . I think, most importantly, if the senior Senator from Kentucky does not allow this commonsense reform simply with a vote on the Senate floor about what happened in the House, they are ignoring the rare bipartisan support that we have.[191]

On June 2, 2015, over fierce opposition by McConnell, the Senate passed the USA Freedom Act without amendment by a vote of 67–32. There were forty-four Democrats supporting the bill along with twelve Republicans and one independent, Bernie Sanders of Vermont. Senator McConnell not surprisingly voted no, as did Senators John McCain (R-AZ), Lindsey Graham (R-SC), Charles Grassley (R-IA), Orrin Hatch (R-UT), and Rand Paul, who all supported a stronger bill. No Democrats voted against the bill.[192] President Obama, who strongly supported ending the metadata program, signed the USA Freedom Act into law that same day. The USA Freedom Act is the ten-letter backronym for Uniting and Strengthening America by Fulfilling Rights and Ending Eavesdropping, Dragnet-Collection and Online Monitoring Act. As noted, with passage of this act, the NSA, within six months or by December 2015, would no longer be able to collect phone records; however, it could access them through telecommunications companies with an FISC order. Other provisions of the law are extended through 2019.

Also, while the USA Freedom Act ends the government's bulk collection of domestic phone records, it *does not* end the collection of other data, such as emails and the content of Americans' international phone calls. Thus, the act represents a very modest policy drift, and therefore, Americans' privacy rights are still very much at risk.

Some former NSA career bureaucrats criticized the bill, referring to it as the "Free-dumb Act." William Binney, for example, has continued to speak out against the NSA's data collection policies, arguing that the Freedom Act does not go far enough to protect Americans' privacy. Giving the NSA access to personal records via phone companies does nothing more than maintain the status quo, according to Binney and the others.[193]

The Executive Branch Rides Again

Notwithstanding President Obama's desire to end the metadata collection program, shortly after he signed the law he applied to the FISC to restart the bulk collection of data for six months. Recall that the law provided for the program to end by December 2015. The six-month "orderly" transition period was intended to provide the NSA with time to move to the new system whereby the phone companies would maintain phone records. However, the law was silent on whether the NSA could actually continue collecting *bulk* data during that six-month period. The FISC approved the Obama administration's request. Marc Raimondi, a spokesperson for the Justice Department, justified the action: "As we've repeatedly stated before, we believe the program is lawful."[194] Freedom-Works immediately filed a motion in the FISC for an injunction; the motion was rejected.[195]

The ACLU also challenged the FISC action, pointing to the ruling of the Second Circuit Court of Appeals in *ACLU v. Clapper*, discussed earlier, that the surveillance program was illegal. The FISC responded, opining that the Second Circuit ruling was wrong. FISC Judge Michael Mosman, George W. Bush's appointee to the U.S. District Court of Oregon, stated that "Second Circuit rulings are not binding on FISC, and this court respectfully disagrees with that court's analysis, especially in view of the intervening enactment of the USA FREEDOM Act."[196]

The ACLU returned to the Second Circuit seeking an injunction to prevent the government from collecting metadata for another six months, but was dealt another blow. In *ACLU v. Clapper* the court ruled, "While we find that Appellants' claims are not moot at this time, we decline to disturb the decision by Congress to provide for a 180-day transition period to put an orderly end to the telephone metadata program. We therefore deny the motion for a preliminary injunction."[197]

In addition, on November 9, 2015, Judge Richard Leon, who wrote a scathing indictment against the government for its surveillance program in the *Klayman v. Obama* case discussed previously, was asked by the D.C. appeals court to weigh in. He wrote,

> With the Government's authority to operate the Bulk Telephony Metadata Program quickly coming to an end, this case is perhaps the last chapter in the Judiciary's evaluation of this particular Program's compatibility with the Constitution. It will not, however, be the last chapter in the ongoing struggle to balance privacy rights and national security interests under our Constitution in an age of evolving technological wizardry. Although this Court appreciates the zealousness with which the Government seeks to protect the citizens of our Nation, that same Government bears just as great a responsibility to protect the individual liberties of those very citizens.[198]

Yet even here, Judge Leon only ordered the NSA to stop collecting phone records for one Verizon customer: Klayman and his law firm. The ruling has more symbolic value, as its practical importance is minimal. So the government was able to continue with its metadata program through, theoretically, December 2015. Nonetheless, as noted earlier, even though the "orderly" transition period has since expired, telecommunications companies are able to retain and access the data on their customers, and the NSA can compel these companies, with a warrant from the FISC, to provide the agency with these data. In effect, NSA spying has not ended.

In sum, the USA Freedom Act does make some changes to the 2001 Patriot Act and its various amendments, but it still amounts to a small policy drift, thus leaving intact the government's mass surveillance program.[199] The many passionate debates around the act show a high level of interest across branches of government, but in the end their actions led to little real policy change. As noted, the NSA can still access Americans' phone records, providing they use "a specific selection term" on the basis of "reasonable articulable suspicion" that the call is linked to a "foreign power engaged in international terrorism."[200] In addition, the law requires that FISC decisions be declassified for the first time if they are "significant."

And, as noted, under the 2015 act the government is still allowed to collect other data from Americans, such as emails and the content of international phone calls. Internet searches may also still be vulnerable. Senator Paul argued that even with passage of the Freedom Act, the government maintains massive surveillance powers; he said that "the government's reach into individuals' lives remained too intrusive."[201] And we still do not know the extent to which innocent persons have been placed on watch lists or detained for a suspicious phone call.

We have also learned that the federal government has continued to mislead the American people by claiming that mass surveillance has been effective in counterterrorism. The New America Foundation, a Washington-based nonprofit group, found that bulk data sweeps have not enhanced the government's efficacy in protecting America's borders. That is, the NSA has not been able to demonstrate that the bulk phone data policy has deterred a terrorist attack, and much of the evidence it obtained could have been acquired in a timely manner by conventional court orders.[202]

More recently, a heavily redacted report issued in 2015 by the inspector general (IG) of the Justice Department also found that there is no empirical evidence showing that increased surveillance by government agencies has been effective in staving off terrorist attacks. FBI officials and agents who were interviewed by the IG revealed that the surveillance program was not instrumental in its efforts to hunt down terrorists. According to the report, "The agents we interviewed did not identify any major case developments that resulted from the records obtained in response to Section 215 orders."[203] The report also indicated that the FBI tripled its bulk data collection under Section 215 of the Patriot Act, which led to surveilling of Americans who were not even targets of terrorism investigations. The FBI acknowledged that "the data includes records of U.S. persons who were not the subject of or associated with the subjects of authorized investigations."[204] The IG's report also stated that "we identified factual inaccuracies the Department made in several of the reports we reviewed, including incorrectly identifying the number of U.S. persons in a document and providing the FISA Court with incorrect information."[205] The IG's investigation made it clear that for years the FBI had failed to comply with legal requirements under the Patriot Act.

The *New York Times* observed that "indiscriminate bulk data sweeps have not been useful. In the more than two years since the NSA's data collection programs became known to the public, the intelligence community has failed to show that the phone program has thwarted a terrorist attack. Yet for years intelligence officials and members of Congress repeatedly misled the public by claiming that it was effective."[206]

Even more disconcerting is that individuals under government surveillance are still able to purchase weapons in the United States. On June 12, 2016, a lone gunman who pledged allegiance to ISIS killed forty-nine people and injured fifty-three others inside Pulse, a gay nightclub in Orlando, Florida. The FBI had the gunman under surveillance for almost a year. Some reports maintained that the gunman was a lone wolf terrorist. Whether he was or not, at the time of the massacre, he had been dropped from the FBI watch list. Nonetheless, individuals on watch lists pass background checks for gun purchase 91 percent of the time.[207]

Conclusions

There is a tendency to morally and ideologically judge past events from contemporary times; it is a human fallibility. When Americans perceived a grave threat to national security after 9/11, many were willing to allow the government to do whatever was necessary to keep us safe. We pick and choose when it is acceptable to put our complete faith and trust in government to do the right thing. But today, in light of the passage of time and the revelations of new information, we are able to criticize what we did then: accept the wholesale abridgement of our privacy rights.

Some make the argument that for a temporary time when the country faces an intractable crisis, people are willing to submit to the rule of the state, even though it means sacrificing our civil liberties. For example, in *How Patriotic Is the Patriot Act?*, Amitai Etzioni argues that a

> reasonable deliberation about our national security is the recognition that we face two profound commitments: protecting our homeland and safeguarding our rights. Those who, in effect, seek to suspend major parts of the Constitution and its Bill of Rights until we win the war against terrorism must realize that this is a long-term war and, hence, *provisions that might apply for a very short period, during a dire state of emergency,*

cannot be applied here. To live for any length of time without rule of law that makes us what we are is not an option, nor should it be.[208]

He goes on to acknowledge, however, that there is always a need for trade-offs.

The horrifying image of the collapsing Twin Towers in New York City will forever be etched indelibly in the collective minds of Americans. In 2001 we were willing to accept a temporary suspension of our constitutional rights during that "dire state of emergency." But, as Etzioni points out, the foundation of our freedoms that make us who we are cannot be shattered on any enduring basis. Opinion polls seem to bear out the shift in ideology over time. As noted at the beginning of this chapter, a Gallup poll in January 2002 indicated that close to 50 percent of Americans supported the government's war on terror, even if civil liberties were violated. Polling conducted in June 2015 shows a vastly different picture: only 30 percent said that the government should take all steps to fight terrorism, even if our civil liberties are compromised, and 65 percent said that the government should take steps only if it protected our civil liberties.[209]

The Patriot Act and its subsequent amendments or extensions, including the FISA Amendments Act of 2008, represent major drifts from early policies and laws intended to ensure the privacy rights of Americans under the Fourth Amendment. These drifts were aggressively pursued by the Bush administration and to a certain degree the Obama administration; every branch of the federal government worked together to support the surveillance policy, which ensured its durability. The administrative machinery of the FBI and particularly the NSA implemented the substantive policy goals of each president. As Nathan and Calabresi and Yoo would argue, the president was able to secure executive control of the bureaucracy, thus allowing for policy gains administratively that would not be sufficiently attainable through legislation.[210] And despite repeated concerns about the Patriot Act's effects on Americans' privacy rights, Congress, including Democrats and Republicans, continued to pass extensions to the act. There seemed to be a rare display of bipartisanship in Congress to maintain the provisions of the Patriot Act. Even the courts, most of which were presided over by Democratic-appointed judges, as well as the FISC, allowed the government to continue spying on the American people. Thus, going beyond a unitary executive branch or administrative presidency approach, every branch of the federal government worked to maintain the Patriot Act and its various revisions in the putative war on terrorism.[211] And the media, by inflating the sense of danger associated with terrorist attacks, stoked Americans' fears, and hence their desire for safekeeping by the government. Political expediency trumped constitutionalism. This exemplifies the institutional model of policy making. The formal institutional and legal powers of each of the three branches of government promoted the specious political interest of national security at the expense of the essential, cherished value of liberty.

But this leads to questions of how democracy is best served. To the extent that the three branches of the federal government continually allowed the American people to be spied on illegally, was democratic rule compromised? Were our elected leaders truly acting in the best interests of Americans or their constituents? Or were they more concerned about being labeled "unpatriotic" if they didn't support the eponymous law? Legal and constitutional challenges to the government's surveillance programs were made by various policy players and stakeholders to secure the individual freedoms guaranteed under the U.S. Constitution. But these largely failed. So a host of political players did participate in the policy process, but does this in itself represent democratic rule? Our political leaders would respond with a resounding "yes" because they would claim that the outcome supported the broad and virtuous goal of national security, which is after all in the best interest of everyone. And the practical outcome of democratic rule is that there were winners and losers in the policy process. In this case, the American people are the losers, as our privacy rights have been violated. It is the losers who will justifiably question whether democracy has been best served.

With passage of the USA Freedom Act, which represents a minor drift, a realistic question remains: Given that the government bypassed the law as it continued to spy on the American people with each subsequent iteration of the Patriot Act, will the executive branch through the NSA and the FISC circumvent the new law to continue its surveillance activities? Indeed, we are learning that whenever terrorists strike other countries, executive branch officials will decry efforts to contain or limit mass surveillance. In November 2015, just after terrorists attacked the city of Paris, John Brennan, director of the CIA, speaking about Snowden's disclosure in 2013, "denounced what he called 'hand-wringing' over intrusive government spying and said leaks about intelligence programs had made it harder to identify the 'murderous sociopaths' of the Islamic State."[212] Brennan and other executive branch officials are eager to return to a program that gives the federal government carte blanche in surveillance for the sake of national security.

And, indeed, this was France's response to the terrorist attacks of November 2015. President François Hollande declared a state of emergency following the attacks, providing the French government with exceptional powers, including the authority to conduct warrantless searches of homes, impose preventive detention on citizens, restrict the right to peaceful assembly, and strip dual-national citizens of their French citizenship. There is no judicial oversight to these executive actions. And the actions have not yielded information that could be linked in any way to terrorism.[213]

Broader questions will continue to arise. Will the federal government surveil Muslims in the United States or elsewhere in the wake of the terrorist attack in Paris as well as that in Brussels in March 2016? Will other countries surveil Americans? And will Americans support such efforts? With sustained threats from ISIS, will the U.S. government push for renewed efforts to surveil the American people as it did after the 9/11 attacks? With isolated terrorist attacks such as that in San Bernardino, where a husband-and-wife team killed fourteen people at a developmental disability center in December 2015, will there be further drifts in surveillance policy?[214] The response by then President-elect Donald Trump was to bar all Muslims from entering the United States, a xenophobic, alarmist reaction at best. While there may be a collective desire to keep our borders safe, empirical evidence shows that depriving Americans of their constitutional right to privacy by spying on us is not the answer, nor has it proved effective in averting potential terrorist attacks.

In 2017, with a Republican president and Republican majorities in both houses, it is likely that the surveillance policy drifts will remain stable. During the presidential campaign, Trump stated that he strongly supports phone metadata collection by the NSA and the reauthorization of the Patriot Act. He said that security should be our main goal. He also stated that "protecting America from terrorist attacks would require more surveillance of Muslims and 'people that have to be tracked.'"[215] He went on to speculate that "many Americans 'would be willing to give up some privacy in order to have more safety'" and he also "called for 'closing that internet up' to keep terrorist groups like Islamic State from using 'our internet.'"[216] A week after his inauguration, President Trump issued an executive order that closed the U.S. borders to refugees, among others, from seven Muslim nations in an effort to prevent acts of terrorism on American soil. Even those holding green cards with permanent residence in the United States were barred from entering. Yet, since 9/11, no one has been killed in a terrorist attack in the United States by anyone who emigrated from or whose parents emigrated from those seven countries targeted by the executive order.[217] After massive protests across the country, President Trump lifted that part of the executive order applying to those holding green cards, declaring they were exempt from the order.[218]

As president, Trump also filled the vacant seat of Antonin Scalia, conservative justice of the U.S. Supreme Court, who died suddenly and unexpectedly in January 2016. Trump's nominee, Neil M. Gorsuch, was confirmed by the Senate mostly along party lines. This ensures that a conservative majority will remain intact on the High Court. In effect, all three branches of the federal government, as was the case during the Bush and Obama administrations, will ensure the durability of surveillance policy in this nation.

Civil Rights Law and Policy Drifts

Pay Equity and LGBT Employment

The passage of the Civil Rights Act of 1964 was a milestone for the modern civil rights movement. The most sweeping law since Reconstruction, it prohibits discrimination based on race, color, religion, and national original in public places (e.g., hotels, libraries, swimming pools), education, and employment. In the realm of employment, it also prohibits discrimination based on sex.[1] Passage of the bill was not easy, and debate continues to this day around the interpretation and reach of Title VII of the act, which proscribes employment discrimination.[2] Despite the stability and durability of the Civil Rights Act, several amendments have been made to the act as a result of political maneuvering by various stakeholders in the policy process.

This chapter examines two policy drifts in the area of civil rights. First it will examine drifts to pay equity policy under Title VII of the Civil Rights Act of 1964 as amended, illustrating the complex, sometimes ignoble interactions between the stakeholders over whether women should be paid equitable wages compared with men.[3] The U.S. Supreme Court's 2007 decision in *Ledbetter v. Goodyear Tire Co.* ignited the policy drift.[4] The chapter also examines policy drifts aimed at protecting lesbian, gay, bisexual, and transgender (LGBT) employees in the workplace.[5] Because there continues to be resistance to employment protections for LGBT workers, the chapter also shows that policy drifts around pay equity appear more stable or durable, thus ensuring that the policy drifts will continue to work for women as they seek equitable wages.

The chapter begins with a brief review of the specific protections advanced for women and people of color since Reconstruction. It then examines the politics surrounding efforts to restrict and then restore equitable pay for women. The chapter then turns its attention to efforts aimed at passing a civil rights law for lesbian, gay, bisexual, and transgender employees, formally known as the Employment Non-Discrimination Act (ENDA). In particular, it illustrates how President Obama, frustrated by an intransigent Congress, initiated a number of important policy drifts in the area of LBGT rights. The protection of LGBT individuals has been considered the new civil rights issue.

Federal Employment Discrimination Law and Policy

Table 3.1 provides a summary of the civil rights laws and policies (including drifts) prohibiting employment discrimination based on various characteristics from the Reconstruction era to the present. Notwithstanding the earlier provisions, it wasn't until the Civil Rights Act of 1964 that serious consideration was given to nondiscrimination laws and policies. Even here, it took a ruling by the U.S. Supreme Court for the law to be effectively implemented. Briefly, in 1971 the Court issued a landmark decision in *Griggs v. Duke Power Co.*[6] In this case, African Americans sued the power company over a policy that prevented them from transferring into higher-paying jobs in other departments. The company was organized into five departments. All of the lowest-paying jobs were in the labor department, where the highest-paying job paid less than the lowest-paying job in the other four departments. African Americans were segregated in the labor department. On July 2, 1965, the day the Civil Rights Act became effective, Duke Power added a new employment requirement for applicants and job incumbents: in order to be hired in or transferred to any department other than labor, passage of two aptitude tests was required. This new policy worked to keep African Americans in the labor department. Griggs filed a class-action suit against Duke Power. In a unanimous ruling, the *Griggs* Court opined that Title VII of the Civil Rights Act of 1964 "proscribes not only overt discrimination but also practices that are fair in form, but discriminatory in operation."[7] The Court went on to say that if the exclusionary employment practices "cannot be shown to be related to job performance, the practice is prohibited."[8] The *Griggs* decision represented an important policy drift by prohibiting not only overt discrimination but covert as well.

Interestingly, sex was initially not intended as a protected class of Title VII of the 1964 act. It was added by Representative Howard Smith, a conservative Democrat from Virginia, in an effort to gut the entire bill. Smith

TABLE 3.1. Civil Rights Laws and Policies

Law/Policy	Provisions/Coverage
Civil Rights Act of 1866, Section 1981	Provides that "all persons shall have the Same right . . . to the full and equal benefit of the laws . . . as is enjoyed by white citizens."
Fourteenth Amendment to U.S. Constitution (1868)	Requires all states and their political subdivisions to provide equal protection of the laws to all persons in their jurisdictions.
Civil Rights Act of 1871, Section 1983	Prohibits persons acting "under color of any statute, ordinance, regulation, custom or usage" from depriving any citizen or person within the jurisdiction of the U.S. of any rights, privileges, or immunities secured by the Constitution.
Ramspeck Act (1940)	Prohibits discrimination in federal employment based on race, color, or creed.
Executive Order 8802 (1941)	Prohibits discrimination based on race, color, religion, or national origin within the federal service and defense production industries.
Equal Pay Act (1963)	Requires employers to pay women and men equally for doing the same work—equal pay for equal work.
Civil Rights Act of 1964, Title VII	Prohibits discrimination on the basis of race, color, religion, gender, and national origin in private-sector employment.
Executive Order 11246, as amended (1965)	Prohibits employment discrimination based on race, color, religion, gender, and national origin by federal government and federal contractors and subcontractors.
Age Discrimination in Employment Act (ADEA), as amended (1967)	Prohibits employment discrimination based on age.
Equal Employment Opportunity Act of 1972 (amends Title VII of CRA of 1964)	Extends Title VII protection to state, local, and federal government employees and workers in educational institutions.
Vocational Rehabilitation Act of 1973	Prohibits federal government and its contractors from discriminating against persons with disabilities.
Vietnam Era Veterans' Readjustment Act (1974)	Requires the federal government and its contractors to promote employment opportunities for Vietnam-era veterans.
Pregnancy Discrimination Act of 1978 (amends Title VII of CRA of 1964)	Prohibits discrimination based on pregnancy.
Americans with Disabilities Act (1990)	Forbids private, state, and local government employers from discriminating on the basis of disability.
Civil Rights Act of 1991	Overturns several negative U.S. Supreme Court decisions issued in 1989 on EEO and affirmative action; establishes a Glass Ceiling Commission to study the artificial barriers to the advancement of women and persons of color in the workplace.
Family and Medical Leave Act (1993)	Requires public- and private-sector employers to provide workers with up to 12 weeks of unpaid leave for family responsibilities.
Americans with Disabilities Act Amendments Act (ADAAA) of 2008	Amends the ADA to widen coverage of persons with disabilities.
Lilly Ledbetter Fair Pay Act of 2009	Overturns U.S. Supreme Court decision in *Ledbetter v. Goodyear Tire & Rubber Co.* (2007), which made it more difficult to win equal pay lawsuits.

Note: This table does not address affirmative action policies.

did not support any type of civil rights legislation; along with a coalition of House members from the South, he worked to prevent passage of the bill. But because momentum for a civil rights bill was so immense at the time, the act passed, now with protections for women in the workplace.[9]

Certainly, there have been a number of other policy drifts resulting from ideological, social, and political forces. Table 3.2 illustrates, for ex-

TABLE 3.2. The Civil Rights Act of 1991 Overturns the U.S. Supreme Court's 1989 Decisions

Case	Supreme Court's 1989 Ruling	Civil Rights Act of 1991
Wards Cove Packing Co. v. Atonio (Title VII)	Plaintiffs must show that adverse impact was intentional, i.e., that the employment practice resulting in disparities was used not out of business necessity, but for illegal reasons.	Plaintiffs required to demonstrate adverse impact. Employer must then "demonstrate that the challenged practice is job-related for the position in question and consistent with business necessity."
Patterson v. McLean Credit Union (42 USC Section 1981)	42 USC Section 1981 of the Civil Rights Act of 1866 is limited to hiring and some promotion decisions, but does not extend to harassment on the job, discriminatory firing, or other post-hiring conduct by the employer.	42 USC Section 1981 of the Civil Rights Act of 1866 covers all forms of racial bias in employment.
Martin v. Wilks (Title VII)	White male firefighters can challenge, without time limitations, affirmative action consent decrees settling employment discrimination dispute, even if they were not original parties to the consent decree.	The act prohibits challenges to consent decrees by individuals who had reasonable opportunities to object to the decrees at an earlier date.
Lorance v. AT&T (Title VII)	Women challenging the legality of a collective bargaining seniority system must file suit within the first 300 days of the system's adoption.	Employees may challenge a seniority system when it affects them, as well as when the system is adopted.
Price Waterhouse v. Hopkins (Title VII)	In "mixed-motive" cases (those where lawful and unlawful factors motivated the employment decision), the employer can avoid liability by demonstrating that the same action would have been taken without the discriminatory motive. The burden of proof rests with the employer.	*Any* intentional discrimination is unlawful, even if the same action would have been taken in the absence of the discriminatory motive.
EEOC v. Aramco (Title VII)	Coverage of Title VII of the Civil Rights Act of 1964 as amended does not apply outside the territorial jurisdiction of the U.S.	The act extends coverage to U.S. citizens employed by American companies abroad.

Source: Norma M. Riccucci, *Managing Diversity in Public Sector Workforces* (Boulder: Westview, 2002).

ample, how Congress responded to a series of regressive rulings by the U.S. Supreme Court in 1989 by passing the Civil Rights Act of 1991. A separation of powers move restored equal employment opportunity law to its standing prior to those 1989 decisions.

As seen in the last entry of table 3.1, the Lilly Ledbetter Fair Pay Act of 2009, equal pay for women is the most recent political flare-up around civil rights issues. The act was a response to the U.S. Supreme Court's ruling in *Ledbetter v. Goodyear*.

The *Ledbetter* Case

In 1979 Lilly Ledbetter was hired as a supervisor by the Goodyear tire assembly department in Gadsden, Alabama. She assumed that she was being paid the same salary as her male counterparts, and all salaried employees were given or denied raises based upon their supervisor's evaluation of their performance. In 1998 Ledbetter was sent an anonymous note informing her that her salary was lower than that of her male counterparts, including those with far less seniority. Ledbetter was being paid $3,727 per month, while the lowest-paid male supervisor received $4,286 per month and the highest-paid earned $5,236. Within a few weeks of learning of this disparity, Ledbetter filed a discrimination complaint with the U.S. Equal Employment Opportunity Commission (EEOC). Her formal administrative complaint stated that Goodyear was paying her a discriminatorily low salary because of her gender in violation of Title VII of the Civil Rights Act of 1964. That charge was eventually tried by a jury. Ledbetter alleged that over the years, several supervisors had given her poor evaluations because of her gender, and consequently, her pay had not increased as it would have if she had been evaluated fairly. Ledbetter introduced sufficient evidence at the trial to establish that discrimination against women managers at the Gadsden plant and not performance inadequacies on her part accounted for the salary differential. The jury found in her favor, and the U.S. district court entered a judgment for back pay and damages. The U.S. Circuit Court of Appeals for the Eleventh Circuit, however, reversed. The U.S. Supreme Court granted certiorari to resolve the pivotal issue in the case: the proper application of time limits in filing claims under Title VII for pay disparities.

In *Ledbetter*, Goodyear argued that the pay discrimination claim was time-barred under Title VII's 180-day rule. Under Title VII, a charge of discrimination must be filed within a specified period—either 180 or 300 days, depending on the state—"after the alleged unlawful employment practice occurred." Ledbetter maintained that each unequal paycheck she received constituted a new violation of Title VII and therefore the time period for filing a claim should be reset accordingly. In a 5–4 decision led by the conservative wing (as discussed below), the High Court rejected this argument, reasoning that even if employees suffer continuing effects from past discrimination, their claims are time-barred unless filed within the specified number of days of the original discriminatory act. Writing for the majority, Justice Samuel Alito argued that the

> EEOC charging period is triggered when a discrete unlawful practice takes place. A new violation does not occur, and a new charging period does not commence, upon the occurrence of subsequent non-discriminatory acts that entail adverse effects resulting from the past discrimination.[10]

Alito concluded that Ledbetter should have filed suit within 180 days of receiving the first unequal paycheck, notwithstanding the fact that she had no knowledge that her wages were lower than those of her male counterparts.

Interestingly, for its ruling in *Ledbetter*, the Court relied extensively on a 1989 ruling of the Rehnquist Court that was subsequently *invalidated* by the Civil Rights Act of 1991 (see table 3.2). Justice Alito continually pointed to the Court's 1989 ruling in *Lorance v. AT&T Technologies*.[11] In that case, women challenging the legality of a seniority system were told that they must file suit within the first three hundred days of the system's adoption. In *Lorance*, three women were promoted to the nontraditional job of "tester" at an AT&T plant. About a year after the first woman was promoted, the union and AT&T renegotiated the seniority provision for this particular job title. Seniority for testers would now be determined by time in the job title or position rather than by length of plantwide service. A few years later, an economic downturn forced the plant to make demotions. Because the women testers had the least amount of seniority based on the new time-in-position system, they were all demoted. (They would not have been demoted had the former plantwide seniority system been in place.) The *Lorance* Court ruled against the women, arguing that their claim was invalid because they had not filed their suit within three hundred days of the new seniority system's adoption.

Even though seniority was not the issue in *Ledbetter*, a provision of the 1991 Civil Rights Act clearly expresses the intent of Congress to preclude or preempt the type of narrow, strict interpretation of Title VII as reflected in Alito's opinion. In passing the 1991 act, Congress agreed with the dissenting Supreme Court justices in *Lorance* that the majority ruling was at odds with the purposes of Title VII. Thus, while the 1991 act addressed only seniority systems, the *Ledbetter* decision contravened the scope of protection intended by Title VII and other civil rights statutes.

The *Ledbetter* Court also rejected other relevant precedents that have interpreted Title VII as well as the Equal Pay Act of 1963 in such a way that each time an unequal paycheck is issued, a new discriminatory act is considered to have been committed. Supreme Court Justice Ruth Bader Ginsburg alluded to this in her dissent from the majority's decision:

> On questions of time under Title VII, we have identified as the critical inquiries: "What constitutes an 'unlawful employment practice' and when has that practice 'occurred'?" . . . Our precedent suggests, and lower courts have overwhelmingly held, that the unlawful practice is the *current payment* of salaries infected by gender-based (or race-based) discrimination—a practice that occurs whenever a paycheck delivers less to a woman than to a similarly situated man.[12]

Justice Ginsburg's dissent went on to say that treating the actual payment of a disparate wage as a discriminatory act "is more faithful to precedent, more in tune with the realities of the workplace, and more respectful of Title VII's remedial purpose."[13] She also concluded her dissent by urging Congress to correct the majority's decision: "Once again, the ball is in Congress' court. As in 1991, the Legislature may act to correct this Court's parsimonious reading of Title VII."[14] Justice Ginsburg was so disturbed by the Court's decision that she took the rare step of reading aloud her twenty-page dissenting opinion from the bench.[15]

The *Ledbetter* Court also ignored the High Court's unanimous 1986 ruling in *Bazemore v. Friday*.[16] That case involved pay inequities between white and black employees.[17] Even though the discriminatory pay system began prior to passage of Title VII of the Civil Rights Act of 1964, the *Bazemore* Court found that the employer perpetuated pay inequities and "was under an obligation to eradicate salary disparities based on race that began prior to the effective date of Title VII."[18] Justice Brennan, writing for a majority Court, argued that "each week's paycheck that delivers less to a black than to a similarly situated white is a wrong actionable under Title VII."[19] Parenthetically, the composition of the Court in 1986 was very different from what it was in 2007. The year 1986 marked the end of the of the Burger Court, which was known for a number of liberal rulings, despite the fact that Chief Justice Burger was appointed by President Nixon.[20]

Finally, in rendering the ruling, the *Ledbetter* Court rejected the view of the U.S. Equal Employment Opportunity Commission (EEOC), which has interpreted Title VII to permit workers to challenge unequal pay each time it is received. According to the EEOC's Compliance Manual, "Repeated occurrences of the same discriminatory employment action can be challenged as long as one discriminatory act occurred within the charge filing period."[21] With respect specifically to compensation, the manual goes on to say, "An aggrieved individual can bring a charge up to 180/300 days after receiving compensation that is affected by a discriminatory compensation decision or other discriminatory practice, regardless of when the discrimination began."[22] In fact, according to the EEOC, Title VII requires employers to eliminate pay disparities attributable to a discriminatory system, even if that system has been discontinued. Given the EEOC's long-standing interpretation of Title VII in this way, it actively supported Ledbetter in the lower courts.

While a number of briefs were submitted in support of Lilly Ledbetter, a number were also filed in support of Goodyear, including one by the Bush administration, which argued in favor of a time bar. The administration stated that "an employee must challenge a pay decision within 180 or 300 days of its occurrence, and an employee may not circumvent that limitations period by challenging a paycheck received many years later on the theory that it perpetuates the effects of an unchallenged pay decision that occurred outside the limitations period."

The administration concluded by urging the *Ledbetter* Court to uphold the appeals court ruling, which "properly held that [Ledbetter's] claim is time-barred."[23]

The *Ledbetter* decision was reached along ideological lines, with the conservative bloc (Justices Alito, Scalia, Kennedy, and Thomas and Chief Justice Roberts) in the majority and the liberal bloc (Justices Sotomayor, Ginsburg, Breyer, and Kagan) in the minority. Justice Alito, who wrote for the Court, is a George W. Bush appointee, as is Chief Justice Roberts. Justice Thomas was appointed by his father, George H. W. Bush. Justices Scalia and Kennedy were appointed by President Reagan. The liberal members were appointed by Democratic presidents: Justices Ginsburg and Breyer by President Clinton, and Justices Sotomayor and Kagan by President Obama.

Some members of Congress were willing to take on the High Court on this policy drift. In 2007, as an immediate response to the *Ledbetter* ruling, the 110th Congress introduced the Lilly Ledbetter Fair Pay Act. This act sought to supersede the Court's decision, which represented a severe blow for women's pay equity.

Congress Takes Action

The Ledbetter bill was introduced to the House on June 22, 2007, by George Miller (D-CA). Not surprisingly, there was a lively debate, mostly along partisan lines. Miller urged his colleagues to pass the bill, arguing that

> discrimination is anathema to everything this country stands for. It is anathema to the promise that is America. Regrettably, the recent Supreme Court's recent [*sic*] Ledbetter v. Goodyear decision threatens to turn back the clock on the progress we have made since the passage of the Civil Rights Act of 1964 more than 40 years ago. The Supreme Court's decision in Ledbetter severely restricts the right of employees to challenge pay discrimination. It ignores the realities of the workplace, prior precedent, and the clear intent of Congress. Justice Ginsburg's dissent in this narrowly divided 5–4 decision called on Congress to reverse this decision, and that is what we are here to do today. . . . The Lilly Ledbetter Fair Pay Act[] is narrowly tailored and designed to restore the law on pay discrimination

as it was before the Supreme Court's decision, the law as it was for some 35 years, the law as it was reaffirmed in circuit court after circuit court, as it was affirmed by the Congress of the United States. This bill restores the law so that the 180-day statute of limitations clock runs when a discriminatory pay decision or practice is adopted, when a person becomes subject to the pay decision or practice, or when a person is affected by the pay decision or practice, including whenever she receives a discriminatory paycheck. In other words, every discriminatory paycheck is a violation of the act. That is as the law was for these many, many years. That is what we seek to do.[24]

Immediately following Miller's remarks, a number of Republicans took issue with the bill. For example, Representative Howard "Buck" McKeon (R-CA) exhorted,

I rise in opposition to this ill-considered and over-reaching legislation. Proponents of this bill claim it simply reverses a May 29, 2007, U.S. Supreme Court decision and further clarifies congressional opposition to wage discrimination against employees in the workplace. In reality, however, it will set into motion unintended consequences that its supporters simply are not willing to acknowledge. . . . I believe, [this] is where the two parties diverge on the bill before us. We aren't taking sides for or against discrimination in the workplace; rather, we're staking out different positions on fair and equitable justice and the rule of law.[25]

which are?

McKeon then warned of a potential veto: "the Bush administration last week threatened to veto, should the bill ever arrive at his desk. Specifically, the administration noted that the legislation 'would serve to impede justice and undermine the important goal of having allegations of discrimination expeditiously resolved.'"[26]

Several women spoke out against the bill, including Representatives Nancy Boyda (D-KS) and Marsha Blackburn (R-TN). Boyda, who ultimately voted against the bill, did not see the issue in gender terms. She argued that this

is not a gender issue; all employees should have an equal chance of getting a just wage. . . . I believe that Congress must find a way to fix the problem that the Ledbetter decision poses for employees who have experienced discrimination. However, I do not believe that this bill was the best way to accomplish that. By not establishing any deadlines after the initial hire date, Congress has now gone too far; similar to the Supreme Court decision, they have ignored the realities of the average employment environment. I agree that employees need more time than 180 days, but I also believe that employers need to be afforded some timeline as well.[27]

Blackburn, who ultimately did not cast a vote, stated that the act would do much more than overturn the High Court's decision:

> What this change would do would serve to impede justice and undermine the important goal of having allegations of discrimination expeditiously resolved. The bill essentially limits the 1964 Civil Rights Act statute of limitations regarding almost every claim of discrimination available under Federal law and potentially broadens the scope and application of the civil rights laws to entirely new fact patterns, practices and claims.[28]

Most Republicans were concerned with the impact of the bill on private enterprise. Comments by Representative Todd Tiahrt (R-KS) are illustrative:

> How can a company defend itself when the accused offenders left the company decades before? The answer is—they can't. . . . This legislation will not end pay discrimination, but it will certainly encourage frivolous claims and lawsuits. It is inevitable that under this legislation employees will sue companies for reasons that have little if anything to do with the accused discrimination.[29]

Just as the Bush administration supported Goodyear in the *Ledbetter* case, it also opposed legislation to restore pay equity for women. According to the statement the administration filed in the House against the Ledbetter Act,

> The Administration supports our Nation's anti-discrimination laws and is committed to the timely resolution of discrimination claims. For this and other reasons, the Administration strongly opposes the Ledbetter Fair

Pay Act of 2007. [It] would allow employees to bring a claim of pay or other employment-related discrimination years or even decades after the alleged discrimination occurred. [It] constitutes a major change in, and expanded application of, employment discrimination law. The change would serve to impede justice and undermine the important goal of having allegations of discrimination expeditiously resolved.[30]

On July 27, 2007, the Bush administration issued a Statement of Administration Policy (SAP) on the bill indicating that if passed, the president would veto it.

What makes the Bush administration's position even more indefensible is that it ignores the hostile work environment created by Goodyear. In her testimony before the House Committee on Education and Labor on June 12, 2007, Lilly Ledbetter revealed that her time at Goodyear was difficult and that she had previously filed a sexual harassment action with the EEOC:

I tried to fit in and to do my job. It wasn't easy. The plant manager flat out said that women shouldn't be working in a tire factory because women just made trouble. One of my supervisors asked me to go down to a local hotel with him and promised if I did, I would get good evaluations. He said if I didn't, I would get put at the bottom of the list. I didn't say anything at first because I wanted to try to work it out and fit in without making waves. But it got so bad that I finally complained to the company. The manager I complained to refused to do anything to protect me and instead told me I was just being a troublemaker. So I complained to the EEOC. The company worked out a deal with the EEOC so that supervisor would no longer manage me. But after that, the company treated me badly. They tried to isolate me. People refused to talk to me. They left me out of important management meetings so I sometimes didn't know what was going on, which made it harder to do my job. So I got a taste of what happens when you try to complain about discrimination.[31]

She continued,

According to the Supreme Court, if you don't figure things out right away, the company can treat you like a second-class citizen for the rest of your career. And that is not right. The truth is, Goodyear continues to treat me like a second-class worker to this day because my pension and my Social Security is [sic] based on the amount I earned while working there. Goodyear gets to keep my extra pension as a reward for break-ing the law. My case is over, and it is too bad that the Supreme Court decided the way that it did. I hope, though, that Congress won't let this happen to anyone else. I would feel that this long fight was worthwhile if at least at the end of it I knew that I played a part in getting the law fixed so that it can provide real protection to real people in the real world.[32]

The remark by Representative Ric Keller (R-FL) that followed Ledbet-ter's testimony was gratuitous at best: "There is an old saying, hard cases make bad law. That applies here. Do we throw out the statute of limita-tions in employment cases because *a nice lady* waited 19 years to file a lawsuit? Common sense tells you the answer is no."[33]

With over two hundred organizations pushing for the bill, it was passed by the Democratic-controlled House on July 31, 2007, by a vote of 225–199, along almost entirely partisan lines.[34] Of the 225, 223 were Democrats and two were Republican men—Don Young (AK) and Chris-topher Shays (CT). Of the 199 nays, six were Democrat and 193 were Republican. The Democrats voting no were Bud Cramer (AL), Allen Boyd (FL), Tim Mahoney (FL), Dan Boren (OK), Nick Lampson (TX), and one woman, Nancy Boyda (KS).[35] The bill, as seen below, went next to the Senate.

The 2008 Bid for the Presidency

The Ledbetter Act of 2007 became part of the 2008 campaign for the presidency, despite the fact that economists and pollsters talked mostly about a recession and consumers' concerns about the security of their jobs. The Democrats lauded Senator Barack Obama's support of the Ledbetter bill and chastised Senator John McCain's opposition to the proposed law. On McCain's campaign tour through poverty-stricken towns and cities, he stated that he opposed the proposed Ledbetter Act because it would lead to more lawsuits: "I am all in favor of pay equity for women, but this kind of legislation, as is typical of what's being proposed by my friends on the other side of the aisle, opens us up to lawsuits for all kinds of problems." He suggested that what was needed was more education and training, rather than pay equity: "They need the education and training, particularly since more and more women are heads of their households, as much or more than anybody else."[36]

Senator Hillary Clinton, also running for president in 2008, criticized McCain's lack of support for the pay equity bill: "Senator McCain has yet again fallen in line with President Bush while middle-class families are falling by the wayside. . . . Women are earning less, but Senator McCain is offering more of the same."[37]

Gail Collins wrote a highly critical editorial for the *New York Times* on April 26, 2008, arguing that

this is a man who told the folks in Youngstown, Ohio—where most of the working single mothers cannot make it above the poverty line—that the answer to their problems is larger tax deductions. . . . Having delivered his objections to the Ledbetter bill this week, McCain went on to tell reporters that . . . "it's hard for [women] to leave their families when they don't have somebody to take care of them." . . . Was McCain saying that it's less important to give working women the right to sue for equal pay than to give them help taking care of their families? There have been many attempts to expand the Family and Medical Leave Act to protect more workers who need to stay home to take care of a sick kid or an ailing parent. . . . We also have yet to hear a McCain policy address on how working mothers are supposed to find quality child care. If it comes, I suspect the women trying to support their kids on $20,000 a year are going to learn they're in line for some whopping big income-tax deductions. Let them eat dinner mints.[38]

It is unclear as to whether McCain's opposition hurt his presidential race and whether Obama's support for the bill helped him win the election. It was clear, however, that independent and moderate Republican women were seen as a key swing voting bloc for the presidential race.[39] And in fact, Obama's campaign was geared in part to this bloc of voters. Two issues were targeted by his campaign strategists: reproductive choice and equal pay.[40]

The Senate Kills the 2007 Bill

The senators campaigning for the presidency were absent for the vote on the proposed Ledbetter Act. Their vote wouldn't have made a difference; nor did the fact that the Senate was controlled by Democrats. On July 20, 2007, Senator Ted Kennedy (D-MA) introduced a nearly identical bill to the House's in the Senate, entitled the Fair Pay Restoration Act (S. 1843). This bill was referred to the Senate Committee on Health, Education, Labor, and Pensions, where hearings were held. The bill had forty-three co-sponsors. Nine months later, on April 21, 2008, Senate majority leader Harry Reid (D-NV), in the wake of a threatened GOP filibuster, filed a cloture petition on the motion to proceed to the bill.[41] On April 23, 2008, cloture was invoked and failed. The vote was 56–42, far short of the 60 needed to block a GOP-led filibuster.[42] The Democratic-controlled Senate failed to muster enough votes to keep the Ledbetter bill alive.

Senator Kennedy stated in response to the vote,

> I am deeply disappointed we were not able to get the required 60 votes. . . . I think most of us who have been around this institution for some time and who have been involved in the civil rights issue understand if you don't have a remedy, you don't have a right. This debate was about restoring a right to Lilly Ledbetter, her right to be treated fairly in the workplace and the rights of millions of others too. Those who are disabled, elderly, people in our society of various national origins, those of particular religious faiths, and women all are threatened by the underlying Supreme Court decision. That has to be altered. It has to be changed. I welcome the fact that our majority leader has sent a powerful signal by indicating that we will come back and revisit this issue. This issue is about fairness. It is about equity.[43]

Others were happy to see the bill die. Senator John Isakson (R-GA) stated that

> everyone within the sound of my voice needs to understand something. This debate today is not about allowing, favoring, or supporting discrimination. It is about preserving the Civil Rights Act . . . , because the Civil

Rights Act stated clearly that if a complaint was filed, it needed to be filed within 180 days of the act of discrimination, or as, as [*sic*] current EEOC practice allows, 180 days from the date which a reasonable person should have known. . . . Some will argue . . . about hidden, or concealed, discrimination, whereby a person might not become aware they are being victimized. Essentially, you can rope-a-dope someone and fool them. Current EEOC practice clearly states that it is 180 days from the time a reasonable person should have known or would have known they were discriminated against.[44]

In a preemptive move to prevent Republicans from griping about possible financial implications of the bill, the Congressional Budget Office (CBO) issued a cost estimate indicating that the bill would not significantly impact the number of discrimination filings with the EEOC or increase the costs incurred by the EEOC or the federal courts. The CBO also stated that "enacting the bill would not affect revenues or direct spending."[45]

Renewed Efforts to Pass the Ledbetter Act

On January 6, 2009, Representative Miller reintroduced the Lilly Ledbetter Fair Pay Act to the 111th Congress. Both the House and Senate were still controlled by Democrats. In fact, in the November 2008 elections the Democrats picked up a number of seats, and as a corollary, the Republicans lost seats. The House comprised 256 Democrats and 178 Republicans.[46] In the Senate there were 57 Democrats, 41 Republicans, and two independents—Bernie Sanders (VT) and Joe Lieberman (CT)—generally caucusing with the Democrats.[47]

In addition to the Ledbetter Act of 2009, Representative Rosa DeLauro (D-CT) introduced on January 6 the Paycheck Fairness Act, which would strengthen equal pay laws and help close the wage gap with measures that would prevent unequal pay in the first place. Specifically, it would amend the Equal Pay Act of 1963 to revise remedies for, enforcement of, and exceptions to prohibitions against sex discrimination in the payment of wages.[48] It would impose harsher penalties for pay discrimination and prohibit employers from retaliating against employees who share salary information with each other. This bill was voted on separately from the Ledbetter Act. After much debate, the House voted to pass the Paycheck Fairness Act on January 9, 2009, with a vote of 256–163.[49] The Senate did not pass this bill.

On the same day, the House considered the Ledbetter Act. As with the 2007 bill, there was debate on both sides, with Democrats once again arguing that pay discrimination against women must end, and Republicans claiming that the bill is flawed and would result in a series of frivolous, open-ended lawsuits that would be harmful to business. But now there was a president in office, Barack Obama, who was very supportive of pay equity measures and promised to sign the bill. On January 9, 2009, the House passed the Ledbetter Act with a vote mostly along partisan lines, 247–171.[50] There were 244 Democrats and three Republicans supporting the combined bill. Fifteen House members did not participate in the vote.

The Republicans voting to support—all men—were Chris Smith (NJ), Ed Whitfield (KY), and Don Young (AK); Young had voted to support the 2007 bill; Whitfield and Smith had both voted against the 2007 bill. Smith, who has served New Jersey's 4th District since 1981, was presumed to be voting more progressively since his district was gerrymandered in this very blue Garden State.[51] Whitfield also crossed party lines to vote in support of the 2009 bill, stating, "I believe strongly that individuals should receive equal pay for equal work. Race, gender, religion and ethnicity should never play a role in determining one's salary for a job. What's more, the law should protect individuals from such discrimination and allow recourse for restitution. The Lilly Ledbetter Fair Pay Act will do just that and I am pleased to support this landmark legislation."[52]

Five Democrats, all men, voted against the act: Dan Boren (OK), Allen Boyd (FL)—who both voted against the 2007 bill—Bobby Neal Bright (AL), Travis Childers (MS), and Parker Griffith (AL), all three of whom were not in office in 2007. Nancy Boyda (D-KS), who opposed the bill in 2007, was no longer in Congress, having been voted out in 2008.

Senator Barbara Mikulski reintroduced the Ledbetter Act to the Senate on January 8, 2009, and on January 13, Senate majority leader Reid filed a cloture petition on the motion to proceed to the Ledbetter Act; two days later the Senate voted 72–23 to invoke cloture only on the Lilly Ledbetter Fair Pay Act of 2009 as a standalone measure; it detached the Paycheck Fairness Act, which it said it would consider at another time.[53]

One of the most interesting, shrewd developments was an alternative bill introduced by Senator Kay Hutchinson (R-TX), the Title VII Fairness Act, which would completely derail the Ledbetter Act. The bill she introduced would not create the "pay-check accrual" rule called for by the Ledbetter Act, but would, in effect, maintain the Supreme Court's *Ledbetter* ruling. Hutchinson's bill would create a narrow, complicated new exception for workers who can prove that they did not know and did not have reason to suspect discrimination within 180 days of the original discriminatory decision. The bill, in short, would benefit businesses, not employees.[54] Although this bill was never acted upon by either house of Congress, several Republican members of the Senate urged passage of the bill.[55]

Senator John Isakson (R-GA), who opposed the bill in 2007, drawing on his southern roots, made an impassioned plea to his colleagues to oppose the act:

> I grew up in the South when the civil rights era came and the civil rights laws were passed. . . . I am proud and appreciative of what it has helped us to accomplish. . . . Obviously, with the votes that have taken place and the failure of the Hutchison amendment, it is pretty obvious which direction the bill is going. So it is time we ask ourselves one question: Is it fair to reach back to the 1960s, repeal a statute of limitations that applied for over 45 years, and open the possibility of a plethora of cases that have not been filed to now being filed or, asked another way: Is it fair, after a game has been played, to change the rules in order to change the outcome?[56]

Isakson was one of many Republican senators who believed that the Ledbetter Act would be harmful to business. Senator Jim DeMint of South Carolina went so far as to say that it would create a chilling effect on the hiring of women:

> I am afraid the Ledbetter bill is another example that the majority in the Senate doesn't understand the American economy or how businesses create jobs or how freedom works for all of us to create a better quality of life. Recessions are caused by uncertainty. This bill creates more uncertainty for the very businesses we need to create the jobs and to keep the jobs we have in our country today. Why would we pass a bill, or even be talking about it, in the middle of a recession, that many have said is the worst we

have ever seen in our lifetime? This bill will also create a lot of unintended consequences that will do the exact opposite of what it is intended to do. I was in business for well over 20 years before I came to Congress. *Once you create more liability for hiring a woman* or know that liability is going to exist for years, employers are going to figure out a way to get around that. This is more likely to discourage the employment and the promotion of women because it creates an indefinite liability.[57]

On January 22, 2009, the Senate passed the act, 61–36. Thirty-six Republicans voted against; no Democrats opposed the act. In support were fifty-four Democrats, five Republicans, and two independents—Bernie Sanders (VT) and Joe Lieberman (CT). The five Republicans voting for the act were Lisa Murkowski (AK), Susan Collins and Olympia Snowe, both of Maine, Arlen Specter (PA), and surprisingly, Kay Hutchinson (TX), who had offered an alternative bill that would have killed the Ledbetter Act.[58]

The Senate's version of the Ledbetter bill was returned to the House for a vote. On January 27, 2009, the House passed the Senate's bill by a vote of 250–177; six did not vote. The same five Republican representatives voting no on the Ledbetter Act on January 9 also voted against the act on January 27. Interestingly, Representative Leonard Lance (R-NJ), who voted no on January 9, voted to support the act on January 27. It is uncertain what caused Lance to change his vote in such a short span of time. He was up for reelection in 2010, and his district was moving away from a Republican base toward a more competitive district, so perhaps he perceived some advantage to switching his vote in support of the Ledbetter Act.[59] Representative Don Young (AK) did not cast a vote. Representatives Chris Smith (NJ) and Ed Whitfield (KY) once again voted to support the act.[60] On January 29, 2009, in a significant civil rights action, President Obama signed the first new law of his administration, the Lilly Ledbetter Fair Pay Act.

[handwritten marginal note: All about how it impacts them—Not in what is right.]

More Drifts in Pay Equity Policy

With passage of the Ledbetter Act, the policy drift on the issue of pay equity as a result of the Supreme Court's *Ledbetter* ruling was rendered temporary. However, other policy drifts have occurred as a result of action by the executive branch. Presidents tend to issue executive orders or memoranda to circumvent the lack of action on the part of Congress. For example, Congress has yet to act on the Paycheck Fairness Act, which was killed by the Senate in 2009. It was reintroduced in Congress in 2011, 2012, 2014, and 2015, but again failed each time in the Senate, where Republicans continued to argue that the act is bad for business and would result in job loss.[61] President Obama vowed to continue his fight for passage of the act, and dealt with an intransigent Senate through executive actions.

A perpetual problem regarding equal pay laws is that women often do not know that they are being underpaid, as was the case with Lilly Ledbetter, and thus cannot take action to challenge pay inequities. In many cases, private-sector employees such as Ledbetter are asked to sign contracts that prevent them from discussing salaries with other workers. Such contractual obligations promote a culture of secrecy that tends to work against women. Recognizing this conundrum, President Obama took two executive actions in 2014 to strengthen enforcement of equal pay legislation and help fight pay discrimination. Executive Order 13665 is focused on pay transparency by prohibiting federal contractors from retaliating against workers who discuss their pay.[62] And his presidential memorandum "Advancing Pay Equality through Compensation Data Collection" requires federal contractors to submit to the U.S. Department of Labor data on compensation paid to their employees by gender and race.[63] The memorandum states that "Effective enforcement of [the Equal Pay Act of 1963] is impeded by a lack of sufficiently robust and reliable data on employee compensation, including data by sex and race. The National Equal Pay Task Force, which I created to improve enforcement of equal pay laws, identified this lack of data as a barrier to closing the persistent pay gap for women and minorities."[64] Data collection by the Department of Labor is intended to address this enduring problem.

In January 2016 President Obama advanced another executive action requiring companies with a hundred or more employees to report to the EEOC how much they pay their employees by race, ethnicity, and gender.[65] This will assist the EEOC in its investigations of pay discrimination across the country. Importantly, these executive actions are not as far-reaching as legislation, but they serve as an important bridge to legislation, and they also signal to Congress the president's support for pay equity.

The Paycheck Fairness Act was reintroduced to both chambers of Congress in 2017, but has not yet been acted upon.[66] The Ledbetter Act was a victory for women's pay because it restored the interpretation of the law that a wage discrimination claim accrues whenever discrimination *affects* an employee. By overturning the 180-day statute of limitations for women to contest pay discrimination, it restores workers' day in court to challenge pay inequities. On the other hand, the Paycheck Fairness Act would prevent unequal pay from happening at the outset. It would close the wage gap between women and men working the same jobs, would require organizations to report pay information data to the EEOC, and would allow for class-action lawsuits.[67] Today, women earn around eighty cents for every dollar men earn for comparable work. In 2007 it was seventy-seven cents. In April of every year since 1996, the United States has celebrated Equal Pay Day to raise public awareness of how far women need to work into the year to earn what men earned in the previous year.[68] April 14 marked Equal Pay Day in 2015, revealing that women needed to work an extra four months to earn the same wages as a male counterpart.[69]

Compared to other nations across the globe, the United States, according the Organization for Economic Co-operation and Development (OECD), ranked twenty-fourth out of thirty-five for pay inequities in 2014.[70] The OECD measures the gender pay gap as the difference between male and female earnings as a percentage of male earnings. The smallest gender pay gap was in New Zealand at 5.62 percent, and the largest was in South Korea at 36.6 percent. The OECD average is 15.46 percent. In the United States the gap was 17.91 percent, higher than in countries such as Belgium (6.41 percent), Denmark (7.8 percent), Spain (8.65 percent), Italy (11.11), France (14.05 percent), and the United Kingdom (17.48 percent).

Table 3.3 illustrates the extent of pay differentials by gender in every state in the United States as well as Washington, D.C. As the data show, there is variability in the pay gap across the states. Washington, D.C., has the highest earnings ratio, close to 90 percent, indicating that while there is still a pay differential, the gap is lowest in this region of the country. The lowest earnings ratio is in Louisiana, where women earn only sixty-five cents to every dollar earned by men. In Alabama, where Lilly Ledbetter worked, women make 72.6 percent of what men earn on the dollar.

TABLE 3.3. Median Annual Earnings, Full-Time Employment, by Gender and State, 2014

	Women ($)	Men ($)	Earnings Ratio (%)		Women ($)	Men ($)	Earnings Ratio (%)
Alabama	32,136	44,245	72.6	Nebraska	35,101	44,533	78.8
Alaska	46,288	57,318	80.8	Nevada	35,993	42,294	85.1
Arizona	36,916	43,945	84.0	New Hampshire	42,052	55,617	75.6
Arkansas	31,161	39,916	78.1	New Jersey	48,943	60,870	80.4
California	42,486	50,539	84.1	New Mexico	32,473	41,561	78.1
Colorado	41,690	50,898	81.9	New York	44,781	51,580	86.8
Connecticut	50,706	61,385	82.6	North Carolina	35,481	41,857	84.8
Delaware	41,278	50,976	81.0	North Dakota	36,087	50,624	71.3
Florida	34,768	40,971	84.9	Ohio	37,140	47,737	77.8
Georgia	36,468	44,623	81.7	Oklahoma	32,186	43,803	73.5
Hawaii	40,162	46,786	85.8	Oregon	38,801	47,194	82.2
Idaho	31,019	42,624	72.8	Pennsylvania	39,905	50,412	79.2
Illinois	40,898	51,652	79.2	Rhode Island	41,469	50,765	81.7
Indiana	34,846	46,273	75.3	South Carolina	33,719	41,991	80.3
Iowa	36,522	47,202	77.4	South Dakota	32,048	42,034	76.2
Kansas	36,162	46,951	77.0	Tennessee	34,009	41,661	81.6
Kentucky	33,704	42,203	79.9	Texas	36,428	46,235	78.8
Louisiana	31,586	48,382	65.3	Utah	34,351	50,937	67.4
Maine	36,137	45,784	78.9	Vermont	39,322	46,911	83.8
Maryland	50,481	59,085	85.4	Virginia	42,445	52,864	80.3
Massachusetts	50,459	61,611	81.9	Washington	41,926	54,358	77.1
Michigan	37,419	50,157	74.6	West Virginia	31,712	45,272	70.0
Minnesota	42,066	51,625	81.5	Wisconsin	37,481	47,518	78.9
Mississippi	31,465	40,850	77.0	Wyoming	35,652	51,926	68.7
Missouri	35,311	45,273	78.0	Washington, D.C.	61,718	68,932	89.5
Montana	31,696	42,679	74.3				
				U.S.	38,941	48,745	79.9

Source: Calculated from U.S. Census Bureau, American Fact Finder, American Community Survey (ACS), factfinder.census.gov, accessed November 11, 2015.

Passage of the Ledbetter Act reflects the shared powers model of policy drifts. It illustrates the maneuvering of institutional power among the three branches of government to influence pay equity policies. Democrats in Congress, along with the support of President Obama and over two hundred organizations, were able to overcome the political opposition from a majority of U.S. Supreme Court justices, Republicans in Congress, and such organizations as the U.S. Chamber of Commerce, the Society for Human Resource Management, the National Association of Manufacturers, the College and University Professional Association for Human Resources, and the Associated Builders and Contractors. In addition, President Obama relied on his unitary executive powers to regulate pay inequities in the absence of legislative support for the Paycheck Fairness Act.

In addition to pay equity, another civil rights issue has been on the forefront in recent years: the employment rights of lesbian, gay, bisexual, and transgender (LGBT) persons. The following section examines the efforts to pass a national law to protect LGBT individuals in the workplace. Frustrated by a Congress that repeatedly failed to pass federal legislation, President Obama relied on his executive powers to extend job protections to LGBT individuals working for the federal government or federal contractors. Unlike pay equity, which derives from a stable civil rights law, Title VII, there is no federal law to protect LGBT employees in the workplace. Thus, President Obama circumvented Congress and pursued an executive strategy of initiating policy drifts to benefit LGBT workers. As will be seen, however, executive actions do not carry the same weight as law, making the policy drifts more susceptible to change, and ultimately less sustainable.

LGBT Employment Rights

The years 2013 and 2015 were historic for LGBT rights. In 2013, in a 5–4 decision, the U.S. Supreme Court in *United States v. Windsor* struck down the constitutionality of the Defense of Marriage Act (DOMA), signed into law by President Clinton in 1996, which in defining marriage as an institution between a man and a woman effectively denied federal recognition of same-sex marriages.[71] In 2015, in a 5–4 ruling, the Court went even further in *Obergefell v. Hodges* when it upheld the constitutionality of same-sex marriages.[72] These two decisions were milestones for LGBT individuals and reflected a cultural transformation in America's relationship to at least gays and lesbians.[73] Same-sex couples can now marry in all fifty states. Yet they still do not have federal employment protection in all fifty states. It is only at the state level that we see some LGBT employment protections. As seen in table 3.4, only nineteen states and the District of Columbia have laws to protect the employment rights of LGBT workers in both the public and private sectors.[74] Other states have set restrictions on the protections they offer.

Civil rights laws are enacted at the federal level of government to ensure uniformity so that every state provides the same protections for all workers. Article VI of the Constitution makes federal law "the supreme Law of the Land." Thus, any federal law, including any regulation issued by a federal agency, takes precedence over any conflicting state law. Moreover, even state constitutions are subordinate to federal law.[75] Prior to federal civil rights laws, the states either offered no protections, such as in the South, or passed fair employment practice laws with varying degrees of coverage. Around twenty-two states enacted such laws to protect workers from employment discrimination based on race, color, religion, and national origin.[76] Gender was not included as a protected class. When the federal government steps in to pass a national law, it is signaling that the issue is of paramount importance to the entire country, not simply a single state. Federal laws symbolize a nation's commitment to a particular issue and ensure that every citizen will be protected. The different status of federal and state law reflects the concept of federalism or states' rights, which has been a politically contentious issue since the founding of this nation.[77] As mentioned at the beginning of this chapter, many southern states, represented by both Democrats and Republicans, resisted passage of the federal Civil Rights Act of 1964, arguing that states should have the power essentially to regulate race relations. States in the South operated under Jim Crow laws, which perpetuated legalized racial segregation even after the Fourteenth Amendment was ratified and concomitant federal civil rights laws were passed (see table 3.1). African Americans were forced to use separate, generally substandard drinking fountains, restrooms, and dining areas; they were forced to the backs of buses and faced inordinate discrimina-

TABLE 3.4. LGBT Antidiscrimination Laws

Public & Private Sectors (Sexual Orientation & Gender Identity*)	Public & Private Sectors (Sexual Orientation Only)	Public Sector Only (Sexual Orientation & Gender Identity*)	Public Sector Only (Sexual Orientation Only)
California	New Hampshire	Indiana	Alaska
Colorado	New York	Kentucky	Arizona
Connecticut	Wisconsin	Michigan	Missouri
Delaware		Pennsylvania	Montana
District of Columbia		Virginia	Ohio
Hawaii			
Illinois			
Iowa			
Maine			
Maryland			
Massachusetts			
Minnesota			
Nevada			
New Jersey			
New Mexico			
Oregon			
Rhode Island			
Utah			
Vermont			
Washington			

* "Gender identity" refers to self-identification apart from biological sex or gender.
Source: Human Rights Campaign, "Map of State Laws and Policies," June 2015, www.hrc.org, accessed November 12, 2015.

tion in the workplace. Whites in southern states did not want a federal law to change their predilections, behaviors, culture, or lifestyle.

Civil rights protections for LGBT individuals have not yet gained the level of support or commitment for federal legislation. Indeed, until the Clinton presidency, politicians feared referring openly to gays or lesbians for fear of retaliation during reelection cycles. There has been a movement since 1994 to introduce a federal law, the Employment Non-Discrimination Act (ENDA), but the efforts have failed.[78] A federal law is obviously needed if LGBT individuals are to have full employment protections, which in turn ensure economic and social stability.

The 1994 ENDA

A survey conducted by the Pew Research Center of 1,197 LGBT adults revealed that 21 percent said they faced workplace discrimination.[79] In another survey, over half of LGBT workers nationwide stated that they hide who they are in the workplace to avoid harassment or discrimination.[80] And a national survey of 1,200 registered voters (not solely LGBT) found that 63 percent favored a federal law that protects gay and transgender people from employment discrimination; only 25 percent opposed it.[81]

Yet there is no federal law protecting LGBT individuals from employment discrimination. Efforts to pass a federal law date back to 1994, when ENDA was first introduced in Congress. But it failed to gain enough support for passage into law.[82] Of course, the cultural and social contexts of this time period are obviously relevant. Bill Clinton, who campaigned on a promise to end discrimination against gays in the military, was elected president in 1992. At the time, President Ronald Reagan's 1982 policy or directive was still on the books. It read in part,

> Homosexuality is incompatible with military service. The presence in the military environment of persons who engage in homosexual conduct or who, by their statements, demonstrate a propensity to engage in homosexual conduct, seriously impairs the accomplishment of the military mission. The presence of such members adversely affects the ability of the Military Services to maintain discipline, good order, and morale.[83]

Gays or bisexuals would be immediately discharged from the military.

Popular support for the LGBT movement was just beginning to gain some momentum, and 1994 marked the first year that LGBT History Month was celebrated.[84] Democrats were in control of both houses of Congress, but there was bipartisan resistance to altering existing military policy. In addition, there was a portentous 1993 decision by a U.S. district court judge in *Meinhold v. U.S. Department of Defense.*[85] In May 1992 Volker Meinhold, an airborne sonar analyst for the Navy, admitted he was gay in an interview on ABC's *World News Tonight*. He was subsequently discharged from the Navy and filed suit. As district court judge Terry Hatter Jr., a Carter appointee, argued, Meinhold "was discharged not because he engaged in prohibited conduct, but because he labeled himself as gay."[86] The court ruled that the Department of Defense could not discharge or deny "enlistment to any person based on sexual orientation in the absence of sexual conduct."[87] Hatter also issued a temporary injunction against the Navy and ordered Meinhold reinstated.

On appeal, a three-judge panel of the Ninth Circuit, two Republican appointees and one Democratic appointee, ruled unanimously that the Navy could not discharge Meinhold simply because he said he is gay.[88] While the court deferred to the Navy's judgment that homosexual conduct "seriously impairs the accomplishment of the military mission," it rejected the argument that a declaration of homosexuality was reason enough for discharge.[89] The court noted that "no similar assumption is made with respect to service members who are heterosexual" unless they are guilty of such prohibited conduct as adultery, sodomy, bigamy, indecent assault, or prostitution.[90] The Department of Defense did not appeal the decision; in March 1996, after almost twenty years of service, Meinhold retired from the Navy with full military honors and was awarded the Navy Achievement Medal.[91] A "don't ask, don't tell" policy was in the offing.

President Clinton was still intent on a complete elimination of discrimination on the basis of sexual orientation in the military. He issued a draft executive order that was circulated to Congress and high-level military personnel, who generally opposed any modification to existing policy. General Colin Powell, for example, who chaired the Joint Chiefs of Staff at the time, opposed allowing gay men and lesbians to serve openly in the military. Powell stated that the "presence of homosexuals in the force would be detrimental to good order and discipline, for a variety of reasons, principally relating around the issue of privacy."[92] He also stated that if gays and lesbians were allowed to "exist openly in the military, [it] would affect the cohesion and well-being of the force. It asks us to deal with fundamental issues that society at large has not yet been able to deal with."[93] But then Powell seemed to suggest that the government should simply stop asking about sexual orientation: "a possible solution [is] we just stop asking," and there would no longer be any "witch hunting."[94]

But many military officials were opposed to any compromise. Commander Craig Quigley, for example, a Navy spokesperson, made this very specious, offensive claim: "Homosexuals are notoriously promiscuous. . . . If homosexuals are allowed to declare their sexual orientation openly . . . heterosexuals who showered with gay men would have an uncomfortable feeling of someone watching."[95] General H. Norman Schwarzkopf, who would eventually make some concessions, stated that "open homosexuality is the problem" and that "allowing declared gay men and lesbians to serve in the armed forces would result in disheartened troops."[96]

Most members of Congress did not support lifting the ban on gays and lesbians in the military at this time. But after extensive hearings held by the Senate and House Armed Services Committees, a congressional consensus emerged over what Sam Nunn (D-GA), chair of the Senate's committee at that time, dubbed, presumably based on Powell's statement and the *Meinhold* case, a "don't ask, don't tell" approach.[97] Here, the Department of Defense would not be able to inquire about the sexual orientation of a prospective candidate for the military and the candidate would not be able to reveal his or her sexual orientation. If the candidate did come out as gay or lesbian, he or she would be discharged. Gays and lesbians would be required to stay hidden and cloaked in secret subterfuge. Although President Clinton sought to completely lift the ban on gays and lesbians in the military, his hands were tied. It seemed obvious during his first term that amid a potential bipartisan backlash, he would need to strike a compromise with Congress and military leaders. The "don't ask, don't tell" policy took effect in 1994 and remained in effect until its repeal in 2010. The policy epitomizes the politics of discrimination around LGBT issues. It was a minor policy drift that was not beneficial to gays or lesbians in the military.[98]

The reluctance of Congress to end discrimination in the military certainly signaled its lack of support for a law that would end discrimination against LGBT individuals in the workplace. On June 23, 1994, Representative Gerry Studds (D-MA) introduced to the Democratic-controlled House the Employment Non-Discrimination Act (ENDA). It would protect at least gays and lesbians in the workplace; the proposed law did not contain a provision for gender identity, which is intended to protect transgender employees. The bill had a total of 108 co-sponsors, from every region in the country, including the South. There were 103 Democrats, four Republicans, and one independent.[99] On July 19 it was referred to the Subcommittee on Select Education and Civil Rights, where it died.[100] The subcommittee did not hold any hearings on ENDA.

Senator Ted Kennedy (D-MA) introduced the bill to the Democratic-controlled Senate also on June 23, 1994, with twenty-nine co-sponsors, mostly Democrats, from all regions of the country.[101] This bill also did not contain a provision for gender identity. Like the House bill, it died in committee. In the hearings on July 29 before the Senate Committee on Labor and Human Resources, there seemed to be some support. Senator Kennedy, who chaired the committee, said in his opening statement,

> From the beginning, civil rights has been the great unfinished business of America, and it still is. . . . Federal law now rightly prohibits job discrimination because of race, gender, religion, national origin, age, and disability. Establishing these essential protections was not easy or quick. But they have stood the test of time, and they have made us a better and a stronger Nation. We now seek to take the next step on this journey of justice by banning discrimination based on sexual orientation. At the press conference introducing this legislation, Coretta Scott King said: "I support the Employment Non-Discrimination Act of 1994 because I believe that freedom and justice cannot be parceled out in pieces to suit political convenience. As my husband Martin Luther King, Jr., said, injustice anywhere is a threat to justice everywhere." . . . This bill is not about granting special rights. It is about righting senseless wrongs. What it requires is simple justice for gay men and lesbians who deserve to be judged in the workplace like all other Americans by their ability to do the work.[102]

Other Democrats on the Senate committee also rose in support of ENDA, including Senators Wellstone (MN) and Simon (IL). Senator Claiborne Pell (D-RI), a co-sponsor of the bill, was not present at the hearings but offered this in his prepared statement to the committee:

> It is unfortunate that in 1994 this Nation is still debating the issue of discrimination. Didn't we learn anything from the Civil Rights movement of the 1960's? Haven't we learned not to judge others based on who they are or what they are? Unfortunately, there are still too many of our fellow

citizens who go to work every day in fear of losing their jobs for reasons having nothing to do with their job performance.[103]

One Republican member of the committee, Senator Nancy Kassebaum (KS), was willing to express some opposition. She began by stating that she looked forward to the day when "it is the content of the character that is the basis for judgement." But then she surprisingly questioned whether legislation was the most appropriate way to address discrimination based on sexual orientation:

> As the chairman knows, and others, perhaps, I have always questioned just how much we can do by law to end intolerance, to help us reach that point where we judge by character and not on other factors that should not be used in judging the ability of one to do his job and his work and take his place in society. But that is what this hearing is about; how do we and how should we address this issue.[104]

Interestingly, the conservative former senator Barry Goldwater (R-AZ) entered a prepared statement to the committee offering his support for ENDA:

> You don't have to look very far to see there's a lot of support out there for this kind of legislation. In 1992, I worked with a broad-based bi-partisan coalition to pass an ordinance prohibiting job discrimination based on sexual orientation here in Phoenix. We had the support of the civil rights, religious, and business communities. Even large companies like US West were on our side. In spite of this wide support, some people said the world would end if the ordinance passed. But it didn't. Phoenix businesses haven't collapsed. In fact, they haven't suffered one bit as a result. And that shouldn't be surprising. In states that have laws protecting gays and lesbians from job discrimination, officials report less than a 5% increase in job discrimination. As US West put it, this kind of legislation presents no danger to firms who don't discriminate.[105]

A number of gay and lesbian workers who were fired based on their sexual orientation appeared before the Senate committee to convey their experiences. For example, Cheryl Summerville of Georgia gave an impassioned statement:

> I am from a small town in rural west Georgia called Bremen. . . . I worked [at Cracker Barrel] for almost 4 years and always had excellent performance evaluations. I got awards and promotions. I enjoyed my job at Cracker Barrel, and I thought I had a real bright future ahead of me. . . . One day in January of 1991, that all came to an end. The chairman of Cracker Barrel, the Corporation, had a memo sent around directing managers to fire all employees "whose sexual preferences fail to demonstrate normal heterosexual values." When I heard it, I could not believe it. What would happen to me? What would happen to my family? I was scared. . . . I could not afford to lose my job. . . . So after nearly 4 years of committed service with Cracker Barrel, including raises and personal achievement awards, I was fired for being a lesbian—something that has nothing to do with my ability to do my job and do it well. On my separation notice, they wrote, "This employee is being terminated due to violation of company policy. This employee is gay." . . . If I lived in Massachusetts or Minnesota, the State law would have protected me against being fired for being gay. But not in Georgia. What Cracker Barrel did was perfectly legal under the laws of Georgia, and most States. . . . Federal law did not cover me, either. Senators, what happened to me is not fair, and it is not right.[106]

Senator Howard Metzenbaum (D-OH) was very supportive but noted that not all members of the Senate would advocate for this issue. "Ms. Summerville," he stated, "it was very difficult for you to testify, but it was very important. I think there are many of us in Congress—I am not sure if there is a majority—who feel as strongly as this Senator does, that any kind of discrimination is just wrong."[107] He went on to say, "It is immoral what is happening to those persons who are gay or lesbian, and I think we have a responsibility to do something about it. I will not be here in the Senate very long, but I hope that before I leave it, I will be a party to making a change so that discriminating against people who are gay or lesbian is just as illegal as discriminating against people on the basis of race, creed, national origin, or other bases."[108]

Ernest Dillon, a gay postal employee who was forced to quit his job in Detroit because of repeated harassment, also testified before the Senate committee:

> I wish I did not have a story to tell, but I do. . . . I began working for the postal service in Detroit in 1980. It was a good job, a job I was extremely grateful to have. . . . Then, in 1984, things changed. A coworker, suspecting I was gay, began to make anti-gay remarks to me. . . . Whether I was gay or not was not anybody's business, and it certainly did not have anything to do with my job. I did my job, and I did it well. But the insults soon escalated into more serious harassment. . . . To earn a living, I had to endure constant verbal abuse, and try to keep focused while finding outrageous things written about me, plastered on the walls of the office and in the trucks—nasty things, vulgar things, hurtful and hostile things. I reported these incidents to my supervisors and to my union representative. My supervisors said there was nothing they could do to help me until my harasser actually "did something." . . . I am a black man from Detroit, and I have seen much bigotry before. I had been taught at a young age that you do not run from prejudice. You persist in the face of it. You work hard, you persevere, and eventually it pays off. More than anything else, I had been taught to believe that in America, if you do your job well, you have the right to keep it. Then, 1 [sic] day while on the job, my coworker cornered me, and I thought he would kill me. He threw me down on the floor, kicked me, and beat me until I was unconscious. He left me in a pool of blood, with two black eyes, a severely bruised sternum, and gashes in my forehead. When I regained consciousness, a supervisor rushed me to the medical unit and then to the emergency room.[109]

Dillon went on to say that he had endured physical, emotional, and psychological damage for another three years, but was forced to quit because the post office offered no protection. He filed suit, and his case wound its way up to the U.S. Court of Appeals for the Sixth Circuit, which ruled that there was no federal law that could protect him. Dillon paraphrased the Circuit Court's ruling: "Dillon's coworkers deprived him of a proper work environment because they believed him to be homosexual. Their comments, graffiti, and assaults were all directed at demeaning him solely because they disapproved vehemently of his alleged homosexuality. These actions, although cruel, are not made illegal by Title VII."[110]

Not surprisingly, there were also statements and testimony in opposition to ENDA. For example, Robert H. Knight of the Family Research Council argued that the law would be detrimental for children and families from the standpoint of religion and morality:

> As a pro-family organization, we see the Employment Non-Discrimination Act as less about tolerance than about the government forcing acceptance of homosexuality on tens of millions of unwilling Americans. The bill essentially takes away the rights of employers to decline to hire or promote someone who openly acknowledges indulging in behavior that the employer or his customers find immoral, unhealthy and destructive to individuals, families and societies. Employers would lose the right to include character in their assessment of a prospective employee, and that would be tyranny. . . . Martin Luther King Jr. said that a just society would judge people not by their skin color but by the content of their character, and character involves behavior. Many employers believe that homosexual behavior is immoral and they recognize that it has been discouraged in every successful culture in the world. The issue here is not job discrimination. It is whether private businesses will be forced by law to accommodate homosexual activists' attempts to legitimize homosexual behavior. If this bill becomes law, for the first time in history Americans will be told that they must hire people they believe to be committing immoral acts precisely because they commit those acts. This interferes with freedom of association, freedom of speech and freedom of religion.[111]

As noted, the bill did not make it out of the Senate committee. Of the seventeen members of the committee, only five were present for the hearings, far short of a quorum needed to move the bill forward. Those present were Senators Kennedy, Metzenbaum (D-OH), Simon (D-IL), Wellstone (D-MN), and Kassebaum (R-KS). Interestingly, even those members of the committee who were co-sponsors of the bill *were not present* for the hearings. These include Senators Claiborne Pell (D-RI), Jim Jeffords (R-VT), Christopher Dodd (D-CT), Tom Harkin (D-IA), Barbara Mikulski (D-MD), and Jeff Bingaman (D-NM).[112]

Protections for LGBT individuals in 1994 would, therefore, be left to the patchwork of laws or policies developed by the states. At that time, there were only eight states that enacted antidiscrimination laws to protect gay and lesbian workers: California, Connecticut, Hawaii, Massachusetts, Minnesota, New Jersey, Vermont, and Wisconsin. Governors of eleven states issued executive orders doing the same for public employees: Colorado, Louisiana, Maryland, Michigan, New Mexico, New York, Ohio, Oregon, Pennsylvania, Rhode Island, and Washington. And about a hundred cities and counties across the country had ordinances prohibiting discrimination based on sexual orientation in public employment.[113]

Subsequent Efforts to Pass ENDA

Since 1994, ENDA has been introduced in every Congress except the 109th. In virtually every instance, the bill never made it through congressional committees. There have been three notable exceptions. The first was on September 5, 1996, when Senator Ted Kennedy reintroduced ENDA to the Republican-controlled Senate.[114] On September 6 a floor action to consider the bill was laid before the Senate by unanimous consent.[115] But on September 10 it failed, 49–50. Forty-one Democrats and eight Republicans voted in favor. The Republicans voting in favor included Lincoln Chafee (RI), William Cohen (ME), Al D'Amato (NY), Mark Hatfield (OR), Jim Jeffords (VT), Alan Simpson (WY), Olympia Snowe (ME), and Arlen Specter (PA). Forty-five Republicans voted against, as did these five Democrats: Robert Byrd (WV), Jim Exon (NE), Wendell Ford (KY), Howell Heflin (AL), and Sam Nunn (GA).[116]

Senator Orrin Hatch (R-UT) was one of the detractors voicing opposition.[117] He argued that "special protected status in the law" was not needed for gays and lesbians:

This bill deals in a blunderbuss way with an issue much more complex than issues raised by legislation addressing race, ethnicity, and gender. Sexual orientation involves conduct, not immutable nonbehavioral characteristics. . . . Skin color is a benign, non-behavioral characteristic. Sexual orientation is perhaps the most profound of human behavioral characteristics. Comparison of the two is a convenient but invalid argument. . . . It is totally indefensible to say that a black person should be denied the right to teach children of any race in any of our public or private schools. But should the Senate run roughshod over the concerns of parents and educators about having homosexuals teach their kids?[118]

The bill never reached a floor vote in the House.[119] It eventually died in the House Subcommittee on the Constitution; like the Senate, the House was controlled by Republicans at this time.[120]

In April 2007 the openly gay Representative Barney Frank (D-MA) introduced ENDA to the 110th Congress.[121] The bill died in the House Subcommittee on the Constitution, Civil Rights and Civil Liberties, primarily because it contained a provision on gender identity. It was the first time, since ENDA had first been introduced, that the bill sought to protect workers based on gender identity. But when Frank reintroduced the bill in September 2007, now without the language on gender identity, it passed the Democratic-controlled House by a vote of 235–184.[122] There were 200 Democrats and 35 Republicans who supported the bill; 159 Republicans and 25 Democrats voted against it.[123]

The bill was placed on the Senate's legislative calendar on November 8 and 13, but it was never acted upon.[124] The Senate at this time was controlled by Democrats. The bill was not supported by President George W. Bush, either, who issued a Statement of Administration Policy promising to veto the bill if it reached his desk. Bush, who ran as a compassionate conservative, may not have supported LGBT employment protections, but, in his own words, he drew the line at physical violence: "I'm not going to kick gays. I think it is bad for Republicans to be kicking gays."[125] It seemed clear that the country had still not garnered enough political backing, even from Senate Democrats, to support the passage of a federal law guaranteeing employment protections to LGBT workers.

The last time ENDA made it out of a congressional committee was in 2013. On April 25, 2013, Representative Jared Polis (D-CO) introduced ENDA to the Republican-controlled House.[126] This version of the bill had a provision for gender identity. The House at this point under the leadership of its Speaker, John Boehner (R-OH), seemed confused as to which committee the bill should be referred, notwithstanding the fact that there had been no confusion in previous sessions when ENDA was introduced. It was referred to the Committee on Education and the

Workforce, but also the Committees on House Administration, Oversight and Government Reform, and the Judiciary. Perhaps this was a delaying tactic by the Speaker. Boehner subsequently referred the bill to the Subcommittee on the Constitution and Civil Justice. Then, on July 8, it was referred to the Subcommittee on Workforce Protections, where, not surprisingly, it died.[127]

But the Democratic-controlled Senate moved further on the bill. On April 25, Senator Jeff Merkley (D-OR) introduced Senate Bill 815.[128] This version, like the House's, had a gender-identity provision. The bill was referred to the Senate Committee on Health, Education, Labor, and Pensions, which, due to previous years' support for and testimonials in favor of the bill, did not hold hearings. The committee's report began by stating,

> Thousands of hardworking Americans have lost their livelihoods simply because of who they are or who they love, and millions more go to work every day facing that threat. The committee believes the Federal Government should not permit unfettered bigotry to go unchecked, leading to the loss of jobs, fear in the workplace, economic instability, and personal hardship, while allowing employers and the economy to lose competent, qualified workers. Employment decisions should be made on individual merit and performance, not extraneous factors such as sexual orientation or gender identity. The committee believes that sexual orientation and gender identity are irrelevant to a person's ability to do his or her job and they only become factors when people's biases and prejudices determine employment actions such as hiring and firing. Just as it is unacceptable to fire or refuse to hire a person based on his or her race, sex, national origin, religion, age or disability, it is unacceptable to base employment decisions on an employee's or applicant's sexual orientation or gender identity.[129]

The committee also pointed to hundreds of companies that continued to endorse ENDA. For example, Kenneth Charles, vice president at General Mills, testified that "ENDA will be good for business and good for American [sic] by helping businesses attract and retain talent, helping provide a safe, comfortable and productive work environment, free from any form of discrimination, and helping create a culture that fosters creativity and innovation that is vital to the success of all businesses."[130]

Similarly, Robb Webb, chief human resources officer at Hyatt, testified that "we believe that including sexual orientation and gender identity protection in workplace non-discrimination legislation will have a positive impact on our country's ability to compete on the world stage."[131] In addition, although religious organizations are not covered by ENDA, many religious organizations offered support for ENDA. Nearly fifty religious organizations wrote to the Senate committee endorsing the bill.[132] Their statement read in part,

> As a nation, we cannot tolerate arbitrary discrimination against millions of Americans just because of who they are. Lesbian, gay, bisexual and transgender (LGBT) people should be able to earn a living, provide for their families and contribute to society without fear that who they are or who they love could cost them a job. . . . We call on you to pass this important legislation without delay. . . . Any claims that ENDA harms religious liberty are misplaced. ENDA broadly exempts from its scope houses of worship as well as religiously affiliated organizations. This exemption—which covers the same religious organizations already exempted from the religious discrimination provisions of Title VII of the Civil Rights Act of 1964—should ensure that religious freedom concerns don't hinder the passage of this critical legislation.[133]

In addition, President Obama issued a Statement of Administration Policy on November 4 urging the Senate to pass ENDA:

> The Administration strongly supports Senate passage of S. 815 because the bill would establish lasting and comprehensive Federal protections against employment discrimination on the basis of sexual orientation or gender identity. This bipartisan legislation is necessary to ensure that strong Federal protections exist for lesbian, gay, bisexual, and transgender workers no matter where they live. Workers should not fear being fired from their jobs, harassed at their workplaces, or otherwise denied the chance to earn a living for themselves and their families, simply because of sexual orientation or gender identity. This legislation would, for the first time in this Nation's history, make explicit in Federal law such guarantees, which are consistent with America's core values of fairness and equality. Passage of this bill is long overdue.[134]

Several senators opposed the passage of ENDA, primarily on religious grounds and implications for the provision of restrooms. Although the term "morality" was never used, it seemed part of the subtext. Republican senators Lamar Alexander (TN), Mike Enzi (WY), John Isakson (GA), Rand Paul (KY), Pat Roberts (KS), and Tim Scott (SC) explained,

> We voted against this legislation when the committee considered it and continue to oppose this legislation. . . . S. 815 makes no provisions for, nor seems to in any way acknowledge the potential for nefarious abuse of employment protections and gender-specific area access privileges. This oversight creates a gaping hole which could leave employers powerless and confused about how to prevent abuse and protect fellow employees, customers, and others present at the workplace. Among other workplaces, we are concerned about the application of S. 815 in schools, preschools, and other institutions serving children. Issues with the use of shared facilities by transgender students have already arisen in several States under State laws unrelated to ENDA. Under these State statutes the courts have largely dismissed the concerns of schools, teachers, parents, and fellow students regarding safety issues for the peers of transgender students, setting a precedent that leaves these groups powerless to raise or resolve such concerns. . . . We are concerned that this will be repeated in workplaces around the country. . . . For some employers, the mandates of this legislation would conflict with deeply held religious beliefs. As reported, the bill singles out specific classes of employers for total exemption based on religious beliefs, but disregards others whose religiously-based opposition to the bill's mandates may be just as sincere. In our view, there is little basis for this distinction. The bill raises additional concerns with us because, in creating a new protected class, it actually affords that new class with rights that are elevated above those granted to existing protected classes of race, sex, national origin, religion, age and disability. . . . Finally, we oppose S. 815 because the legislation is not necessary. As noted, 17 States and the District of Columbia have adopted similar legislation, as well as a number of cities. Some large employers have also adopted voluntary provisions. . . . That is their choice, and in our system of government they are thankfully free to make it.[135]

On November 4, 2013, the Senate agreed, 61–30, to the cloture motion to proceed to consideration of ENDA. And on November 7 the Senate agreed to invoke cloture. On that day, it voted to pass ENDA, 64–32; 4 did not vote. No Democrats voted against the bill, and ten Republicans voted to support it.[136] A message on the Senate action was sent to the House on this same day, urging the House to reconsider the bill. After referral to several committees, the Republican-controlled House took no further action, thus killing the ENDA of 2013.[137]

After almost twenty years, Congress was still unable—or perhaps un-willing—to pass legislation that would protect LGBT employees in the workplace. Frustrated by the lack of progress, President Obama skirted Congress and used his power as chief executive to initiate policy drifts in the form of executive orders that would extend employment protec-tions to at least LGBT employees of the federal government. As will be discussed, because executive orders are more vulnerable to change when a new party takes over the White House, their durability remains uncertain.

President Obama Initiates Policy Drifts

A campaign promise in 2008 by Obama, once dubbed "the first gay president," was to take action on ENDA. He stated that "as president, I will place the weight of my administration behind the enactment of . . . a fully inclusive Employment Non-Discrimination Act to outlaw workplace discrimination on the basis of sexual orientation and gender identity."[138] However, as we saw above, both Democrats and Republicans in Congress have resisted passing legislation that prohibited discrimina-tion against LGBT citizens. Although the Democrats prevailed in 2007 when ENDA passed in the House, and then again in 2013 when ENDA passed in the Senate, there simply has not been enough support to pass the law. In defiance of Congress and its inability, failure, or reluctance to enact a law to protect LGBT individuals in the workplace, President Obama took executive action to address LGBT employment rights, thereby creating a significant policy drift in this area of civil rights.

Although executive action is more limited than statutory laws, Pres-ident Obama took a number of steps to provide LGBT workers with employment protections. One of his first presidential memoranda was issued in June 2009 in response to the 2007 resignation of Michael Guest, the first openly gay ambassador, from the State Department.

Guest, a Foreign Service officer since 1981, served as U.S. ambassador to Romania during the Bush presidency, from 2001 to 2004. President Obama wrote that Guest

> believed that the country he served was failing to implement the principles of equality it espoused abroad. His partner was ineligible for training provided to Ambassadorial spouses; he bore the costs of his partner's transportation to his placements abroad; and his partner did not receive the overseas benefits and allowances given to spouses of Ambassadors. It is too late to prevent Ambassador Guest from having to make the choice he made, but today I am proud to issue a Presidential Memorandum that will go a long way toward achieving equality for many of the hardworking, dedicated, and patriotic LGBT Americans serving in our Federal Government. . . . Extending equal benefits to the same-sex partners of Federal employees is the right thing to do. It is also sound economic policy. Many top employers in the private sector already offer benefits to the same-sex partners of their employees; those companies recognize that offering partner benefits helps them compete for and retain the brightest and most talented employees. The Federal Government is at a disadvantage on that score right now, and change is long overdue.[139]

President Obama's memorandum directed federal agencies to extend virtually all benefits to the same-sex partners of federal employees. He explained that not all benefits could be offered: "Unfortunately, my Administration is not authorized by existing Federal law to provide same-sex couples with the full range of benefits enjoyed by heterosexual married couples. That's why I stand by my long-standing commitment to work with Congress to repeal the so-called Defense of Marriage Act. It's discriminatory, it interferes with States' rights, and it's time we overturned it."[140]

In addition, President Obama appointed John Berry as director of the U.S. Office of Personnel Management (OPM), the office responsible for the federal government human resources program and system. He was the highest-ranking openly gay official in U.S. history. He served as OPM director from April 13, 2009, to April 13, 2013, when Obama nominated him to serve as ambassador to Australia; he was confirmed to this post by unanimous consent of the U.S. Senate in August 2013.

In June 2010 President Obama issued a presidential memorandum entitled "Extension of Benefits to Same-Sex Domestic Partners of Federal Employees," which went even further than his 2009 directive. It ensured that children of same-sex partnerships were covered, and provided an expansive view of "family." It provided a number of additional benefits to partners of federal workers, including travel and relocation assistance, childcare subsidies, and certain retirement benefits.[141]

And President Obama fulfilled his campaign promise to repeal the "don't ask, don't tell" policy. He worked with Congress and military personnel to end this regressive policy. His secretary of defense, Robert Gates, and Joint Chiefs chair Michael Mullen both urged immediate repeal. Along partisan lines, it passed the House by a vote of 250–175, and the Senate 65–31.[142] On December 22, 2010, Obama signed the Don't Ask, Don't Tell Repeal Act.[143] Although Congress was unwilling to support a federal law to protect LGBT workers from employment discrimination, it was willing to allow at least gays and lesbians to serve openly in the military. The Repeal Act did not apply to transgender persons. In July 2015 the Pentagon announced that it was considering a policy to allow transgender persons to serve in the military, and by June 2016 it had adopted such a policy, allowing transgender Americans to serve openly in the military for the first time.[144]

Other actions taken by the Obama administration in 2010 in support of LGBT individuals include the following:

- In January 2010 the Office of Personnel Management added gender identity to the equal employment opportunity policy governing all federal jobs. In September 2011 it issued additional guidance to federal managers regarding the equal treatment of transgender workers.
- In March 2010 the IRS clarified that domestic partners (and their children) can be designated beneficiaries for VEBA funding/payment purposes.
- President Obama issued a presidential memorandum in April 2010 directing the Department of Health and Human Services to issue regulations requiring all hospitals receiving Medicaid and Medicare to prohibit discrimination in visitation against LGBT people. The HHS issued regulations that went into effect in 2011.

- In June 2010 the Office of Personnel Management published a final rule allowing same-sex domestic partners of federal employees to apply for long-term care insurance, and to take funeral and sick leave to care for a domestic partner.
- In June 2010 the Department of Justice issued an opinion clarifying that the criminal provisions of the Violence Against Women Act related to stalking and abuse apply equally to same-sex partners.
- In June 2010 the Department of State revised the standards for changing a gender marker on a passport, making the process less burdensome for transgender people.
- In June 2010 the Department of Labor issued guidance clarifying that an employee can take time off under the Family and Medical Leave Act to care for a same-sex partner's child, even where the partner does not have a legal or biological relationship to that child.[145]

Obama's "ENDA" in the Federal Government

Although Congress has repeatedly failed to pass a national law protecting LGBT workers from employment discrimination, President Obama used his executive powers to provide such protection as broadly as legally and constitutionally permissible. For example, on July 21, 2014, he signed Executive Order 13672, amending Executive Order 11246, to prohibit federal contractors and subcontractors from discriminating on the basis of sexual orientation or gender identity. The executive order also amends E.O. 11478 (1969) and E.O. 13087 (1998) to include gender identity as a protected class in the federal civilian workforce.[146] These represent significant policy drifts on LGBT employment rights. At the signing of his executive order, Obama stated, "It doesn't make much sense, but today in America, millions of our fellow citizens wake up and go to work with the awareness that they could lose their job, not because of anything they do or fail to do, but because of who they are—lesbian, gay, bisexual, transgender. And that's wrong." He went on to say that because of their "passionate advocacy and the irrefutable rightness of [their] cause, our government—government of the people, by the people, and for the people—will become just a little bit fairer."[147]

President Obama's press release went even further:

America is built on the fundamental promise that if you work hard, and play by the rules, you can get ahead. But today, millions of Americans in most states in the country go to work every day fearing that they could lose their jobs simply because of who they are or who they love. No current federal law adequately protects lesbian, gay, bisexual, and transgender (LGBT) workers from employment discrimination. This is completely contrary to our values as Americans—and it's also bad for business.[148]

President Obama's aims and ideology were also reflected in cases where his federal agencies went beyond congressional action or statutory law, holding that discrimination against a transgender individual is sex discrimination and therefore prohibited under Title VII of the Civil Rights Act as amended. This rule, a major policy drift, is derived from the adjudicatory powers of the Equal Employment Opportunity Commission (EEOC). In 2012 the EEOC issued a decision in *Macy v. Holder* holding that discrimination in the workplace based on gender identity is illegal under Title VII.[149] In this case, Mia Macy, a former Phoenix police officer, presented as a man when she applied for a position with the DOJ's Bureau of Alcohol, Tobacco, Firearms and Explosives. She was promised the job subject to a background check, but when she revealed that she was in the process of transitioning from male to female, she was told the position was no longer available. She later learned that another person had been hired for the position.[150] Drawing on the U.S. Supreme Court's 1989 ruling in *Price Waterhouse v. Hopkins*, the EEOC began by arguing that "six members of the Supreme Court in *Price Waterhouse* agreed that Title VII barred 'not just discrimination because of biological sex, but also gender stereotyping—failing to act and appear according to expectations defined by gender.'"[151]

The EEOC continued,

That Title VII's prohibition on sex discrimination proscribes gender discrimination, and not just discrimination on the basis of biological sex, is important. If Title VII proscribed only discrimination on the basis of biological sex, the only prohibited gender-based disparate treatment would be when an employer prefers a man over a woman, or vice versa. But the statute's protections sweep far broader than that, in part because the term "gender" encompasses not only a person's biological sex *but also the cultural and social aspects associated with masculinity and femininity.*[152]

In a unanimous ruling, the EEOC asserted that

when an employer discriminates against someone because the person is transgender, the employer has engaged in disparate treatment "related to the sex of the victim." . . . This is true regardless of whether an employer discriminates against an employee because the individual has expressed his or her gender in a non-stereotypical fashion, because the employer is uncomfortable with the fact that the person has transitioned or is in the process of transitioning from one gender to another, or because the employer simply does not like that the person is identifying as a transgender person. In each of these circumstances, the employer is making a gender-based evaluation, thus violating the Supreme Court's admonition that "an employer may not take gender into account in making an employment decision."[153]

The EEOC also drew on the following cases in rendering its decision in *Macy*: *Schwenk v. Hartford* (2000), *Smith v. City of Salem* (2004), and *Glenn v. Brumby* (2011), where the federal courts ruled that discrimination against an individual for gender-nonconforming behavior violates Title VII's prohibition against sex stereotyping.[154] The courts did not rule that transgender status is a protected class, but they did rule that Title VII protects persons from discrimination by their employers if they fail to act in accordance with their perceived sex or gender.[155] Importantly, however, the EEOC in *Macy* held that discrimination based on gender identity is *illegal* under Title VII.

Rulings by the EEOC are significant because they represent a form of rulemaking by an administrative agency.[156] That is, through adjudication, an administrative agency is effecting policy or creating policy drifts. In the case of *Macy*, the EEOC is instructing its staff, including private-sector investigators, that gender-identity discrimination is prohibited under Title VII.

Consistent with the EEOC's decision in *Macy*, Attorney General Eric Holder in December 2014 announced that the U.S. Department of Justice (DOJ) would now interpret Title VII's prohibition against sex discrimination to cover gender identity, including transgender status. Recall that Holder was the defendant in *Macy*, supporting the decision by the DOJ's Bureau of Alcohol, Tobacco, Firearms and Explosives not to promote Macy. Although statutory law is not changed by Holder's interpretation, it is certainly an indication of the powerful reach of an administrative agency, particularly where its views mirror that of the president. It could affect how the DOJ supports a transgender plaintiff in lawsuits brought against employers.

Indeed, in March 2015 the DOJ and the EEOC filed a lawsuit against Southeastern Oklahoma State University and the Regional University System of Oklahoma for violating Title VII by discriminating against a transgender employee on the basis of her sex and retaliating against her when she complained about the discrimination. It is the first time the DOJ has filed such a suit. Dr. Rachel Tudor began working for the university as an assistant professor in 2004. Tudor presented as a man at the time of her hire. In 2007 Tudor, consistent with her gender identity, began to present as a woman at work. As an assistant professor, Tudor performed well, and in 2009 she sought tenure and promotion to associate professor. She was denied tenure and promotion despite a positive recommendation by the Faculty Tenure and Promotion Committee, which based its decision on the traditional academic standards of teaching, scholarship, and service. The committee's decision was overruled by the vice president of academic affairs, Dr. Douglas McMillan, who had previously inquired with the university's Department of Human Resources as to whether Tudor could be terminated because her lifestyle "offends his Baptist beliefs."[157] She was fired in 2011, and the DOJ filed suit alleging that Tudor was denied tenure and ultimately fired because of her sex. Tudor joined that lawsuit shortly afterward. In July 2015 the federal district court judge in Oklahoma denied the university's motion for dismissal of the case.[158]

The DOJ and the EEOC explicitly decided to collaborate on efforts to interpret Title VII as protecting transgender employees. The *Tudor* lawsuit was brought by both agencies in a "joint effort to enhance collaboration between the EEOC and the Justice Department's Civil Rights Division for vigorous enforcement of Title VII."[159] Acting Assistant Attorney General Vanita Gupta of the Civil Rights Division went on to say that the

Department of Justice is committed to protecting the civil rights of all Americans, including transgender Americans. . . . Discrimination against employees because of their gender identity, gender transition, or because they do not conform to stereotypical notions about how men and women should act or appear violates Title VII. Retaliating against an employee for complaining about unlawful discrimination, as happened in this case, is also unacceptable under Title VII.[160]

Jenny R. Yang, chair of the EEOC, agreed. According to Yang, "This is a tremendous example of how collaboration between EEOC and the Department of Justice leads to strong and coordinated enforcement of Title VII. . . . This case furthers the EEOC's Strategic Enforcement Plan, which includes coverage of lesbian, gay, bisexual and transgender individuals under Title VII's sex discrimination provisions as a national enforcement priority."[161]

The collaboration between these two federal agencies speaks to the powers of administrative agencies in policy drifts. As noted in chapter 1, the administrative presidency and unitary executive authority refer to the actions taken by the president and political appointees to shape or reshape public policies and programs in the absence of congressional approval.[162]

In addition to the *Tudor* lawsuit filed by the EEOC and the DOJ, in late 2014 the EEOC, for the first time, filed lawsuits against two private-sector organizations for gender-identity discrimination. In one case the EEOC asserted that an organization of health care professionals based in Lakeland, Florida, discriminated against its director of hearing services, Brandi Branson, in violation of Title VII, because she was transitioning from male to female. Branson was fired, argued the EEOC in *EEOC v. Lakeland Eye Clinic*, because she was transgender.[163] The case was ultimately settled out of court in April 2015; Lakeland Eye Clinic agreed to pay Branson $150,000, and also agreed to train both employees and management on transgender discrimination and develop and implement a new gender discrimination policy.[164]

In a second case, *EEOC v. R. G. & G. R. Harris Funeral Homes*, the EEOC filed a lawsuit on behalf of a funeral director, Aimee Stephens, who was fired because of her transgender status and gender transition, and based on gender-based stereotypes.[165] The district court decision, issued in 2015, argued that

> transgender status is not a protected class under Title VII. Thus, if the EEOC's complaint had alleged that the Funeral Home fired Stephens based solely upon Stephens's status as a transgender person, then this Court would agree with the Funeral Home that the EEOC's complaint fails to state a claim under Title VII. But the EEOC's complaint also asserts that the Funeral Home fired Stephens "because Stephens did not conform to the [Funeral Home's] sex- or gender-based preferences, expectations, or stereotypes."[166]

Thus, the court found that the EEOC had successfully argued a sex-stereotyping gender discrimination claim under Title VII.[167]

In effect, according to the courts, transgender status is not protected under Title VII, but the law does protect a transgender person to the extent they do not act in accordance with their perceived sex or gender. It is the act of sex stereotyping that is illegal, reinforcing the argument made by the *Price Waterhouse* Court in 1989, mentioned previously, which is somewhat ironic. As noted, six members of the High Court supported the view that sex stereotyping is proscribed by Title VII. But the Court majority ruled against Ann Hopkins on the grounds that there was a "mixed-motive" in Price Waterhouse's denial of a partnership. In a mixed-motive case, Price Waterhouse could argue, which it did, that Hopkins would not have been promoted to partnership even in the absence of sex discrimination. Price Waterhouse argued that Hopkins didn't wear makeup, or didn't walk and talk femininely, and wasn't feminine enough for a partnership. But it then claimed that these depictions of Hopkins were not the real reason she did not get the partnership. The High Court bought Price Waterhouse's argument (see table 3.2).[168]

Pushing the boundaries of Title VII further, in 2015 the EEOC held in a 3–2 ruling along party lines in *Baldwin v. Anthony Foxx, Department of Transportation* that discrimination against an individual because of that person's sexual orientation is discrimination because of sex and therefore prohibited under Title VII.[169] In this case, Baldwin worked as a temporary supervisory air traffic control specialist at the International Airport in Miami, Florida. He applied for but was turned down for a permanent position as a front line manager (FLM) at the airport; the permanent FLM position was never filled. Baldwin alleged that he was not selected for this position because he is gay. Baldwin stated that his supervisor, who was involved in the selection process, made several negative comments about Baldwin's orientation. Baldwin stated, for example,

> that in May 2011, when he mentioned that he and his partner had attended Mardi Gras in New Orleans, the supervisor said, "We don't need to hear about that gay stuff." He also alleged that the supervisor told him on a number of occasions that he was "a distraction in the radar room" when his participation in conversations included mention of his male partner.[170]

The EEOC ruled that

> sexual orientation is inseparable from and inescapably linked to sex and, therefore, that allegations of sexual orientation discrimination involve sex-based considerations. One can describe this inescapable link between allegations of sexual orientation discrimination and sex discrimination in a number of ways. Sexual orientation discrimination is sex discrimination because it necessarily entails treating an employee less favorably because of the employee's sex. . . . [This] is a legitimate claim under Title VII that sex was unlawfully taken into account in the adverse employment action.[171]

One final example of how Obama's administrative agencies induced policy drifts in the absence of congressional action can be seen in a rule issued by the U.S. Department of Labor. In February 2015, before the U.S. Supreme Court upheld the constitutionality of same-sex marriages in *Obergefell v. Hodges*, the U.S. Department of Labor issued a rule revising its definition of "spouse" under the Family and Medical Leave Act (FMLA) of 1993. The FMLA allows eligible employees of covered employers to take unpaid, job-protected leave for specified family and medical reasons for up to twelve weeks. The rule amends the regulatory definition of spouse under the FMLA to cover "same-sex spouses residing in States that recognize such marriages. . . . Similarly, . . . the definition of spouse as a person of the opposite sex as defined in DOMA is no longer valid."[172] In light of *Obergefell*, same-sex spouses in *any* state can now take FMLA leave to care for their spouse or family members.

In sum, the administrative presidency model explains how the Obama administration took a series of progressive actions in support of LGBT rights when Congress refused to.[173] Although controversial, this model, similar to unitary executive branch theory, rests on constitutional and statutory principles. While the U.S. Constitution does not explicitly state that a president can issue executive orders, memoranda, or rules, these are implied powers. Article II, Section 3, of the Constitution provides that the president shall "take Care that the Laws be faithfully executed." Also the Administrative Procedures Act of 1946 acknowledges the president's authority to issue executive orders in that it states that all executive orders must be published in the *Federal Register*.[174] To be sure, executive orders can be challenged by congressional actions as well as in court by Congress or other parties, including states.[175] For example, in 2013 the Obama administration issued a rule to delay the implementation of the employer mandate under the Affordable Care Act. Republicans in Congress responded by filing suit against the administration for this delay, but also because the Obama administration was paying subsidies to insurance companies that were never appropriated by Congress. Republicans argued that the administration was violating Article I, Section 1 of the Constitution, which grants Congress "all legislative powers."[176] In 2016 a federal district court ruled in favor of the House, opining that Congress had never appropriated funds to pay cost-sharing subsidies to health insurers.[177] The decision is likely to be appealed unless, of course, the Affordable Care Act is gutted by President Trump. Indeed, one of Trump's first executive orders instructed his administration to chip away at the act.[178]

In addition, in 2014 President Obama instructed the Department of Homeland Security to issue directives that extended various protections to immigrants.[179] Texas and twenty-five other states, all with Republican governors, immediately filed suit to enjoin implementation of those directives. The U.S. federal district court in Texas issued an injunction halting implementation nationwide. The injunction was upheld by the U.S. Court of Appeals for the Fifth Circuit.[180] In 2016 the U.S. Supreme

Court issued a 4–4 ruling in *United States v. Texas*.[181] The death of Justice Scalia in early 2016 left the Court one member short. The absence of a majority ruling leaves in place the appellate court ruling that blocked Obama's immigration plan. In short, executive orders or actions can be challenged in court.

The Equality Act of 2015

In 1974 Representatives Bella Abzug (D-NY) and Ed Koch (D-NY) introduced the Equality Act of 1974, which sought to amend Title VII of the Civil Rights Act to include sexual orientation as a protected class. It was never passed, but it gave way to ENDA, which, as seen earlier, also never passed. Notwithstanding, some members of Congress, with President Obama's support, have been attempting to amend the Civil Rights Act of 1964 to include protections that ban discrimination on the basis of sexual orientation and gender identity in employment, housing, public accommodations, credit, and education. It seemed a long shot, given that Congress has been unwilling to pass ENDA, which would protect LGBT individuals in the workplace.

On July 23, 2015, Representative David Cicilline (D-RI), who is openly gay, introduced H.R. 3185, the Equality Act of 2015, to the Republican-controlled House. It would amend Title VII to include sexual orientation and gender identity. It had 170 co-sponsors, all Democrats, from every region of the country.[182] Since it was introduced, it has been referred to several House committees; however, no action has yet been taken. The Human Rights Campaign has been a driving force for this law.

On this same day, Senator Jeff Merkley (D-OR) introduced the Equality Act of 2015 to the Republican-controlled Senate. It had 39 co-sponsors: 36 Democrats, one Republican—Mark Steven Kirk of Illinois; and two independents—Bernie Sanders of Vermont and Angus S. King Jr. of Maine.[183] The Senate, too, has not yet taken action on this bill.

President Obama has been a strong supporter of the act. White House press secretary Josh Earnest noted that the "unfortunate reality is that, while LGBT Americans can legally get married, millions remain at risk of being fired or denied services for who they are or who they love because the majority of states still lack explicit, comprehensive non-discrimination protections."[184]

The Equality Act of 2015 has received support from a host of corporations, such as Apple, Dow Chemical, Levi Strauss, American Airlines, Facebook, General Mills, Google, and Nike.[185] But a number of conservative and religious groups vowed to fight against passage of the bill. For example, Andrew T. Walker, director of policy studies for the Ethics and Religious Liberty Commission of the Southern Baptist Convention, stated that the

> Equality Act represents the most invasive threat to religious liberty ever proposed. Were it to pass, its sweeping effects on religious liberty, free speech, and freedom of conscience would be historic. . . . Were this bill to become law, traditional Christian, Jewish, and Muslim sexual morality would immediately be treated as suspect and contrary to federal law. This breathtaking attempt to relocate historic religious belief outside the bounds of polite culture is unacceptable and would have negative consequences for millions of Americans.[186]

Even a few advocates for LGBT issues have expressed reservations about the Equality Act, mainly in its intent to amend the very established Civil Rights Act. For example, Wade Henderson, president of the Leadership Conference on Civil and Human Rights, a group seeking to mobilize African American support for the bill, stated that "some are concerned about opening up, arguably, the most important statute Congress has ever enacted for the issue of racial discrimination."[187] Nevertheless, Henderson pledged to help assuage those concerns within the civil rights community.

Other groups felt that the proposed amendments to the Civil Rights Act did not go far enough to protect LGBT individuals. For example, Heather Cronk, co-director of the LGBT grassroots group GetEQUAL, explained that "we've been really clear that we don't support amending the Civil Rights Act because there's so many potential downfalls, but also because amending the Civil Rights Act actually doesn't fully protect LGBTQ folks in the unique way that we need, and so we continue to advocate for a standalone bill."[188]

The Equality Act did not pass the 114th Congress and it seems unlikely that the 115th Congress will pass the act, even with support from various interest groups. Despite the political, social, and cultural shifts in Americans' attitudes toward LGBT individuals, there continues to be strong opposition to national policies protecting LGBT employment rights. And it is doubtful that President Trump will push a Republican-controlled Congress into taking action on this bill. Also noteworthy, it is unlikely that more states or localities will adopt employment protections for LGBT persons, since citizen groups have developed a number of strategies to oppose such measures. For example, in Houston, Texas, voters in 2015 flatly rejected an ordinance that would prohibit discrimination against LGBT individuals in city employment, housing, contracting, and business services. The city's openly lesbian mayor, Annise Parker, fought hard against conservatives who blocked the measure. Opponents speciously framed the issue as the "bathroom ordinance," provoking fear that "gender identity protection would allow sexual predators to enter women's bathrooms."[189] Opponents picketed outside polling places with placards that read, "NO Men in Women's Bathrooms." And television ads sponsored by the opponents "depicted a young girl being followed into a bathroom stall by a mysterious older man."[190]

This issue has been largely waged by the states, with the lower federal courts weighing in on the side of transgender students.[191] But the power struggle over transgender students' rights was elevated to new heights when the state of North Carolina pushed a showdown with the federal government over the rights of transgender people to use the bathroom that corresponds with their gender identity. Although the topic is beyond the scope of this chapter, which addresses LGBT employment, a cursory review of this case is instructional as it is an important civil rights issue; moreover, it has implications for the employment rights of workers. Briefly, in early 2016 North Carolina passed a law, generally referred to as HB2, that banned local governments in the state from enacting antidiscrimination measures to protect LGBT individuals; it also restricted which bathrooms transgender students may use, which was the key element of HB2. The state law was a political reaction to an antidiscrimination law passed by the city of Charlotte in February 2016. The Charlotte ordinance expanded employment protections to cover sexual orientation and gender identity. One element of the ordinance was to allow trans people to use the restroom of their choice.

The Obama administration's Justice Department argued that North Carolina's law was in violation of federal civil rights law. Recall that, beginning with Eric Holder, the Justice Department has included gender identity and transgender status as a basis for discrimination claims under federal civil rights law. The U.S. Department of Education, under the Obama administration, similarly viewed the state law as a violation of Title IX. North Carolina was warned that if it did not repeal the law, it may be ineligible for billions of dollars in federal aid for highways, housing, and schools.[192] When North Carolina failed to back down, the Justice Department sued the state. The then governor of North Carolina, Pat McCrory (R), responded by filing a lawsuit against the Justice Department accusing it of overreaching its federal authority. He argued that "the Obama administration is bypassing Congress by attempting to rewrite the law."[193]

Shortly afterward, officials from eleven states also filed a lawsuit challenging the Obama administration's transgender bathroom policy.[194] In August 2016 a U.S. federal district court judge for the Northern District of Texas issued a ruling blocking the Obama administration's enforement of new guidelines that would allow trans students across the country to use the bathroom that corresponds with their gender identity.[195] Although limited in scope, this decision represents a blow to the Obama administration's efforts on transgender bathroom access.

On the other hand, a U.S. federal court judge from the Middle District of North Carolina issued a ruling, albeit limited, that the University of North Carolina system cannot enforce that section of the "bathroom bill" restricting which bathrooms trans students can use.[196] The partial ruling, however, is limited to only the people who brought one of the lawsuits over HB2. The court made clear that bathroom provisions violate Title IX as interpreted by the U.S. Department of Education, which redefined sex to include gender identity.

In addition to North Carolina, other states have developed explicit policies that have been harmful to LGBT employment. For example, in February 2015 Republican Governor Sam Brownback of Kansas rescinded an eight-year-old executive order issued by his predecessor, Governor Kathleen Sebelius, that protected LGBT individuals in state government from employment discrimination. Brownback argued that "any such expansion of 'protected classes' should be done by the legislature and not through unilateral action."[197]

Then, in July 2015, in response to the Supreme Court's *Obergefell* ruling in June, Governor Brownback issued an executive order that in effect promotes discrimination against LGBT people by allowing taxpayer-funded religious groups, including those providing social services, to discriminate against LGBT individuals without fear of legal reprisal.[198] An agency could argue on religious grounds, for example, to refuse to place a child with lesbian or gay parents. Brownback's executive order also states that clergy cannot be compelled to preside over a gay or lesbian marriage. This portion of the executive order was somewhat gratuitous, as ecclesiastics have always retained this right. It seems certain that this policy can only generate a slew of lawsuits.[199]

In sum, a national law or policy that protects LGBT individuals from employment or other forms of discrimination may be a long time coming. Perhaps Representative Barney Frank (D-MA), who introduced ENDA to the House in 2007, got it right when he once observed that "there is more resistance to protection for people who are transgender than for people who are gay, lesbian and bisexual. . . . This is not a good fact," he observed, "but ignoring bad facts is a bad way to get legislation passed."[200] Notwithstanding, political stakeholders, including elected officials, bureaucrats, interest groups, and even various religious organizations, are intent on continuing the fight for LGBT civil rights.

Conclusions

This chapter illustrates the different strategies or approaches to explain policy drifts on the issue of civil rights. Notably, the Civil Rights Act of 1964 has been particularly stable. It is inconceivable that the law could be repealed, thus stripping civil rights protections in the venues of employment, education, or public accommodations. But sporadic episodes of instability stemming from social or political upheaval have produced efforts to change the interpretation of the law and protections to those covered by the law (women and people of color). As discussed, regressive U.S. Supreme Court rulings in 1989 that sought to limit the scope of Title VII ultimately led to the 1991 amendments to the Civil Rights Act. And the High Court's *Ledbetter* decision, which would make it more difficult for women to achieve pay equity, was, after a good deal of wrangling by Congress, counteracted by the Lilly Ledbetter Fair Pay Act.

Perhaps the best theory to describe policy drifts with respect to pay equity is punctuated equilibrium. Pay equity policy remains relatively stable until punctuated by frenetic political activity.[201] This activity creates an abrupt change to existing policy, without complete eradication. This is then followed by bursts of activity by other stakeholders punctuating the political process to restore stability to the policy or law.

A potential deleterious drift, arising from the Supreme Court's *Ledbetter* decision, was averted by different stakeholders working to ensure that women are paid equitably. Democrats in Congress as well as President Obama were particularly instrumental in passing the Lilly Ledbetter Act. The shared powers model here shows how the democratic machinery, through checks and balances, operates to ensure that various interests participate in the process, even though in the end, women are the primary beneficiaries of this law, as it was originally intended. Nonetheless, everyone benefits from the stability and integrity that pay equity policies produce.

Yet efforts to push for even greater gains for women's pay have been stalled, mainly by Congress. As noted, the Ledbetter Act is critical in that it restores workers' rights to legally challenge pay inequities. On the other hand, the Paycheck Fairness Act would work against the occurrence of unequal pay. Both Democrats and Republicans have not been supportive of this act, no doubt in acquiescence to business interests, which benefit from paying women wages and salaries that are lower than men's. In effect, the powerful, elite special interest group collectively known as big business remains in control of pay structures that promote inequalities between women and men. As discussed in chapter 1, pluralism tends to operate at the expense of not simply women, but all those who support the promise of equality for all, which is, putatively, the American way.

Policy drifts and gains for LGBT individuals in the workplace, on the other hand, have materialized largely due to an administrative presidency or unitary executive strategy. The path dependency model fits here in that institutional inertia produces a resistance to change. Incremental changes to past policies promote policy continuity. While legislating pay equality at the federal level has had a long history, LGBT employment protections have not garnered enough attention or support, perhaps because society has been very slow to offer tolerance or acceptance of LGBT lifestyles. Consider, for example, that it wasn't until 1973 that the American Psychiatric Association removed homosexuality from its list of mental disorders. It is the shifting of attitudes among the populace that has gradually resulted in behavioral shifts. But we have not yet reached a point where society is willing to lend broad support for a national law to protect LGBT employment rights. With Congress's unwillingness to pass a national law, President Obama has exerted his executive control and authority to provide LGBT individuals with some protections.

But unilateral action by the president has led to concerns about whether democracy is thwarted. If Congress or the Supreme Court has not been willing to extend job protections to LGBT employees, should the president act alone to do so? Some question the legitimacy of the unitary or administrative presidency model of governance. As noted in chapter 2, many have argued that unitary executive authority undermines American democracy.[202] For example, in *Madison's Nightmare: How Executive Power Threatens American Democracy*, Peter Shane argued that the results of George W. Bush's unilateral presidency

> were hugely dysfunctional government—predictably bad decision making in the domains of military planning, foreign policy, and national security; contempt for the rule of law among government lawyers; presidential efforts to generate a phony appearance of legitimacy for executive resistance to accountability; and presidential usurpation of administrative agency decision making that is costly both economically and in terms of the health and safety of the American people.[203]

To be fair, of course, there is always an impulse to question the legitimate use of unitary executive authority when your party is not in power. Republicans will view executive privilege as executive imperialism when a Democrat is in office, and vice versa. Political partisanship trumps the question as to whether politics and concomitant law and policy are good or bad. Yet, interestingly enough, when Trump was campaigning for the presidency, he vowed to overturn all of President Obama's executive orders; in particular, LGBT activists expressed concerns that Trump would roll back the progress made during the Obama administration over LGBT rights.[204] In fact, once elected, President Trump was poised to gut Obama's executive order protecting LGBT employees, but at the urging of his daughter Ivanka and son-in-law Jared Kushner, he stated that he would leave that order in place.[205] Nonetheless, gay rights groups have remained skeptical of Trump's willingness to embrace their cause.[206] Transgender persons may be even more skeptical, especially in light of President Trump's decision to rescind the Obama administration's directives allowing transgender students the right to use the bathrooms corresponding with their gender identity.[207] Trump also announced that transgender persons could not serve in the military.[208] This, again, points to how policies can drift with changes to the party in control of the White House.

President Obama did rely on his unitary executive powers, but he did so within constitutional and statutory boundaries; his policy drifts are modest in scope, covering only federal employees and contractors. And, as noted, his executive orders granting LGBT citizens certain rights can be challenged in court by Congress. This has not happened. But then, are democratic values undermined when the bureaucracy, independent of Congress or the people, issues rules that effectively create protections for LGBT individuals? Certainly, when the Department of Justice as an extension of presidential authority takes certain actions, such as interpreting Title VII to cover gender identity or transgender status, an important unilateral policy decision or drift ensues. Is democratic rule even more compromised when an agency that is independent of presidential authority acts unilaterally to change public policy? In this chapter, we saw how the EEOC relied on its administrative powers to interpret Title VII in a manner that seems to go beyond legislative intent. Congress never interpreted Title VII to cover LGBT employees.

In a democracy, there are always winners and losers. There is a rich body of scholarship and empirical evidence in public administration illustrating how the bureaucracy serves as a safety net for disenfranchised individuals, such as people of color, who tend to fall through the cracks in terms of policy gains.[209] In this sense, the bureaucracy fulfills democratic goals and principles by representing the interests of those individuals. Frederick Mosher and Paul Appleby, for example, argue that for pragmatic reasons the bureaucracy has been forced to act politically, particularly since Congress is unwilling to take politically risky moves.[210] In effect, bureaucracy has become the fourth branch of government, operating as a political participant within the system of checks and balances. Mosher states that elected representatives are necessary in our political system, but so too are career bureaucrats. He argues that the "accretion of specialization and of technological and social complexity seems to be an irreversible trend, one that leads to increasing dependence upon the protected, appointive public service."[211] Out of necessity, he continues, in order to be compatible with democracy, the public service must reflect the social characteristics of the people and work to serve their needs and interests.[212] Kenneth Meier and Laurence O'Toole also point out that

> administrators properly socialized in the requisites of democratic governance can use their discretion to grease the wheels of the system by facilitating the virtually endless rounds of bargaining characteristic of pluralistic democracy. In this depiction public administrators, as the lead bureaucrats, are necessary . . . partners in pluralistic politics.[213]

In short, the president and the bureaucracy, perhaps mirroring cultural shifts in society, have taken positive steps to provide LGBT employment protections when Congress has not. Even the U.S. Supreme Court may be unwilling to provide such protections. Although the Supreme Court provided lesbians and gays with the right to marry in any state in the Union, it may not be as willing to do the same with employment rights. While the constitutional and legal standards are different, the High Court, given its conservative majority, simply may not support civil rights for LGBT individuals in the workplace. Thus, the president and the bureaucracy have worked together on behalf of these marginalized groups to ensure that their needs and interests are met.

4

The Politics of Climate Control Policy Drifts

Global warming has posed one of the greatest threats to the environment in recent times. According to the U.S. National Oceanic and Atmospheric Administration (NOAA), 2005 and 2010 were tied for the record of the warmest years of the global surface temperature since 1880.[1] Global warming results from the collection of carbon dioxide and other global warming pollutants (e.g., methane and nitrous oxide) in the earth's atmosphere, forming a type of insulation that traps the sun's heat, causing temperatures to rise to unusually high levels. Human activity is the primary cause. For decades, scientists have warned about the dangers of global warming, including its detrimental effects not just on the environment, but on the economic and social conditions of our planet as well.

Notwithstanding the abundance of scientific evidence on global warming, however, certain segments of our society have sought to undermine the credibility of this evidence. Industry groups and many states, for example, are the major naysayers, claiming that the evidence is misleading and that global warming poses no significant threat to the environment or society. This is not surprising, given that efforts to combat global warming will negatively affect the fossil fuel industry, which produces the coal, oil, and gas that contribute to the problem. The existence of global warming has its political skeptics as well, split mainly along party lines. A number of Republicans in Congress have questioned or denied the science surrounding global warming. Senator James Inhofe (R-OK), for example, has called global warming a conspiracy and "the greatest hoax perpetuated on the American people."[2] Senator Ted Cruz (R-TX), a Republican candidate for the 2016 presidential election, stated to the president of the Sierra Club that climate change was not a science but a religion.[3] With global warming thus politicized, efforts to develop or change climate policy have become more demanding and challenging.

There is also a schism along ideological lines. Ultraliberals mistrust the science around global warming and balk at certain technologies such as nuclear power that have the ability to produce great amounts of electricity while emitting virtually no greenhouse gases. A 2014 poll by the Pew Research Center found that support for nuclear power is more popular with Republicans than Democrats: 50 percent of Republicans back the use of nuclear power as a strategy to combat global warming, whereas only 28 percent of Democrats supported such action.[4]

This chapter examines the politics surrounding policy drifts in the area of climate change. In particular, it focuses on one critical, contemporary policy drift: the Obama Clean Power Plan, a historic and important step in reducing global warming. A host of policy players, particularly individual states, are stakeholders in the process as well as outcomes. As will be seen, shared beliefs and values led policy players to form advocacy coalitions. These coalitions, consisting of state governments and their allies (business and fuel interest groups), fight for certain values and work against those coalitions that oppose them. And although the issues are not new, global warming has become more salient in recent years, particularly in light of the landmark 2007 U.S. Supreme Court ruling in *Massachusetts v. EPA*, which held that greenhouse gases are air pollutants covered by the Clean Air Act, and thereby are subject to regulation by the EPA.[5]

The chapter begins with a brief review of the concepts of global warming and the greenhouse effect. It then examines the politics surrounding efforts to regulate climate change in light of the *Massachusetts* decision; this ruling was an important trigger for drifts in environmental policy and in turn a battle between the federal government, particularly the EPA, and the states on the right to regulate greenhouse gas emissions. The chapter also shows that policy drifts around global warming lack sustainability because they are not tied explicitly to any federal law. Instead, the drifts are driven by administrative actions, the states, and the courts. To the extent that there is a change in stakeholder structure—namely, the party controlling the White House—administrative actions under the party in control can undo any drifts made during previous administrations. Thus, the strategy that best explains this is administrative federalism.

Global Warming and the Greenhouse Effect

The greenhouse effect is one of the contributing factors to climate change or global warming. The greenhouse effect refers to trace gases such as carbon dioxide that accumulate in the atmosphere and prevent heat from escaping. Unlike global warming, the greenhouse effect is a natural process that happens constantly, due to sunlight and the atmosphere. It is vital for maintaining life on our planet; without it, earth would be uninhabitable.[6] However, an excess of greenhouse gases counteracts the positive effects of the process. As Dianne Rahm points out in *Climate Change Policy in the United States,*

> The greenhouse effect, first detected in 1896, is responsible for making the planet Earth habitable by preventing all the solar radiation that enters the atmosphere from radiating back into space. The link between the excessive buildup of greenhouse gases in the atmosphere and human activities was first described in the 1930s. It is this extreme buildup of greenhouse gases that is causing the warming of our planet.[7]

The United States and China are the largest producers of greenhouse gases, because their wealthy economies have been built on the consumption of energy, which in turn leads to greenhouse gas emissions. Yet in the United States, there is no federal law that explicitly requires public or private organizations to curb their impact on climate change.[8] Rather, it is a federal agency, the EPA, that at least since 2011 has relied on such statutes as the Clean Air Act of 1970 in its efforts to regulate greenhouse gases.[9] The Clean Air Act does not explicitly address climate, nor does it authorize regulation to address global warming.[10] Responsibility for climate change laws and policies in the United States has instead devolved to the states.[11] As Barry Rabe points out,

> The United States has been widely condemned for its repeated inability to forge bold national strategies to address climate change. This opprobrium targets the limited capacity of federal government institutions to devise policies to stabilize and reduce American greenhouse gas emissions, as well as their inability to assume a credible leadership role in

international treaty deliberations. . . . Federal inertia has had a largely unanticipated effect of shifting the locus of most climate-related policy development to subfederal levels, producing a patchwork quilt of state and local government policies. Even those policies adopted by the federal government have been . . . heavily reliant on states for either initial policy development or central roles in implementation, leading to a remarkably decentralized governance approach for an issue generally framed as a "global" problem.[12]

Why has it been so difficult to forge national laws to curb the pollutants that are responsible for global warming? The short answer to this question, as we will see in the following section, is—not surprisingly—politics.

Efforts to Stall Climate Change Policy in the United States

There has been an overwhelming amount of scientific evidence in recent years showing the harmful effects of global warming on the environment and human health.[13] In April 2016 the White House released a study, *The Impacts of Climate Change on Human Health in the United States: A Scientific Assessment*, that points to the health effects of climate change.[14] It provides evidence that global warming could negatively affect the human respiratory and cardiovascular systems, and could lead to an increase in allergies, asthma, and deaths by the proliferation of insect-borne diseases. Such claims are not new, but the report, reviewed by the National Academies of Sciences, Engineering, and Medicine, provides the strongest evidence to date on the effects of climate change on human health.

But as noted earlier, there continues to be a good deal of skepticism about this evidence, which has thwarted the ability of policy makers to regulate climate change. "Climategate," for example, was a contributing factor to the questioning of scientism around climate change.[15] In 2009 a university server at the Climatic Research Unit of the University of East Anglia in the United Kingdom was hacked, exposing thousands of emails between prominent American and British climate researchers. Skeptics of climate change interpreted the text of the emails as evidence that global warming itself is a hoax perpetrated by a scientific conspiracy. Based on the emails, they claimed that scientists were manipulating climate data. In one email exchange, for example, a scientist wrote of "using a statistical 'trick' in a chart illustrating a recent sharp warming trend." In another email, a climatologist at the U.S. National Center for Atmospheric Research writes, "The fact is that we can't account for the lack of warming at the moment and it is a travesty that we can't." A climatologist at NASA stated, "Science doesn't work because we're all nice."[16] These scientists maintained, however, that the emails were taken out of context and amounted to nothing more than a smear campaign, particularly since the disclosure of the hacked emails was timed to occur several weeks before the 2009 Copenhagen Summit on Climate Change.[17] It is uncertain as to whether the email breach propagated by the skeptics had a negative effect on the summit.[18] Nonetheless, the Copenhagen Summit resulted in nothing more than an agreement among the participating countries that the problem of global warming continues to be a threat and must be addressed accordingly.[19]

Richard Lazarus observed that

> many people, businesses, and political leaders would prefer to be climate sceptics, no matter how overwhelming the scientific evidence to the contrary. That is why they will readily embrace almost any available excuse—even some extra snowflakes—to ignore the problem. Justice Antonin Scalia, during the oral argument in *Massachusetts v. EPA*, expressed what is probably the unstated feeling of many Americans when, acknowledging that he was "not a scientist," he added that "[t]hat's why I don't want to have to deal with global warming, to tell you the truth."[20]

In short, global warming skeptics have been known to hinder any progressive movement on climate policy.

Interestingly enough, however, even when strong scientific evidence of climate change and environmental degradation was lacking, one policy or regulatory approach that was relied upon by federal agencies in the early years was the "precautionary principle."[21] As Nicholas Ashford and Charles Caldart explain, a precautionary approach is taken when uncertainties run high.[22] They note that regulatory action is called for "when the available (yet imperfect) data are sufficiently suggestive of harm."[23] Since the 1992 United Nations Conference on Environment and

Development (or the Rio Declaration), the precautionary principle or approach has been recognized international environmental law. Principle 15 of the declaration holds,

> In order to protect the environment, the precautionary approach shall be widely applied by States according to their capabilities. Where there are threats of serious or irreversible damage, lack of full scientific certainty shall not be used as a reason for postponing cost-effective measures to prevent environmental degradation.[24]

The point here is that many nations at least on paper supported measures to combat global warming even in the absence of scientific data on climate change. Today, however, the call for scientific evidence has become a necessity if nations are to develop and implement concrete policies aimed at climate change.

The absence of federal law on climate change can also be attributed to the political battles within and the intransigence of the U.S. Congress.[25] As Hari Osofsky and Jacqueline Peel argue, the "U.S. Congress is generally too politically divided to take significant action supporting or opposing climate change regulation. Even on the rare occasions when it unites on this issue, it does not do so in a way that could survive presidential veto."[26] Moreover, there are skeptics among congressional leaders, the preponderance of whom are Republicans. Indeed, attitudes toward global warming cleave along party lines. In a 2015 poll conducted by the Pew Research Center, 71 percent of Democrats and independents who lean Democratic believe that the planet is warming; only 27 percent of Republicans and those who lean Republican hold this view.[27] But the unwillingness of Congress to pass a law regulating climate change goes beyond skepticism. For one thing, the oil and gas industries expend an inordinate amount of money lobbying Congress. The total amount of contributions to congressional campaigns by the fossil fuel industry in 2013–2014 was $326 million. In that same time period, the total amount of fossil fuel subsidies provided by Congress totaled $33.7 billion.[28]

Encouraging Congress—or other nations around the globe, for that matter—to tackle global warming is a political conundrum because our economies and high standards of living depend on the processes, materials, and products that produce greenhouse gases. Moreover, efforts to curb greenhouse gases will have a disproportionately negative effect on the people living in those countries that emit the least amount of greenhouse gases.[29] The irony is that developing countries need the very greenhouse-emitting materials to improve the development of their economies and standard of living. In any case, global warming does far more damage to poor nations than to wealthy ones.[30] Yet developing countries bear the brunt of the costs of policies to curb global warming. Evidence shows, for example, that "even if environmental costs were distributed equally to every person on earth, developing countries would still bear 80% of the burden (because they account for 80% of world population). As it is, they bear an even greater share, though their citizens' carbon footprints are much smaller."[31]

But this does not make the problem intractable. As Dennis Parker explains, "The challenge is how to initiate scientifically sound long-term measures but avoid hasty steps that would undermine the foundations of the global economy. All nations would benefit from an assessment of the impact of emission reduction targets and timetables on their standard of living as well as their driving habits and industrial progress."[32] He goes on to say that this is a global issue, whereby every nation "should determine how proposed climate change measures will impact their nation's economy and quality of life."[33]

The U.S. Congress has been unwilling to sign on to various global agreements aimed at curbing greenhouse gas emissions unless developing countries agree to an equal burden in terms of targets for emissions reductions.[34] Developing countries counter that industrialized countries are the greatest contributors to global warming and are better equipped to shoulder the lion's share of the costs of reductions.[35] A prime example of this quid-pro-quo prerequisite for climate change policy is the 1997 Kyoto Protocol, as will be addressed in the following section. Also, even if the United States signs a protocol, its ratification, as with most treaties, generally occurs after it is submitted to and approved by the U.S. Senate (but see the discussion below on the Paris Agreement).

Finally, Senate procedural rules around the filibuster have been a major impediment to legislation aimed at combating global warming.

A filibuster is a tactic whereby long-winded speeches by a senator are used to delay or prevent action on a piece of legislation.[36] Cloture is a process for limiting filibustering, but it can be invoked only when three-fifths of all senators (i.e., sixty) vote for the cloture motion. The filibuster was intended to protect the interests and rights of the Senate minority, providing them with the right to voice their views and opinions. This has worked well for senators who oppose climate change policy. As Tora Skodvin and Steinar Andresen argue, "the minority most affected by climate legislation is empowered by its filibuster capacity and can block policy change in this issue area."[37] As will be seen shortly, the U.S. Senate has effectively blocked passage of climate change policy.

The Kyoto Protocol: Stalled Policy Drifts

The first World Climate Conference was held in 1979 in Geneva (see table 4.1).[38] Its purpose was to ascertain the state of knowledge about climate issues and determine the potential global effects of climate change.[39] Perhaps one of the most important outcomes of this conference is that it ultimately led to the creation in 1988 of the Intergovernmental Panel on Climate Change (IPCC) by the United Nations Environment Programme (UNEP) and the World Meteorological Organization (WMO). The IPCC is the leading international body for assessing climate change, and currently it has 195 member countries.[40] Additional important events leading to the Kyoto Protocol include the 1990 Second World Climate Conference, held in Geneva, and in 1992, the formation of an international treaty—the United Nations Framework Convention on Climate Change (UNFCCC)—to consider measures to limit global temperature increases and the resulting climate change, and to cope with its impacts.[41] The UNFCCC was signed by then president George H. W. Bush and approved by the U.S. Senate. Currently it has 196 countries, including the United States.[42] In addition, in 1995 the first Conference of the Parties (COP) was convened in Berlin. The COP is the official negotiating body of the UNFCCC. All countries that are parties to the UNFCCC are represented at the COP, which meets every year to address measures for reducing atmospheric concentrations of greenhouse gases.

TABLE 4.1. Significant Events in Global Climate Change Negotiations

1979	First World Climate Conference, Geneva
1988	Intergovernmental Panel on Climate Change (IPCC) created
1990	Second World Climate Conference, Geneva
1992	Earth Summit in Rio* United Nations Framework Convention on Climate Change (UN-FCCC) signed
1994	UNFCCC Treaty entered into force with 50 ratifications
1995	First Conference of the Parties (COP 1), Berlin
1997	Kyoto Protocol formally adopted at COP 3, Kyoto
2001	Marrakesh Accords adopted at COP 7, establishing rules for implementing Kyoto Protocol
2001	President Bush rejects the Kyoto Protocol
2005	Kyoto Protocol takes force, COP 11, Montreal
2009	Copenhagen Summit on Climate Change; COP 15 countries submit nonbinding emissions reductions pledges
2013	COP 19, Warsaw; parties to create roadmap for COP 21
2015	COP 21, Paris Agreement

*The Rio pact was approved by the U.S. Senate. It called for industrialized nations to *aim* to reduce greenhouse gas emissions to their 1990 levels by 2000. The goal was not achieved.
Source: Adapted from United Nations, "Climate Negotiations Timeline," www.un.org, accessed February 9, 2016.

One legal instrument of the UNFCCC is the Kyoto Protocol, adopted in Kyoto, Japan, in December 1997.[43] Seen as one of the first serious efforts to curb global warming, it set targets and timetables for thirty-seven industrialized countries and the European Community to reduce greenhouse gas emissions. Vice President Al Gore, a strong supporter of climate control, negotiated the treaty on behalf of the United States. As David Victor explains in *The Collapse of the Kyoto Protocol*, "on average during the years 2008–2012, emissions from the countries in the European Union must be 8% below the 1990 level. Japan's required cut is 6%, while the United States committed to reduce its emissions to 7% below the 1990 level."[44] It was also expected that nations would agree to caps in the future.[45] On November 12, 1998, the United States signed the Kyoto Protocol. However, acknowledging a major roadblock in Congress, the Clinton administration, which was very supportive of climate control policy, chose not to submit the protocol to the Senate for ratification, particularly in light of the resolution it had passed the year before.

In mid-1997 the Senate passed Senate Resolution 98—or the Byrd-Hagel Resolution, named for its sponsors—a nonbinding measure that states that developing countries must make legally binding commitments to limit the emission of greenhouse gases.[46] Although developing countries ratified the Kyoto Protocol, they have no binding obligations under the treaty.[47] Thus, the Senate would not be open to ratifying the protocol. Briefly, the resolution was introduced by Senators Robert Byrd (D-WV) and Chuck Hagel (R-NE) on June 12, 1997, reported to the Senate by the Committee on Foreign Relations on July 21, 1997, and passed or agreed to by every member of the Republican-controlled Senate without amendments, 95–0, on July 25, 1997.[48]

Interestingly enough, hearings held on Senate Resolution 98 did not involve any opponents to the measure, such as environmental groups, the main proponents for a global treaty on climate control policy. Industry groups, however, along with scientists who denied the existence of global warming, were allowed to present testimony. One of the resolution's co-sponsors, Senator Hagel (R-NE), began by asserting,

> We all want to leave our children a better, cleaner, more prosperous world. I have yet to meet one American or one Member of Congress who wants dirty air, dirty water, a dirty environment or declining standards of living for their children and grandchildren. This debate will not be about who is for or against a clean environment. It never has been. . . . We need to insure that any agreement negotiated and signed by the administration will be fair to America, the world, and that it will not adversely affect America's global competitiveness, our economy, and will not challenge our national sovereignty. . . . We are also interested in why the administration is advocating legally binding emissions reductions for the United States and not for nearly 130 other countries, like China, Mexico, South Korea, Singapore, Indonesia and other countries.[49]

Senator Byrd (D-WV), also co-sponsor of the resolution, added the following:

> Let me begin like this. I will soon be 80 years old. I do not need any scientific analysis to tell me that something is wrong out there, that something is happening. I have seen it in my own lifetime. The winters are

different. The summers are different from what they were when I was a boy. Something is at work out there. I can't explain it, but I think we must understand that there is something going on that is causing the storms, the floods, causing the elements to be so unpredictable. It seems to me that we are all in this boat together, the developed world and the developing world.[50]

He goes on to say that

the developing world must fully participate in the treaty negotiations and commitments and play a meaningful role in effectively addressing the problem of global climate change. . . . The emissions of the developing world continue on their inexorable upward track, even as we, in the OECD group, make the painful and costly adjustments necessary to force down our own emissions. . . . Many of the biggest emitters of greenhouse gases in the developing world have refused to even discuss, let alone seriously consider, taking any emissions limitations commitments upon themselves. In what can only be viewed as an act of environmental irresponsibility, the developing nations have adamantly refused to recognize that they will, over the next 2 decades, become the primary cause of the problem in terms of annual emissions.[51]

Testimony from farm interests, labor representatives, and manufacturers all argued that the Kyoto Protocol would be harmful to workers and business. Bryce Neidig, president of the Nebraska Farm Bureau Federation, for example, stated that farmers "are concerned about higher costs for fuel, energy, vehicles, and equipment. They are concerned about new, burdensome regulations. They are concerned about threats to their competitiveness in world markets where they now must export about one-third of the crops they grow."[52] Richard Trumka, secretary-treasurer of the AFL-CIO, made an impassioned plea about the profound effects the treaty would have on the incomes and job security of American workers as well as the lifestyle of American families. Perhaps most interesting was the testimony of two scientists who refuted the evidence of global warming and maintained that climate changes were modest. Alan Robock, for example, a climatologist for the state of Maryland, stated that "if we look at all of the evidence, it supports that we are having a human impact on climate, but it does not prove it unambiguously because there is so much natural variability and we are trying to see a very small signal so far."[53]

In short, the U.S. Senate sent a clear signal to the Clinton administration that it would not ratify the Kyoto Protocol. It was in fact a preemptive move on the part of Congress. In response, Greenpeace dumped four tons of coal and seven barrels of oil in front of the U.S. Capitol. The United States remains the sole industrial nation not to have ratified the treaty; to date, 129 countries have ratified the pact.[54] The United States has been viewed as a leader in its commitment to environmental policy, and without its involvement, the ability of the treaty to meet its goals was severely hindered.[55] Indeed, inaction by the United States has been viewed as a major obstacle for achieving any global agreement on combating global warming. It was a stunning defeat for President Clinton and Vice President Al Gore. When George W. Bush became president in 2001, he rejected the Kyoto Protocol and in February 2002 he announced a U.S. policy for climate change that would rely on domestic, voluntary actions to reduce greenhouse gas emissions.[56] As noted at the beginning of the chapter, a change in the political party controlling the White House can lead to consequential policy drifts—in this case, drifts that would impede efforts to address the effects of climate change.

Climate Policy and the EPA

Within two months of taking office, President Bush reversed his campaign pledge to seek major reductions in U.S. power plant carbon dioxide emissions. His EPA administrator, Christine Todd Whitman, announced that "we have no interest in implementing that [Kyoto] treaty. . . . If there's a general agreement that we need to be addressing the global climate change issue, [the question is] how do we do it in a way that allows us to make some progress, instead of spending our time committed to something that isn't going to go."[57] While this chapter does not seek to provide a comprehensive review of climate policy under the Bush administration, it does show that its inaction was the catalyst for an important U.S. Supreme Court ruling in *Massachusetts v. EPA*, discussed below, that forced the EPA to regulate greenhouse gas emissions; it represented a significant climate policy drift.[58]

Much has been written about Whitman's short tenure as head of the EPA. Indeed, it was speculated that one of the reasons she resigned her post in June 2003 was that she clashed with President Bush on environmental matters such as greenhouse gas emissions.[59] As many have argued, the Bush administration sought to make environmental policy and regulations more business-friendly.[60] And his approach to regulating the environment was to cooperate with business rather than enforce existing regulations. Whitman, however, was a moderate, and she eventually began to interpret the agenda for environmental regulation in different ways than President Bush did. For example, Bush claimed early on that he did not believe the science on global warming. But Whitman argued publicly that the president "has also been very clear that the science is good on global warming. It does exist. There is a real problem that we as a world face from global warming and to the extent that introducing CO_2 to the discussion is going to have an impact on global warming, that's an important step to take."[61] She indicated that the president was committed to considering carbon dioxide as a pollutant contributing to global warming. These clashes were a major reason that Whitman stepped down as EPA administrator so early on in the Bush administration.[62] Indeed, Whitman made it clear after her return to private life that she is very supportive of the EPA's efforts to combat global warming, and by 2015 was praising the agency's Clean Power Plan.[63]

Subsequent leaders of the EPA under the Bush administration were much less open to regulating carbon dioxide and other pollutants that contribute to global warming.[64] The trigger that set off a critical policy drift was inaction by the EPA in September 2003. The EPA, now headed on an acting basis by George Bush's appointee Marianne Lamont Horinko, refused to issue a rule authorizing the agency to regulate greenhouse gases. Her decision led to the landmark ruling in *Massachusetts v. EPA*, discussed in the next section, which required the EPA to regulate under the Clean Air Act a range of pollutants, including carbon emissions from power plants.

Massachusetts v. EPA: A Significant Policy Drift

In 1999 a coalition of nineteen environmental, public interest, and trade organizations petitioned the EPA to issue a rule under the Clean Air

Act, first passed in 1963, to regulate greenhouse gas emissions from new motor vehicles.[65] At the time, Carol Browner headed the EPA. The petition stated that

> carbon dioxide remains the most important contributor to anthropogenic forcing of climate change; projections of future global mean temperature change and sea level rise confirm the potential for human activities to alter Earth's climate to extent unprecedented in human history. Approximately 90% of U.S. greenhouse gas emissions from anthropogenic sources occurs [sic] because of the combustion of fossil fuel. U.S. mobile sources are responsible for a significant amount of greenhouse gas emissions. In fact, in the United States, the fossil fuel CO_2 emissions from cars and light trucks are higher than the total nationwide CO_2 emissions from all but three other countries (China, Russia, and Japan). This anthropogenic forcing of climate change will affect not only the environment, but will also significantly impact human health.[66]

The petitioners pointed to Section 202(a)(1) of the Clean Air Act as amended to support their request.[67] This section of the act mandates that

> the Administrator shall by regulation prescribe (and from time to time revise) in accordance with the provisions of this section, standards applicable to the emission of any air pollutant from any class or classes of new motor vehicle or new motor vehicle engine, which in his judgment cause, or contribute to, air pollution which may be reasonably anticipated to endanger public health or welfare. Such standards shall be applicable to such vehicles and engines for the useful life . . . whether such vehicle or engines are designed as complete systems or incorporate to devices to prevent the control of such pollution.

Although the Clean Air Act is silent on the regulation of greenhouse gases, the petitioners argued that in the framework of decision making in the United States, the "precautionary principle," as discussed earlier, has been adopted as a regulatory approach.[68] They noted that under the Clean Air Act (CAA), the [EPA] Administrator is permitted to make a precautionary decision to regulate pollutants in order to protect public health and welfare. . . . In addition to the precautionary nature of the CAA, the Administrator has a mandatory duty to regulate greenhouse gas emissions from new motor vehicles under Section 202(a)(1) of the Act. Petitioners urge the Administrator to reduce the effects of global warming by regulating the emission of greenhouse gases from new motor vehicles.[69]

On February 10, 2000, the EPA issued one of its final rules: "Control of Air Pollution from New Motor Vehicles"; this rule, also known as the "gasoline rule," was designed to reduce emissions from new passenger cars and light trucks.[70] And on January 18, 2001, just two days before George Bush was sworn into office as president, the EPA published a final rule—the "diesel rule"—aimed at reducing emissions from heavy-duty engines.[71] Then, on January 23, 2001, the EPA, still under the direction of Carol Browner (Whitman did not become administrator of the EPA until January 31, 2001), issued a proposed rule entitled "Control of Emissions from New and In-Use Highway Vehicles and Engines," aimed at further reducing emissions from motor vehicles.[72] The EPA received close to fifty thousand public comments, the preponderance of which supported the proposed rule.[73] But on September 8, 2003, over two years after the proposed rule was filed, the EPA, now headed on an acting basis by Marianne Lamont Horinko, denied the petition for rulemaking, claiming that the Clean Air Act did not authorize the EPA to regulate greenhouse gases.[74] The EPA went on to say that even if the act did provide such authorization, it "does not impose a mandatory duty on the Administrator to exercise her judgment. Instead, section 202(a)(1) provides the Administrator with discretionary authority to address emissions."[75] The EPA argued that regulating greenhouse gases from motor vehicles would interfere with the U.S. Department of Transportation's (DOT's) fuel efficiency standards. It stated that "the only practical way to reduce tailpipe emissions of CO_2 is to improve fuel economy. Congress has already created a detailed set of mandatory standards governing the fuel economy of cars and light duty trucks, and has authorized DOT—not EPA—to implement those standards."[76]

A number of state as well as local governments joined the coalition of environmental groups to file a lawsuit against the EPA, challenging its refusal to regulate greenhouse gases under the Clean Air Act.[77] State and local governments worked with environmental interest groups because of their shared values in reducing greenhouse gases in their states. The U.S. Court of Appeals for the D.C. Circuit ruled for the EPA on the grounds that it properly exercised its discretion under Section 202(a)(1) of the Clean Air Act to deny a petition for rulemaking.[78] On appeal, the U.S. Supreme Court issued its landmark decision ruling that the EPA does have the authority to regulate greenhouse gas emissions, and it must use it. Writing for the majority, mostly along partisan lines, Justice John Paul Stevens argued that the "EPA has statutory authority to regulate emission of such gases [as carbon dioxide, methane, nitrous oxide, and hydrofluorocarbons] from new motor vehicles."[79] He went on to say that the "EPA has offered no reasoned explanation for its refusal to decide whether greenhouse gases cause or contribute to climate change. Its action was therefore 'arbitrary, capricious . . . or otherwise not in accordance with law.'"[80] The Court made it clear that the EPA is compelled to exercise its regulatory authority: "Under the clear terms of the Clean Air Act, EPA can avoid taking further action *only* if it determines that greenhouse gases do not contribute to climate change or if it provides some reasonable explanation as to why it cannot or will not exercise its discretion to determine whether they do."[81] Acknowledging that the Clean Air Act leaves the determination to act upon the "judgment" of the EPA's administrator, the Court further stated that "the use of the word 'judgment' is not a roving license to ignore the statutory text."[82]

The Court in rendering its decision pointed to the 1984 landmark ruling in *Chevron U.S.A. v. Natural Resources Defense Council*, where the U.S. Supreme Court set forth the legal test for deferring to administrative agencies' interpretations of statutes.[83] The *Massachusetts* Court stated, in light of *Chevron*, "As we have repeated time and again, an agency has broad discretion to choose how best to marshal its limited resources and personnel to carry out its delegated responsibilities."[84]

Finally, it is noteworthy that at least the majority of justices on this Court in 2007 were convinced by the evidence that automobile emissions have an impact on the environment: "Judged by any standard, U.S. motor-vehicle emissions make a meaningful contribution to greenhouse gas concentrations and hence, according to petitioners, to global warming."[85]

The High Court's decision was a victory for the concerned states and environmentalists. It was a direct rebuke to the Bush administration's efforts to derail the regulation of greenhouse gases. In response to the Court's ruling, the EPA, instead of issuing an Advance Notice of Proposed Rulemaking (ANPR), the preliminary step toward promulgating regulations, spent most of 2007 and 2008 internally reviewing the potential impacts if any of climate change to ascertain whether global warming would endanger public health or welfare. In December 2007 the EPA finalized its "endangerment report" and sent it to the White House. An endangerment finding is a necessary precondition under the Clean Air Act to regulatory action by the EPA. In this case, the endangerment finding was that six key greenhouse gases—carbon dioxide, methane, nitrous oxide, hydrofluorocarbons, perfluorocarbons (PFCs), and sulfur hexafluoride—in the atmosphere threaten the public health and welfare of current and future generations.

President Bush would not accept the finding and suppressed the report, and it wasn't until 2009 that President Obama ordered the sequestered document to be released.[86] In effect, the Bush administration ensured that a response to the *Massachusetts v. EPA* ruling would be delayed until the following administration, and it wasn't until April 2009 that the EPA, under the leadership of Lisa Jackson, issued a scientific endangerment finding that greenhouse gases present a danger to the public's health and welfare.[87] After public hearings, the EPA issued its final rule in December 2009 announcing that it would begin the planning phase of regulating greenhouse gas emissions.[88] A series of rules ensued, including the following:

- "Timing Rule," which stated that the earliest that greenhouse gases could be subject to regulation is January 2, 2011;[89]
- "Tailpipe Rule," whereby the EPA and the National Highway Traffic Safety Administration (NHTSA) issued standards for new light-duty vehicles for model years 2012–2016; the rule set the combined average emissions level at 250 grams/mile of carbon dioxide;[90]
- "Tailoring Rule," which set thresholds—emission of 100–250 tons per year of greenhouse gases—for large polluters such as power plants, refin-

eries, and other large industrial plants, while exempting smaller sources like farms, restaurants, and schools emitting less than 75,000–100,000 tons of greenhouse gases per year.[91] The result was a more manageable rule that targeted power plants and other large emitters.[92]

In sum, the Bush administration was successful, at least temporarily, in averting efforts to combat greenhouse gases. Even after EPA officials found that several greenhouse gases threaten the health and welfare of the public, Bush dragged his feet to prevent the agency from taking any action. But with the election of Obama, the Democrats now controlled the White House, and this led to a shift in the nation's response to regulating the emission of greenhouse gases. This, in turn, incited action by the states.

Federalism: The States Fight Back

Not surprisingly, a coalition of states—led by Texas and Virginia—and industry groups immediately challenged the EPA's rules, in particular the endangerment finding, and the timing, tailpipe, and tailoring rules, claiming that the agency did not possess the authority to regulate greenhouse gases.[93] In June 2012 the U.S. Court of Appeals for the D.C. Circuit, repeatedly referring to the High Court's decision in *Massachusetts v. EPA*, upheld the EPA's rules in *Coalition for Responsible Regulation v. EPA*.[94] Regarding the endangerment finding, the appellate court argued that the Clean Air Act "requires EPA to answer only two questions: whether particular 'air pollution'—here, greenhouse gases— 'may reasonably be anticipated to endanger public health or welfare,' and whether motor-vehicle emissions 'cause, or contribute to' that endangerment."[95] The court went on to assert that

these questions require a "scientific judgment" about the potential risks greenhouse gas emissions pose to public health or welfare—not policy discussions. . . . In *Massachusetts v. EPA*, the Supreme Court rebuffed an attempt by EPA itself to inject considerations of policy into its decision. At the time, EPA had "offered a laundry list of reasons not to regulate."[96]

The court opined that the specific rules were neither "arbitrary nor capricious" and were "unambiguously correct." It further found that various state and industry groups lacked standing to sue the EPA. A petition for certiorari was denied by the U.S. Supreme Court on October 15, 2013.[97]

Parenthetically, in a 2014 consolidated case, *Utility Air Regulatory Group v. EPA*, the U.S. Supreme Court upheld most of the EPA's greenhouse gas regulations.[98] It struck down only the tailoring rule, thus overturning that portion of the appellate court's *Coalition* decision.[99] In *Utility*, the Court had the opportunity to strike down the *Massachusetts* decision, but it did not. In effect, as many have pointed out, the *Utility* decision, overall, was inconsequential and has had limited practical impact on the power of the EPA to regulate greenhouse gas emissions.[100]

Massachusetts and *Coalition* represent polar opposites in terms of state action. One coalition of states and environmental groups is supportive of the EPA's efforts to regulate the environment, particularly in regard to global warming. Another coalition, made up of different states and industry groups, sets up roadblocks to prevent the EPA from regulating greenhouse gases. The issue, to be sure, is one of federalism, and it converges with the science, economics, and politics of global warming. States such as California, Massachusetts, New York, Connecticut, and the others joining with the EPA in *Coalition* support the science showing the deleterious effects of greenhouse gases on the planet, and believe that the Clean Air Act gives the executive branch discretion to address new environmental threats to the atmosphere. These states are thus invested in curbing the emission of these gases to protect the health and safety of their citizens, and are committed to promoting renewable energy sources and creating and maintaining sustainable communities.[101] Indeed, California is the second-largest emitter of carbon dioxide, yet it has been a leader in pushing for climate change policy, investing in clean energy and the growth of businesses that contribute to the goal of lowering carbon emissions.[102] Massachusetts has also been a national leader in promoting climate change policies and promoting a clean energy economy. In this sense, a number of states are working with the federal government to implement air pollution reduction programs to protect public health and the environment. After all, the Clean Air Act creates a partnership between the states and the federal government in that the law requires the EPA to establish minimum national standards for air quality, but assigns primary responsibility to the states to ensure compliance with the standards.

The forces of federalism have had the opposite effect on states such as Texas, the largest emitter of carbon dioxide, and other states such as West Virginia, Wyoming, and Kentucky, which are among the largest coal-producing states.[103] It is not surprising, then, that these states refute the scientific evidence for global warming, are averse to the EPA providing estimates of how much greenhouse gases should be reduced, and believe that the federal government has overstepped its power in addressing climate control. They also argue that the EPA regulations are cost-prohibitive. The brief for the twelve states in *Coalition*, led by Texas, argued that the EPA's tailoring rule "is one of the most audacious power-grabs ever attempted by an administrative agency."[104] The Southeastern Legal Foundation filed a brief contending much the same: "This case involves perhaps the most audacious seizure of pure legislative power over domestic economic matters attempted by the Executive Branch" since President Harry Truman seized the nation's steel mills during the Korean War (an act that was nullified by the Supreme Court in 1952).[105]

Interestingly, the appeals court for the D.C. Circuit in *Coalition* ruled, as noted earlier, that the various states and industry groups lacked standing to sue the EPA. But in *Massachusetts*, the U.S. Supreme Court ruled that Massachusetts was a sovereign state and thus should be afforded special deference in its claim to standing. As Linda Greenhouse reasoned, this "new twist on the court's standing doctrine may have been an essential tactic in winning the vote of Justice Kennedy, a leader in the court's federalism revolution of recent years. Justice Stevens, a dissenter from the court's states' rights rulings and a master of court strategy, in effect managed to use federalism as a sword rather than a shield."[106]

In sum, the decisions in *Massachusetts*, *Coalition*, and *Utility* ensure that the EPA has regulatory power under the Clean Air Act, and at least under the Obama administration, it has been willing to use that power to attack the problem of global warming. But as we will see in the following sections, that power has not been sustained over time.

A Failed Attempt by Congress to Pass Legislation

As noted, the U.S. Congress has been reluctant over the last several decades to enact laws aimed at curbing global warming. A brief review of the one bill that came close will illustrate why the EPA and the president have moved forward on administrative policies to regulate greenhouse gas emissions.[107] In June 2009 the House in a very close vote passed the American Clean Energy and Security Act (H.R. 2454), the first effort by either house of Congress intended to address global warming. The provisions of the bill revolved around clean energy, energy efficiency, transitioning to a clean energy economy, and reducing global warming pollution. Regarding global warming, the bill would establish a cap-and-trade system for greenhouse gas emissions and set goals for reducing such emissions from covered sources by 83 percent of 2005 levels by 2050. Under a cap-and-trade system, the government sets limits (caps) on the total amount of greenhouse gases that can be emitted nationally. Companies are then allowed to buy or sell permits to emit these gases. Over time, the cap is reduced to a point where total carbon dioxide emissions are significantly lowered.[108] But for some, it seemed that global warming was secondary in this bill. Henry Waxman (D-CA), one of the co-sponsors of the bill, in presenting the act to the House Energy and Environment Subcommittee, stressed economic issues: "The energy legislation we are considering will create millions of jobs, revive our economy and secure our energy independence. It will also protect our environment."[109] Similarly, Edward Markey (D-MA), also co-sponsor of the bill, stressed economic and security issues:

> Today, Earth Day 2009, we begin the process of writing history as we work to pass new energy legislation that will revitalize our economy, enhance our energy security, create millions of new jobs and end the global warming crisis. . . . We can pass legislation that will create millions of new jobs and reduce our dependence on foreign oil, all in a way that meets our environmental and economic needs.[110]

The question of how other countries would address global warming was a concern in the House, as it had been in the Senate (as discussed above). Representative Diana DeGette (D-CO) argued in response to statements made by Steven Chu, secretary of energy at the time, "So to answer my question, then, in particular with India, but to a lesser degree with China and maybe other developing countries, is their lack of prioritization of this issue reason for us to not move forward?"[111] Not surprisingly, Secretary Chu responded, "No. We have to move forward. Right now the United States and China represent 50 percent of the carbon emissions of the world. And as we go forward, we have to take the leadership position."[112] Similarly Representative Jeff Fortenberry (R-NE) raised concerns that

> the legislation would prompt, as has been addressed earlier, a shift of America's manufacturing and agricultural production to other countries, such as China and India and Brazil, that would not be bound by similar restrictions. . . . Simply by shifting this production overseas, it would likely result in no net reduction in greenhouse gas emissions, and we may actually contribute to an increase inadvertently.[113]

A number of interest groups opposing the proposed law were also concerned with how other countries would curb their greenhouse gas emissions. For example, Bob Stallman, president of the American Farm Bureau Federation, argued that

> there must be some mechanism included in the bill to assure that other countries, particularly China and India, are part of the global climate solution. If that is not done, our country will be engaging in the economic equivalent of unilateral disarmament. . . . When and how will China and India control their own emissions?[114]

Ken Nobis, treasurer of the National Milk Producers Federation and a dairy farmer from St. John's, Michigan, also raised concerns that other countries are not adopting measures to curb greenhouse gas emissions:

> The dairy industry feels very strongly that climate change legislation, if enacted here, similarly has to be enacted around the world. We have learned, very, very well this year, what happens when we are not competitive or if somebody is not buying our product. A year ago, we exported

12 percent of our dairy production, and we had very good prices. This year, that has dropped to seven percent, and that is the primary reason the dairy industry is suffering the economic problems it is suffering this year.[115]

In short, linking regulatory efforts with those of countries such as China and India will continue to hinder progress toward reducing the emissions of greenhouse gases.

Cost was also a factor for opponents. Stallman, for instance, argued that

Congress must not create a hole in America's energy supply. If carbon-based energy is taken out, something else, nuclear for example, must be substituted. We must plug the hole created by the bill or run the risk of Congressionally mandated shortages that will create spikes in energy prices. The agricultural sector, in particular, is poorly equipped to absorb or pass on such costs. Determining the exact economic impact to agriculture of H.R. 2454 is extraordinarily difficult because the range of variables is enormous, and assumptions play a large role in determining the outcome.[116]

Representative Joe Barton (R-TX), a prominent global warming skeptic, raised similar concerns:

Every, every, every estimate that I've seen . . . says that energy costs are going to go up across the board. The electricity costs could go up somewhere between 44 (percent) to 125 percent. Gasoline costs could go up. You name the cost, it's going to go up. How does that affect the unemployment rate? Michigan right now has an unemployment rate of 12 percent. Indiana has an unemployment rate of 10 percent, Ohio's at 9.7 (percent), California and Georgia are at 9.2 percent. Even my great state of Texas where the economy is relatively better off has got an unemployment rate over 6 percent. I mean, if energy prices go up, lots and lots of Americans are going to lose their jobs, and then that in turn is going to cause even more deficit spending on behalf of the federal government. How is that costed into this draft?[117]

And finally, in response to testimony provided by Al Gore, who was very supportive of the bill, Representative Michael Burgess (R-TX) raised the issue of whether human activity really leads to global warming. In a somewhat flippant manner, he stated that "no one who's come before this committee from a scientific basis can show us the smoking gun that mankind [sic] is causing this to happen. You can create relationships between the number of sun spots and the partisan makeup of the Senate [which] can be proven if you're willing to take the time to have the numbers."[118]

Several other opponents to the bill testified before various committees or subcommittees of the House. In a very close vote, the law passed 219–212, with 44 Democrats voting against it and 8 Republicans voting to support.[119] Not surprisingly, it died in the Senate.[120] Electric utilities and coal, gas, and big oil companies heavily lobbied senators to oppose the bill. These industries spent more than $500 million in an effort to prevent the Senate from taking up the legislation.[121]

It seemed clear that any movement on curbing the emission of greenhouse gases would need to be made through the Obama administration and his EPA. With respect to combating global warming, the centerpiece of the Obama's regulatory framework was the Clean Power Plan, addressed in the following section.

Obama and the EPA's Policy Drifts

In June 2013 President Obama announced his Climate Action Plan, which directed the Environmental Protection Agency to develop a broad-based plan to cut the carbon pollution that causes climate change.[122] It served as the blueprint for the EPA's Clean Power Plan (CPP), aimed at reducing carbon dioxide emissions from power plants, the primary driver of global warming.[123] Obama sought to take executive action, relying heavily on the EPA, on the problem of climate change in the absence of a national framework or strategy to effect policy change aimed at ameliorating global warming. Efforts to implement the CPP, often referred to as the global warming rule, set off a firestorm for industry groups and state governments.

On June 18, 2014, the EPA published its proposed rule for the CPP, which seeks to reduce carbon emission by 30 percent by 2030, and sets specific targets for each state.[124] It released the final global warming rule on August 3, 2015 (see table 4.2). As William Scherman and Jason Fleischer point out,

> The EPA asserts that the best system of emission reduction leading to this goal is to "shift" electricity generated from sources that emit more [carbon dioxide] to sources that have fewer or no emissions. As a result, the Clean Power Plan makes the EPA the nation's energy regulator by essentially dictating to the states and their utilities the market share by fuel-type of different generation resources.[125]

In November 2015 the U.S. Senate passed two resolutions, 52–46, seeking to block the EPA from implementing its CPP. They were introduced under the obscure 1996 Congressional Review Act, which allows Congress to block regulatory rules issued by federal agencies through joint resolutions of disapproval.[126] Only a majority vote is needed. In December the House also passed the two resolutions. Shortly afterwards, President Obama vetoed the resolutions.[127] In any case, resolutions brought under the Congressional Review Act are rare, and they have largely been unsuccessful.[128]

TABLE 4.2. Timeline: EPA's Global Warming Rule

August 2015	EPA issues global warming rule (Clean Power Plan)
August 2015	EPA denies state of West Virginia's petition to stay global warming rule
October 2015	EPA's global warming rule is published
October 2015	States petition D.C. appeals court to stay *and* abolish global warming rule (*West Virginia v. EPA*)
January 2016	U.S. Court of Appeals denies states' petition (*West Virginia v. EPA*)
February 2016	U.S. Supreme Court grants states' petition and temporarily blocks implementation of global warming rule (*West Virginia v. EPA*)

Although these particular resolutions were inconsequential, a number of states sued the EPA even before the CPP rule was finalized. For example, in *Oklahoma v. EPA*, twelve states backed by industry groups sued the EPA seeking to block the rule because they were incurring extraordinary expenses to prepare for implementation of a final rule; they claimed that the proposed rule would cause "irreparable harm" because of the amount of time and resources needed to construct new facilities to meet the standards proposed by the rule.[129] The D.C. appeals court ruled against the states, opining that "upon issuance of a final rule, plaintiffs will have a forum in which they can seek judicial review of the emission standards. The Court finds no exceptional circumstances that would warrant judicial intervention at this time."[130]

Once the rule was finalized, a stay request was filed with the EPA by the state of West Virginia; it was denied.[131] And on October 23, 2015, the day the final global warming rule was published, West Virginia along with twenty-three other states petitioned the U.S. Court of Appeals for the D.C. Circuit to not only stay the rule but to abolish it on the grounds that "the States are being immediately and irreparably harmed by EPA's illegal effort to force States to reorder their electrical generation systems. This case involves an unprecedented, unlawful attempt by an environmental regulator to reorganize the nation's energy grid."[132]

On January 21, 2016, the U.S. Court of Appeals denied the states' petition to stay the CPP, arguing that the "Petitioners have not satisfied the stringent requirements for a stay pending court review."[133] In its efforts to expedite the case, the court scheduled oral arguments on the merits of the case for June 2, 2016; the case would go before Judge Karen LeCraft Henderson, a Republican appointee, and Democratic appointees Judges Judith Rogers and Sri Srinivasan. Eighteen states, the District of Columbia, five cities (including New York), and one county pledged support for the CPP and the EPA. A number of environmental groups also planned to intervene in support of the EPA.[134]

But on January 26 the states petitioned the High Court directly to stay the CPP, without waiting for a substantive ruling by the appeals court.[135] In February 2016 Chief Justice Roberts, in an unprecedented move, issued a stay in a briefly worded 5–4 order along ideological lines, temporarily blocking implementation of the CPP.[136] The stay meant that the CPP would not be in effect while the lawsuit over its legality proceeded through the courts. It represented a major setback to President Obama and the EPA in their efforts to regulate the emission of greenhouse gases.

Interestingly, Justice Kennedy had joined the majority opinion in the U.S. Supreme Court's 2007 *Massachusetts* decision, when the Court, it may be recalled, supported the evidence that automobile emissions contribute to global warming. Yet in 2016 Kennedy sided with the majority in *West Virginia*, where the Court issued a stay on the EPA's CPP or global warming rule. Otherwise the ideological makeup of the Court at the time of *West Virginia* did not change, even though its composition changed.[137] Justice Kennedy is the swing vote on the Court, and he has been known to vacillate or flip-flop on a number of issues for no discernible reason.[138] Massimo Calabresi and David Von Drehle point out that "efforts to fit Kennedy's major opinions into a clear, coherent philosophy have met with little success. He generally sides with the court's conservatives but is not tethered to any particular constitutional doctrine. 'There is no grand unified theory for Justice Kennedy's jurisprudence.'"[139]

Although this chapter addresses the policy drifts related to climate change, especially global warming, it would be useful to note an additional policy drift on the EPA's efforts to regulate the environment with its mercury emissions rule (see table 4.3), as it illustrates seemingly contradictory actions by the U.S. Supreme Court. The EPA's Mercury and Air Toxics Standards (MATS) rule, adopted in February 2012, sought to regulate mercury and other hazardous air pollutants from coal and oil-fired power plants.[140] The EPA estimated that its regulations would reduce the emissions of those pollutants by 90 percent and prevent about eleven thousand premature deaths each year. More than twenty states along with industry and labor groups immediately challenged the mercury rule on the grounds that the EPA's rule did not take into account the costs of regulating the pollutants.[141] The Court of Appeals in 2014 upheld the agency's decision not to consider cost.[142] The U.S. Supreme Court, however, siding with the states, reversed in a 5–4 vote along partisan lines, holding that the EPA unreasonably interpreted amendments to the Clean Air Act when it deemed cost irrelevant to the decision to regulate power plants.[143] In *Michigan v. EPA*, Justice Scalia, writing the opinion for the High Court, ruled that "it was unreasonable for EPA to read [the Clean Air Act] to mean that cost is irrelevant to the initial decision to regulate power plants. The Agency must consider cost—including, most importantly, cost of compliance—before deciding whether regulation is appropriate and necessary."[144]

TABLE 4.3. Timeline of EPA's Mercury Rule

February 2012	EPA issues mercury rule (Mercury and Air Toxics Standards, or MATS)
April 2014	U.S. Court of Appeals holds that EPA does not need to consider costs of mercury rule (*White Stallion Energy Center v. EPA*)
June 2015	U.S. Supreme Court rules that EPA must consider costs of mercury rule (*Michigan v. EPA*)
December 2015	D.C. appeals court rejects states' and industry groups' efforts to stay mercury rule
March 2016	Chief Justice John Roberts rejects petition to stay mercury rule

Importantly, the Court's ruling in *Michigan* did not strike down the EPA's mercury rule, but it required the agency to review and rewrite it, taking costs into consideration. After the Court's ruling, the case was sent back to the D.C. Circuit while the EPA conducted a cost analysis on the mercury rule. During that period, the states sought to block federal regulators from enforcing the rule as the case moved forward, citing the financial impact of compliance. In December 2015 the states involved in *Michigan* requested the Court of Appeals for the D.C. Circuit to block the mercury rule while their legal challenge against the EPA proceeded. The request was denied, and the states appealed to Chief Justice John Roberts, who oversees stay requests from the D.C. Circuit. The chief justice can refer those requests to the entire Supreme Court for consideration, but he declined to do so, and in March 2016 he rejected the request on his own authority.[145]

Why did the Court temporarily halt the EPA's global warming rule in February 2016, but not the mercury rule one month later? One theory is that the Court is signaling to concerned parties that it does not want to be inundated with these types of cases. Or the Court is simply more convinced by the science on mercury emissions than that on global warming. Another possible explanation is that Justice Scalia, who wrote for the majority in *Michigan*, had passed away on February 13, 2016; Chief Justice Roberts may have recognized that his death would alter the balance of power on the High Court.[146]

By March 2016, coalitions for and against the global warming rule began public relations campaigns in anticipation of the appellate court ruling on the merits of *West Virginia v. EPA*. Interestingly, the coalition of liberal and environmental advocacy groups modeled its campaign along the lines of the same-sex marriage campaign prior to the

High Court's 2015 decision in *Obergefell v. Hodges*, where it upheld the constitutionality of same-sex marriages.[147] That campaign was aimed at disseminating the message that the issue of same-sex marriage affects individual lives beyond the gay and lesbian communities. The environmental coalition's message was geared toward showing how climate change can directly affect everyone's lives. Social media outlets such as Facebook and Twitter were relied upon to convey the message.[148]

In June 2016 the D.C. appeals court was scheduled for oral arguments on the merits of *West Virginia v. EPA*. However, it rescheduled arguments for September so that the *en banc* court rather than the court's normal three-judge panel could review the case. The appeals court saw this as important enough to warrant attention by the full panel. It is one of the most important environmental cases in almost a decade. On September 27, 2016, the full court heard oral arguments for the case, but as of this writing, it has not yet issued a substantive ruling.[149] And, given the ideology of the Trump administration on the issue of climate control, addressed shortly, it is unlikely that a decision will be rendered. It is also worth noting that the Ninth Circuit appeals court is relatively liberal, where around 58 percent of the active judges sitting on the bench were appointed by Democratic administrations.[150]

Finally, it should be noted that President Obama had committed his administration to lead by example in policies to curb the emission of greenhouse gases that drive climate change.[151] On March 19, 2015, he signed Executive Order 13693, which represents the federal government's commitment to combating global warming. It directs federal agencies to reduce their greenhouse gas emissions by a minimum of 40 percent from 2008 levels by 2025, and to increase electricity generation from renewable energy to 30 percent of total generation. The actions are estimated to save taxpayers up to $18 billion in avoided energy costs.[152]

The Paris Agreement

In December 2015 the Paris Agreement, the first global pact to commit every country to battle global warming, was agreed to by consensus by the participating 195 countries. President Obama's leadership here, as seen in the EPA's CPP or global warming rule, was a key factor in gaining the support of two of the largest polluters in the world, China and

India. The CPP represents the Obama administration's climate pledge. The landmark agreement would be nonbinding, allowing countries to adjust their climate plans in accordance with their domestic circumstances; it was open for signatures at the United Nations in New York between April 22, 2016, and April 21, 2017. On April 22, 2016, 175 countries signed the accord, which is a preliminary step toward reaching the goals of the agreement.[153]

The major goal of the Paris Agreement is to reduce emissions enough so that global temperatures will rise no more than 2 degrees Celsius, or 3.6 degrees Fahrenheit.[154] The participating countries committed to putting forward successive and ambitious nationally determined climate targets and reporting on their progress. President Obama sought to cut emissions to as much as 28 percent below 2005 levels by 2025, mainly through EPA regulations. Importantly, however, although the agreement is nonbinding on such critical aspects as the setting of emissions targets for any individual country, it is binding on such matters as reporting requirements.[155] Also, as noted earlier, the Supreme Court decision to stay the EPA's global warming rule in February 2016 represented a major setback to the Paris Agreement and Obama's domestic climate program, because it questioned the U.S. commitment to reducing greenhouse gases, and as a corollary, that of China and India as well. Until the merits of the claims are decided upon in *West Virginia v. EPA*, the Paris Agreement remains on hold because the CPP is the linchpin of that agreement.[156]

An important distinction must be drawn between the Paris Agreement and the Kyoto Protocol discussed earlier. As noted, the U.S. Senate preempted President Clinton's ability to ratify the pact by passing Senate Resolution 98, or the Byrd-Hagel Resolution, which specified the condition that developing countries must make legally binding commitments to limit greenhouse gas emissions. They did not, and Clinton's hands were tied. But President Obama has treated the Paris pact as a "presidential-executive agreement," which does not require Senate approval; such agreements have historically been entered into by presidents dating back to George Washington.[157]

Article II, Section 2 of the U.S. Constitution specifies that a president can sign an international treaty, but in order to become law, it requires ratification by two-thirds of the U.S. Senate. However, other types of international agreements such as trade deals can be entered into with a "congressional-executive agreement," which requires the approval of a majority in both houses of Congress, a threshold lower than that of Senate approval.[158] Another type is the "presidential-executive agreement," which is approved solely by the president.[159] A number of significant international agreements have been entered into under this model, including the North American Free Trade Agreement (NAFTA), signed by President Clinton in 1993, and the Vietnam peace agreement signed by President Nixon in 1973.[160]

Critics, especially the U.S. Congress, have railed against such agreements, and there continues to be a good deal of uncertainty about them, particularly from a political standpoint.[161] Presidents often pursue these agreements to circumvent the U.S. Congress.[162] In this sense, executive agreements are an international analog to executive orders or, more broadly, the unitary executive or administrative presidency model, discussed in previous chapters. As Gary King and Lyn Ragsdale argue, "executive agreements enable presidents to enhance their autonomy in international affairs and thereby to promote their ability to act as independent policy makers."[163] But executive agreements raise questions about end-runs around the Constitution and the framers' intent for the rules and procedures for treaty making. While Congress seems complicit in allowing presidents to exercise this type of unilateral power, it ultimately holds the power of the purse and thereby controls spending for implementation of any agreement.

The U.S. Supreme Court has consistently upheld presidential-executive agreements, and in general the courts have not struck them down as unconstitutional.[164] However, the scope of presidential power here is unclear. As Louis Henkin argues, "One is compelled to conclude that there are agreements which the President can make on his sole authority and others which he can make only with the consent of the Senate (or of both houses), but neither [the Supreme Court] nor anyone else has told us which are which."[165]

Notwithstanding, the provisions of the Paris Agreement along with constitutional requirements seem to support President Obama's actions. As noted, there are various methods for entering into international treaties. And as Daniel Bodansky points out, Obama was "on relatively firm legal ground accepting a new climate agreement with legal force, without submitting it to the Senate or Congress for approval, to the extent it is procedurally oriented, could be implemented on the basis of existing law, and is aimed at implementing or elaborating the UNFCCC."[166] The Paris Agreement meets these conditions.

Article 4.2 of the Paris Agreement states that "each Party shall prepare, communicate and maintain successive nationally determined contributions that it intends to achieve. Parties shall pursue domestic mitigation measures with the aim of achieving the objectives of such contributions."[167] Article 4.3 further provides that "each Party's successive nationally determined contribution will represent a progression beyond the Party's then current nationally determined contribution and reflect its highest possible ambition."[168] As David Doniger states,

> Article 4 of the Paris agreement doesn't create a new international legal obligation. It reiterates the obligations already contained in Article 4 of the 1992 United Nations Framework Convention on Climate Change. The United States became a party to the Framework Convention after the Senate gave its advice and consent by an overwhelming vote in 1992.[169]

He goes on to explain that

> Article 4 of the Framework Convention obligates the U.S. and every other party to "formulate, implement, publish and regularly update national . . . programmes containing measures to mitigate climate change by addressing anthropogenic emissions by sources and removals by sinks of all greenhouse gases." The U.S. has been reporting periodically on its national program and its mitigation measures for nearly two decades. What's required under Article 3 of the Paris agreement is squarely within the obligations we already assumed under the Framework Convention.[170]

In short, President Obama exercised his authority to enter into an executive agreement on the Paris pact.[171] Another factor that has most recently affected the agreement is the Trump administration. During the presidential campaign, Trump pledged to "cancel" U.S. participation in the Paris Agreement and indeed, suggested he would shrink if not eliminate the EPA. Not even five months into his presidency and four days shy of World Environment Day 2017, Trump withdrew the United

States from the Paris climate accord. He relied in part on the advice of his appointee to head the EPA, Scott Pruitt, who has stated that the science of climate change has not yet been settled, because although there may be some relationship between human activity and climate change, the ability to measure the impact is tenuous at best.[172] But Trump may be naïve about how international agreements actually work. Under the Paris agreement, the United States cannot submit its intention to withdraw until November 2019, and the entire process of withdrawal takes at least four years.[173] By that point, Trump may no longer be in office.

As will be addressed in the concluding section, Pruitt and Trump are beginning to upend the Obama administration's policy drifts that worked to curb global warming. But the important point here, as noted in this chapter, is that party changes to the White House can have significant effects on public policy; and this speaks to the essence of policy drifts. For climate policy, this can be especially pernicious, as the drifts have mostly come from administrative rules and regulations issued by the EPA.

Conclusions

As we have seen in this chapter, environmental policy drifts are developed and implemented as a result of shared powers between a host of stakeholders. Here, the U.S. Congress has been unwilling to develop or implement public policy to address climate change. Perhaps it is an institutional bow to federalism, where many states maintain that environmental policies on such matters as global warming should not operate in the sphere of the federal government but are best controlled by the states. Advocacy coalitions of states supporting this position have relied on the courts rather than Congress to hinder policy drifts aimed at staving off the hazardous effects of global warming. The role of the executive branch has changed with each change of administration. President George W. Bush was willing to push back on climate change policy, whereas President Obama relied on his executive or unitary powers to push for policy drifts on climate change. The power of the bureaucracy, too, can be seen in the actions of the EPA, which has played a central role in efforts to reduce the emissions of greenhouse gases responsible for global warming. Maneuvering to promulgate rules or regulations to combat global warming around the time that President George W. Bush was sworn into office is one example here.

But questions remain on whether the executive branch, especially in the use of presidential-executive agreements, compromises democratic rule. As with the administrative presidency and unitary powers strategy discussed in preceding chapters, there are supporters and detractors of the manner in which the executive branch engages in policy drifts. In the context of climate policy, the question of administrative federalism is raised.[174] Federalism, according to James Madison, has traditionally been viewed as a power struggle between the national government and the states.[175] The Tenth Amendment to the U.S. Constitution reserves to the states the powers not granted to the federal government; however, there has never been clarity as to who has that power.[176] In general, the courts have decided this question.

Administrative federalism, on the other hand, can be construed within the context of the administrative presidency.[177] As Frank Thompson argues, "The administrative presidency rests with the kinds of actions that presidents and political appointees take to reshape public programs in the absence of congressional approval."[178] David Rubenstein goes even further: "Federal agencies are key players in our federalist system: they make front-line decisions about the scope of federal policy and whether such policy should preempt state law. How agencies perform these functions, and how they might fulfill them better, are questions at the heart of 'administrative federalism.'"[179] In this sense, it refers to how administrative agencies affect the balance of power between the federal and state governments.

In the area of climate control, the federal government expects the states and localities to implement the programs and rules established by the EPA, the chief administrative agency responsible for environmental policy.[180] Because Congress fails to act, the president and the EPA will act. This creates tensions between the states and the federal government, particularly for bureaucratic agencies. As we have seen elsewhere in this book, the bureaucracy wields a good deal of policy-making powers; it is sometimes referred to as the fourth branch of government.[181] But when those powers seek to circumscribe or preempt state sovereignty, questions are raised about the constitutionality of the role of the administrative state and its impact on democratic governance.

Much has been written about this issue.[182] As Lisa Schultz Bressman has pointed out, "From the birth of the administrative state, we have struggled to describe our regulatory government as the legitimate child of a constitutional democracy."[183] Early writings on the administrative state warned that government agencies must be driven by democratic principles as opposed to the managerial values of efficiency; that the administrative state must serve democratic ideals.[184] But the evolution of the administrative state over time has established it as a democratic state.[185] Edward Rubin argues that

> many of the basic concepts that we use to describe our current government are the products of social nostalgia. The three branches of government, power and discretion, democracy, legitimacy, law, legal rights, human rights, and property are all ideas that originated in pre-administrative times and that derive much of their continuing appeal from their outdated origins. . . . These concepts are simply not the most useful or meaningful ones that . . . describe contemporary government.[186]

While the U.S. Constitution vests Congress with the lawmaking function, federal agencies are responsible for making vast amounts of administrative law.[187] And as David Rosenbloom has pointed out, federal agencies' powers are inclusive of not simply legislative functions but of judicial and executive as well.[188] He writes that the rise of the administrative state

> represents an effort to reduce the inertial qualities of the system of separation of powers. In essence, all three governmental functions have been collapsed into the administrative branch. Thus, public administrators make rules (legislation), implement these rules (an executive function), and adjudicate questions concerning their application and execution (a judicial function). The collapsing of the separation of powers has been well recognized. . . . A system of checks and balances has devolved to the administrative branch along with the three governmental functions.[189]

John Rohr similarly states that "civil servants 'run the Constitution,' i.e., they reduce its grand principles to practice by their actions both routine and extraordinary."[190] In essence, bureaucrats, as he maintains, manage the separated powers of government.

Gillian Metzger, too, speaks to the significance of administrative law, referring to its use as "constitutionally legitimate."[191] She states that "for federalism to have continued vibrancy as a governing principle, it needs to be 'normalized' and consciously incorporated into the day-to-day functioning of the federal administrative state. Using administrative law to ensure that federalism concerns are met represents a central mechanism for achieving this incorporation."[192] She argues that "administrative law has important federalism-reinforcing features and represents a critical approach for securing the continued vibrancy of federalism in the world of administrative governance."[193] In this sense she sees administrative federalism as the interface of federalism and administrative law.

Interestingly, some have argued that in the context of federalism, federal agencies are in a better position to promote democratic principles than either Congress or the courts.[194] Brian Galle and Mark Seidenfeld argue that "for each of the classic elements of representational democracy—accountability, transparency, and deliberativeness— agencies are in many contexts better suited to consider federalism concerns than are Congress or the federal judiciary."[195] They go on to say that "the issue [with regard to administrative federalism] is not which institution best enables state influence over regulation, but rather which institution fosters state influence that will enhance public welfare, and not simply state officials' opportunities for rent seeking."[196] In the realm of climate control the question becomes, Whose interests are better aligned with the public welfare, the EPA or states opposing climate control?

In addition, the conflicts between the national government and the states provide additional checks and balances in a democratic society. Such conflicts are indeed conducive to "good government."[197] That is, federal law is made by administrative agencies but is ultimately checked along the separation-of-powers doctrine. And recall, also, that the EPA does give states and other stakeholders the ability to participate in rule-making when it issues its Advance Notice of Proposed Rulemaking (ANPR). This ultimately allows for more reasoned policy making.[198] In addition, the Negotiated Rulemaking Act, passed in 1990, encourages but does not mandate negotiated rulemaking, a collaborative process aimed at providing stakeholders more influence over rulemaking.[199] It is a supplement to the 1946 Administrative Procedure Act (APA) rulemaking process, and it does not replace the numerous procedural constraints on agency rulemaking required under the APA. However, as Cary Coglianese finds, while negotiated rulemaking, or "reg-neg," seeks to promote greater democratic legitimacy, it has not necessarily improved the rulemaking process for the EPA, in that it has not led to decreased litigation or more expeditious rulemaking.[200] In any case, Congress continues to possess the ability to intervene in regulating climate control policy, and the states, after all, are very well represented on Capitol Hill, where their lobbyists have easy access to legislators. Thus, rules or regulations promulgated by the EPA allow for state participation, but ultimately, Congress and the courts have the final word over the fate of those rules.

There is great uncertainty in the direction of climate policy under the Trump administration. Just ten weeks into his presidency, Donald Trump signed an executive order calling for a review of the Clean Power Plan in an effort to scuttle efforts to curb greenhouse gas emissions.[201] However, even if Trump and his EPA director, Scott Pruitt, find a way to scrap the plan, they are legally required to come up with another one. Moreover, repeal regulations are not that simple. The EPA is legally required to follow the same rulemaking procedures, with requisite stages of public notice and comment that are used to create regulations. This could take years.[202] Moreover, the CPP continues to be tied up in the courts. The U.S. Court of Appeals for the D.C. Circuit has not yet made a substantive ruling in *West Virginia v. EPA*, and the EPA petitioned the appeals court to hold the case in abeyance until it completes its review of the CPP, per Trump's executive order. This, too, could take years.

In addition, as previously noted, Trump in accordance with EPA Director Pruitt's advice, withdrew the United States from the Paris agreement.[203] Prior to his appointment as head of the EPA, Pruitt was the attorney general of Oklahoma and has been party to several lawsuits against the EPA in its efforts to stem global warming (e.g., *Oklahoma v. EPA*, 2015).[204] He has also joined with other states to nullify the CPP. The *New York Times* discovered that in 2014 Pruitt "helped organize an 'unprecedented, secretive alliance' between Republican attorneys general and large energy companies to attack the EPA—and one of the letters he sent complaining to the agency had in fact been written by industry lawyers."[205] Moreover, although Pruitt believes that the states and not the federal government should regulate the environment, he has not enforced environmental laws in his own state.[206]

An important point to make here is that the policy drifts created by the EPA under Obama's CPP are imperiled by Pruitt, who has been hostile to regulatory efforts to reduce carbon pollution. Current EPA scientists are so concerned that decades of efforts to develop crucial climate measurements could disappear under Pruitt, they downloaded government data onto independent servers in order to protect those data from political interference.[207] This speaks to the power of the bureaucracy. The Trump administration, particularly Pruitt, should not overlook the power of these and other bureaucrats in the EPA, who have spent their entire careers working for government. Through their tenure, expertise, and relationships with Congress and congressional staffers, they can work to obstruct the efforts of those hostile to the mission of their agency. Career bureaucrats are able to obstruct policy efforts by, for example, dragging their feet, leaking information to the press, or threatening to resign. As Marissa Martino Golden states, "bureaucrats can derail [a] president's plans by dragging their feet and stalling until the president forgets about his directive or leaves office."[208]

In addition, Republican members of the U.S. Congress may invoke the 1996 Congressional Review Act, which, as discussed earlier, can be used to dismantle environmental regulations issued under the Obama administration.[209] In effect, Congress can wipe out an entire set of agency rules, providing that President Trump agrees. Again, these actions by the legislative and executive branch of government speak to the essence of policy drifts: there is no finality to the policy process, and even those policies that appear stable can drift in different directions based on changes in stakeholder structure.

The issue of global warming is one of the most significant scientific and technological challenges of our time. It will remain significant for the next several decades. And unless Congress takes a lead role in policy drifts here, presidents and the EPA will continue to play key roles in climate control policy. Administrative federalism, then, will prevail. But who are the winners and losers here, not necessarily in the process but in the outcome? Global warming has garnered enough scientific evidence to indicate its dire consequences for the ecosystem and society, including human health, the environment, agriculture, and animals.[210] How do we respond to images of polar bears and their cubs, for example, seeking refuge from the rapidly disappearing Arctic sea ice due to global warming? Or the images of livestock dying from drought? With respect to human health, Anthony McMichael, Rosalie Woodruff, and Simon Hales point out that "heatwaves, . . . floods, storms, and fires, and various infectious diseases (especially those that are vector-borne)" pose major threats due to global warming.[211] The World Health Organization has estimated that global warming has claimed over 150,000 lives annually over the past thirty years due to respiratory illnesses, cardiovascular disease, infectious diseases, neurological diseases, and malnutrition resulting from crop failures.[212] Industry and the states may benefit economically from stalling efforts to curb greenhouse gas emissions, but their citizens will ultimately pay the price of global warming.

5

Conclusions

Shared Powers, Policy Drifts, and Sustainability

This book examined shared powers in the making of U.S. policy, where policy making was viewed within the framework of policy drifts. Here, unanticipated levers of change such as exogenous economic, political, ideological, or social forces cause modifications to the status quo in public policy, which ultimately lead to policy shifts or drifts. An important thesis of this book is that the policy process is ongoing and continuous. This indeed is the raison d'être of policy drifts. So, for example, as we saw in chapter 4, there were important policy drifts on the issue climate control under the Obama administration. But the Trump administration, which has been more hostile toward environmental regulation, may gut those drifts. On the other hand, if Hillary Clinton had been elected president in 2016, she most likely would have supported and even strengthened those drifts in climate policy initiated by the Obama administration. Hence, the durability or sustainability of policy drifts is highly affected by the party in control of the White House.

We have also seen that shared powers can lead to gains by some groups, which represent a loss to others, but not necessarily on a permanent basis. As illustrated in chapter 3, women were immediately disadvantaged by the U.S. Supreme Court's 2007 *Ledbetter v. Goodyear* decision.[1] But action by the U.S. Congress and President Obama restored pay equity rights for women with the Lilly Ledbetter Fair Pay Act of 2009. In any case, policy drifts carry significant consequences for social, political, and economic change, yet they are vulnerable to change.

This chapter draws out some lessons from the analysis presented in this book. It discusses the implications of shared powers jockeying over public policy for drifts and their outcomes. It illustrates that policy drifts are a rational, coherent part of the dynamics of public policy making. Political uncertainty does not cease once policies drift. A new stimulus for change will arouse interests from relevant stakeholders and new policy drifts will ensue. To the extent that there are no social, political, economic, or ideological forces pushing for change, the most recent drift remains in place. In this sense, some policy drifts may remain more durable or sustainable than others.

The Durability of Policy Drifts

The cases presented in this book indicate that there is no definitive end to the policy process or cycle. It is continuous to the extent that stakeholders challenge an existing policy drift. Policies that seemed settled and durable can drift in unexpected directions in that unanticipated external forces foment change. Yet some drifts and hence their outcomes may remain more durable than others. Durability and stability are in large part a function of the political and legal landscapes surrounding the particular policy. Thus, there is no set formula for predicting the permanence or durability of policy drifts. Nonetheless, policy durability has long been of interest in the study of public policy and politics. It would be interesting to question at this point the potential durability or sustainability of the policy drifts addressed in this book, as some may be more susceptible to change than others.[2]

A good deal has been written about policy stability in a host of contexts, such as policy agendas as well as the broader American political system.[3] For this analysis of policy drifts, the following markers are potentially relevant for determining or gauging policy sustainability: (1) stakeholder structure; (2) stability in the broader policy area; (3) policy feedback; and (4) social constructions of a policy's stakeholders or beneficiaries.

The stakeholder structure may be disposed to permutations to the extent that a drift in policy produces new or incoming stakeholders or policy players who work to restructure, chip away at, or even completely eradicate the drifts. For example, when the Democrats lose the House or Senate to the Republicans—or vice versa—the balance of political power shifts and the wrangling over policies and their drifts can take a completely different direction. The party once in power loses control to the other party, which can affect majority votes as well as the outcome of a cloture motion. Party parity and cohesion are also important factors. In addition, newly elected members of Congress may be pressured by voters or special interests to steer public policy in different directions, and survival of the elected representatives depends to a certain extent on their ability to meet their constituents' demands. Shifts in party control of the presidency and hence administration can also affect the durability of policy drifts. Fluctuations in stakeholder structures or coalitions, then, can significantly impact the sustainability of policy drifts.

Shifts in the political or ideological makeup of the courts can also affect policy durability. District or appellate court judges who are liberal-leaning will interpret laws and policies differently from those who are conservative-leaning. We can virtually always predict the outcome of common law based on the political composition of the U.S. Supreme Court. Politicized policy issues revolving around social, economic, or religious concerns almost always result in polarized 5–4 decisions based on partisanship. Certainly there are exceptions, as we saw in the High Court's decisions on the Affordable Care Act (ACA). In the 2012 *NFIB v. Sebelius* decision, Chief Justice John Roberts in a 5–4 decision surprisingly broke with the conservative bloc to uphold the constitutionality of the individual mandate of the ACA.[4] Three years later, both Chief Justice Roberts and Justice Anthony Kennedy sided with the majority in the 6–3 *King v. Burwell* decision, which upheld a critical component of the ACA: the subsidies used in the federal health insurance exchange.[5] Interestingly, Justice Kennedy was in the dissent in the *NFIB* decision, which would have found the entire law unconstitutional had Justice Roberts not voted with the liberal bloc.

Importantly, however, even when configurations of stakeholders shift or change, those who initially pushed for the drift can strategically frame the policy or its goal in a manner that would prevent further drifts. Rational choice scholars have referred to this as "deck stacking," which ensures policy durability.[6] That is, framing the drift in a particular fashion can encourage stakeholders, new or old, regardless of political philosophy or partisanship, to buy in to the drift, thereby ensuring its survival or sustainability.

Stability in the broader policy area may also ensure some sustainability to policy drifts. Some policies or laws tend to be more bedrock than others. Social Security, for example, has remained durable because it is viewed as a fundamental economic right. Granted, in recent years, it has been targeted for architectural change by conservative factions, especially those eager to privatize the program. Early efforts to partially privatize Social Security did not gain political traction because of bipartisan resistance to change, resistance no doubt linked to the political clout of the highly organized elderly constituency. Although Social Security has been subject to a number of drifts via amendments, overall it has remained remarkably resilient to change.[7]

Another important marker of policy durability that has received a good deal of attention in the political science and public policy literatures, especially regarding welfare, is policy feedback. Theda Skocpol points out that policies or laws, once passed, can restructure political processes and thereby policy outcomes: "As politics creates policies, policies also remake politics."[8] Paul Pierson points out that "the rise of interest groups is one of the clearest examples of how policy feedback from previous political choices can influence contemporary political struggles. Interest groups did not build the welfare state, but the welfare state contributed mightily to the development of an 'interest-group society.'"[9]

Eric Patashnik describes policy feedback as reactions and behavioral change generated by policy reforms or drifts.[10] Unintended beneficiaries of a policy drift, for example, can become advocates of the newly reformed policy. As will be seen shortly, gun enthusiasts may have been unintended beneficiaries of the Patriot Act. For the purposes here, policy feedback refers to all of these markers—specifically, whether and how the immediate outcomes of policy drifts produce positive or negative reactions, new demands, or new stakeholders in support of or against the policy.

Policy feedback can take a number of forms. For example, as the potential impact of policy drifts becomes more evident or apparent, existing stakeholders can shift their attitudes, positions, or behaviors in relation to the drift. New stakeholders may also emerge. One example can be seen in the politically and ideologically motivated undertakings of Ward Connerly and his American Civil Rights Coalition, which promotes the agenda that racial and gender preferences should be eliminated. After Connerly was appointed to the University of California Board of Regents in 1993, he became more familiar with the UC's affirmative action program and the significant policy drift on affirmative action that had occurred years earlier. In 1978 the U.S. Supreme Court, in *Regents of the University of California v. Bakke*, upheld for the first time the principle of affirmative action.[11] By 1995, Connerly had mobilized enough support to mount a general election ballot in California, Proposition 209, to abolish affirmative action in public education, hiring, and contracts in the state. California voters approved the initiative and Connerly went on to successfully back similar ballot measures across the country.

The manner in which a policy's beneficiaries or stakeholders are socially constructed can also affect the sustainability of policy drifts. Society, the media, and political elites are able to characterize persons or groups as either deserving or unworthy of certain rights, benefits, or privileges. Stereotyping of and prejudices against particular groups can help sustain or completely abolish policies or policy drifts. One example here can be seen in the major policy drift, the Personal Responsibility and Work Opportunity Reconciliation Act of 1996 (PRWORA), which ended entitlement to cash assistance for low-income families and replaced Aid to Families with Dependent Children (AFDC) with Temporary Assistance for Needy Families (TANF). The consistent portrayal of beneficiaries of welfare as lazy, irresponsible, and unwilling to work created a major policy shift in how the federal government and the states determine eligibility and provide aid to the poor. Such images of the poor have helped to maintain the policy aims of PRWORA and the overall durability of this policy drift.

In sum, there are a number of markers to gauge the potential durability of policy drifts. To be sure, the applicability of any of these markers depends on the specific policy area or drifts. Political and legal circumstances among others make some indicators more relevant than others. Table 5.1 provides a summary of the policies and policy drifts presented in this book and seeks to ascertain the potential durability or sustainability of policy drifts in each of the three areas.

TABLE 5.1. Charting Shared Powers, Policy Frameworks and Policy Drifts

Policy Domain	Primary Stimulus for Change	Major Stakeholders	Policy-Making Framework	Policy Drifts	Tools/ Strategies	Sustainability/ Durability
Surveillance/ privacy rights	9/11	Congress, president, courts, interest groups	Institutional	Patriot Act and amendments	Secrecy, lack of transparency, unitary executive, deck stacking	Remains stable to the extent terrorism is or is portrayed as a threat and freedom is imperiled
Civil Rights: Pay equity	Supreme Court's *Ledbetter* ruling	Congress, president, courts, interest groups	Punctuated equilibrium	Lilly Ledbetter Fair Pay Act	Separation of powers conflicts and jockeying	Remains stable; linked to Civil Rights Act
Civil Rights: LGBT employment	Social forces (e.g., *Windsor* ruling)	President, EEOC, DOJ, interest groups, Congress	Path dependency	Administrative rules and actions (e.g., executive orders)	Administrative presidency/ unitary executive	Lacks stability; not explicitly linked to federal law; driven by executive actions
Climate control/global warming	Supreme Court's *Massachusetts* ruling	States, EPA, president, courts, Congress	Advocacy coalition	EPA rules and regulations (e.g., global warming rule) via Clean Air Act	Administrative federalism	Lacks stability; not explicitly linked to federal law; driven by administrative actions, states, and the courts

Surveillance Policy

The drifts in surveillance policy as a result of 9/11 led to immense privacy breaches in this nation. Immediately following the 9/11 attacks, the entire country seemed on board when the federal government set in place a broad surveillance dragnet to hunt down the terrorists and stave off future attacks. A major policy drift in the form of the Patriot Act of 2001 launched an almost irreversible movement to invade the privacy of Americans on U.S. territory as well as U.S. citizens abroad, which in the end has done little to combat terrorism or protect our borders. Additional drifts to the Patriot Act reinforced this highly structured and controlled system of intelligence gathering at the expense of Americans' civil liberties. Even in the wake of revelations that our rights were being violated, the policy drifts have remained stable. What explains the utter sustainability of a policy that remains so contentious and embattled?

There has been durability in surveillance policy in large part because national security and freedom have driven the narrative. The policy goal was and is about patriotism, in the name of national security to protect America's freedom. What sitting president or elected member of Congress wants another 9/11 on her or his watch? The deck was stacked by the executive branch of government, which explicitly framed the issue as one of patriotism. Indeed, the name of the law—the Patriot Act—and those of its contiguous policies or laws (e.g., the Protect America Act of 2007) are emblematic of this. The act was about patriotism, in the name of national security to preserve the freedoms we enjoy as Americans.[12] By stacking the deck, the George W. Bush administration ensured that the party in control of Congress was inconsequential. That a Democratic president followed Bush was also irrelevant. The courts, too, even when dominated by judges appointed by Democratic presidents, fell short of gutting the government's surveillance policies and programs, although some were ideologically fervent about privacy rights. Partisanship seemed immaterial. The institutional support from every branch of the federal government legitimized the policies. And so there has been a political aversion to meddling in any effort to redirect policy drifts on this issue.

The Bush administration led the way in its initial drafting of the legislation that was eventually introduced to Congress. Then, President Bush pressured Congress into passing the Patriot Act and its amendments and accused those who balked of being unpatriotic. He went so far as to claim that any further attacks would be on the heads and consciences of those who did not support the Patriot laws. As a senator, Barack Obama may have succumbed to this bullying tactic; he voted in favor of the 2006 amendments to the act. And as president, Obama continued the surveillance programs mandated by the policy drifts. In short, the policy drifts have become entrenched by virtue of the institutional deck stacking by the executive branch and the attendant rubber stamping by all relevant policy players—every branch of the federal government.

The government also ensured a complete lack of transparency in each iteration of its policy drifts. In one case, the secrecy was a stratagem that Congress has employed in many cases and in various policy areas. Recall that the 2010 surveillance policy drift was concealed in an agenda item as part of the Medicare Physician Payment Reform Act of 2010.

The Bush administration was even effective in nudging a major media outlet, the *New York Times*, to suppress information it had gathered on the extent to which the government was spying on Americans.

There has been a modicum of stability in the broader area of surveillance policy to the extent to which the nation has been at war. Although the Fourth Amendment protects the American citizenry from invasions of our privacy rights, public policy has always moved in the direction of allowing those rights to be breached when the nation is battling an enemy. During World War II as well as the Cold War, the federal government surveilled anyone who would compromise tactical military operations or national security. That included spying on presumed communist sympathizers, who were seen as analogs to foreign enemies. Even the 1968 Omnibus Crime Control and Safe Streets Act, the first federal law to restrict wiretapping by requiring a court order, authorized the president to approve warrantless wiretaps in the interest of national security. But much of this early surveillance was aimed at spying on foreign enemies.

The passage of the Patriot Act in response to the 9/11 attacks led to an unprecedented degree of domestic surveillance at the complete expense of Americans' privacy rights. Now the "enemy" no longer had clearly defined boundaries because 9/11 was committed by terrorists, who are ubiquitous and nationless. The relative stability in surveillance policy over the centuries may have been taken as carte blanche by the Bush administration to broaden the boundaries of what constitutes an enemy, and hence institutionalize its domestic surveillance program. This program was perhaps unparalleled until the 2015 and 2016 terrorist attacks in France and Belgium, which led these and other nations to step up their domestic surveillance programs in an effort to avert future terrorist attacks. These new initiatives are raising concerns, not surprisingly, about free speech and privacy.

Policy feedback from the various versions of the Patriot Act brought in new stakeholders who waged political, legal, and ideological battles. The government's surveillance policies were opposed by interest groups as well as high-profile individuals. Some lawsuits were filed by citizens, but most were brought by such groups as the American Civil Liberties Union, cyberspace advocacy groups, and various other nonprofit organizations.[13] As discussed in chapter 2, however, court rulings leaned in favor of the government's surveillance policies. Renewed efforts by several members of Congress to bolster surveillance have also followed the terrorist attacks in Paris and Brussels.

In addition, the Patriot Act and its various iterations may have created unexpected beneficiaries in the form of gun enthusiasts. The policy drifts certainly affected their behaviors. Just after 9/11 there was a spike in the sales of guns nationwide, as Americans feared or anticipated additional attacks; in addition, later terrorist attacks in the United States, which led to amplified rationalizations for surveillance, also resulted in an increase in gun sales. This was the case just after the attacks in San Bernardino and Orlando.[14] A spokesperson for an online ammunition dealer said that just after the San Bernardino attacks, there was a 300 percent increase in sales.[15] And after a gunman killed forty-nine people in the gay night club Pulse in Orlando in June 2016, gun sales increased between 200 and 300 percent.[16] Granted, gun advocates are not necessarily responding to increased surveillance after terror attacks, but rather potential congressional action to pass gun reform. Nonetheless, it represents a form of policy feedback in that it may tangentially relate to policy drifts on surveillance, because a "lone wolf" may be more inclined to purchase guns during these frenzied periods of gun sales. In the end, however, gun advocates may have very little bearing on the durability of surveillance policy drifts.

The social construction of Bradley (now Chelsea) Manning and Edward Snowden is also relevant in terms of policy stability. The media portrayed them as either anti-American or heroes. Although Manning's leaks were not directly related to surveillance policy, Manning called attention to the secrecy surrounding the wars in Iraq and Afghanistan and their concomitant collateral damage—the killing of innocent civilians, including children. She may have been motivated by ideals, but her actions led to a conviction on charges of espionage.[17] Subsequent investigations led to the exposure of the use of waterboarding and other illegal methods the military relied upon when interrogating captured combatants suspected of terrorism. This in turn led to congressional investigations into torture and human rights violations and lobbying efforts to shut down Guantanamo, the prison camp that has been charged with the unconstitutional detainment and interrogation methods of detainees suspected by the federal government of being terrorists. As of this writing, the prison remains open. The same opposition to reforming surveillance policy to ensure that it meets constitutional requirements has worked to keep Guantanamo Bay open.

In 2013 Snowden, who had worked for the CIA and as a contractor for the National Security Agency, exposed the extent to which the NSA was spying on Americans. He revealed the fact that the Obama administration was continuing the massive surveillance program that was abrogating the privacy rights and civil liberties of the American people. Snowden's revelations seemed motivated largely by ideology. He argued that the government was lying to its people and failing to uphold its duties and responsibilities under the U.S. Constitution. High-level, elected officials, he claimed, were abusing their office and were not being held accountable for their actions. This, he maintained, was the ultimate betrayal of the citizenry of this nation.

The social construction of Snowden and Manning was not unanimous, nor was the media's portrayal of these two policy stakeholders. Manning was seen mostly as a traitor, charged with aiding the enemy by exposing sensitive, classified documents. Later accounts portrayed her as having a troubled past, and suffering from depression and mood swings, which led some factions to support her as a "whistleblowing hero."[18] This was due to Manning's struggles with gender identity and decision ultimately to transition to female, as discussed in chapter 2. This, too, may have affected how Manning was construed by society. Snowden was alternately portrayed as a hero, patriot, or traitor. Elected officials consistently called him a traitor, questioning why he did not pursue the formal whistleblower channels, which offer protections as complaints or perceived wrongdoings are disclosed.[19] The U.S. government filed a criminal complaint against Snowden, charging him with espionage and related crimes, but he was granted political asylum in Russia, where he currently holds a residency permit. In both cases, Manning and Snowden perceived Americans to be the beneficiaries of their actions. That is, they were not pursing their own personal gains. Nonetheless, in the end, as we saw in chapter 2, the actions of both Snowden and Manning had relatively little effect on surveillance policy drifts, nor did their social construction as whistleblowers, heroes, or traitors.

For now, surveillance policy appears relatively stable in large part because of the Bush administration's success in stacking the deck. Constancy in underlying motives has protected surveillance policy from drifting. The message seems clear: patriotism trumps privacy rights.

Civil Rights: Pay Equity

This book examined two aspects of civil rights policies and drifts. The first was pay equity, which appears to be somewhat stable or durable due in part to critical shifts in stakeholder structures. First, we saw a lawsuit filed by Lilly Ledbetter on the grounds that she was paid less than her male counterparts at a Goodyear tire plant in Alabama. The U.S. Supreme Court, in a 5–4 decision along partisan lines, ruled that Ledbetter failed to file her lawsuit in a timely manner, and hence was not entitled to restitution. This decision was in fact a drift from previous policy in that the High Court as well as lower courts previously held that unequal pay practices are not necessarily time-barred. One of the strongest explanations for the Court's reversal on this issue is the shift in structure and hence ideological makeup of the Court. In 2007, at the time of the *Ledbetter* ruling, the Court majority leaned much more to the right. Justices Alito, Scalia, Kennedy, and Thomas and Chief Justice Roberts, the conservative bloc, ruled against Ledbetter. The liberal bloc voting for Ledbetter consisted of Justices Sotomayor, Ginsburg, Breyer, and Kagan. The five justices in the majority opinion ignored an important precedent in the 1986 *Bazemore v. Friday* decision, which ruled that an unlawful practice occurs whenever a *current* paycheck may be discriminatory.[20] The *Bazemore* decision was unanimous, and represented one of the last decisions of the liberal-leaning Burger Court. The composition of the Court in 1986 was as follows: Chief Justice Burger and Justices Marshall, Blackmun, Powell, Brennan, White, O'Connor, Rehnquist, and Stevens. In short, a change in the ideological makeup of the Court resulted in a new, more regressive interpretation of Title VII's time limits on filing lawsuits.

After the Supreme Court's *Ledbetter* ruling, a battle was waged between Republicans and Democrats to pass a law that would counteract the ruling. The first attempt to pass the Lilly Ledbetter Fair Pay Act failed in 2007. It passed in 2009. Shifts in stakeholder structure may partially explain why the act passed in 2009. First, Republican president George W. Bush continued to denounce the 2007 act, and repeatedly promised to veto the bill if it reached his desk. In 2009 Democratic president Barack Obama, who supported the bill even while he was a senator, pushed strongly for passage of the act. In addition, the Democrats in the Senate were more successful in mobilizing support for the act in 2009 than they had been in 2007. The Democrats controlled both houses of Congress, and the House passed both the 2007 and 2009 bills. But the Democrats in 2007 were unsuccessful in persuading enough Republicans in the Senate to support a cloture motion. In particular, majority leader Harry Reid fought aggressively to encourage members of both parties to vote in favor of a cloture petition. He was successful in persuading only six Republicans to support it: Norm Coleman (MN), Susan Collins (ME), Olympia Snowe (ME), Gordon Smith (OR), Arlen Specter (PA), and John Sununu (NH). However, because the Senate was short of the sixty votes needed to block a GOP-led filibuster, Reid voted with the Republicans as a procedural tactic to allow him to bring the bill back to the floor in the future. In order for a bill or motion to be reconsidered, someone—generally the majority leader—from the side voting against cloture is required to signal for another vote. It is a strategic move that has been used countless times by many Senate majority leaders.

In addition, changes in the midterm elections of 2008 led to shifts in the voting patterns. The Democrats defeated five Republican incumbents, and they also picked up open seats in Colorado, New Mexico, and Virginia (it was the biggest Senate gain for the Democrats since 1986). In addition, Kay Hutchinson (R-TX) and Lisa Murkowski (R-AK), who did not support the 2007 bill, voted with the Democrats—but perhaps more importantly, with the other women senators—to support it in 2009.[21] The women in the Senate, in particular Barbara Mikulski (D-MD), who championed women's issues throughout her tenure, pushed for a unified women's front. Mikulski was dean of the Senate women, an unofficial post that she created and defined seemingly along the lines of a "women's whip." Mikulski reintroduced the Ledbetter bill to the Senate in 2009 and was committed to its passage, leading the way on the Senate floor and assisting in the defeat of a series of hostile amendments introduced by Republicans. Senator Olympia Snowe (R-ME) was also an advocate for women's issues and one of the original co-sponsors of the Ledbetter bill.[22] For her and the other female Republican senators, at least on the Ledbetter bill, gender trumped party or partisanship.[23] In the end, every woman, both Democrat and Republican, voted in favor of the final bill, which passed 61–36. Ultimately, shifts in stakeholder structure promoted durability in pay equity policy.

Stability in the broader policy area also explains the durability of the policy drifts in pay equity. The Lilly Ledbetter Fair Pay Act amends Title VII of the Civil Rights Act of 1964, and a good deal of the debate in Congress revolved around Title VII's mandate to eradicate discrimination in the workplace.[24] The Civil Rights Act has remained exceptionally durable since its initial passage, having been amended relatively few times. It is inconceivable that the fundamental employment rights enumerated in Title VII would be struck down in any sweeping fashion. Even the U.S. Supreme Court's effort to chip away at provisions for the timeframe for filing a lawsuit was met by resistance from Congress and at least a Democratic president. The long, hard-fought struggle for equality and justice in the workplace continues to be reinforced by champions such as Lilly Ledbetter who have the courage and tenacity to challenge discriminatory practices in the workforce. In short, efforts to effect policy drifts on such civil rights matters as fairness, justice, and equality in employment are thwarted to the extent that they intersect with key provisions of the Civil Rights Act of 1964.[25]

The Ledbetter Act may not have proactively changed the behavior of employers, encouraging them to pay women and men equally, but it did open the courtroom doors to not only women but to African American men as well, who could now sue for equal pay, even with the passage of time.[26] For example, in the 2009 case *Johnson v. Portfolio Recovery Associates*, an African American man, Mark Johnson, was hired at the vice-president level in 2003 at a lower salary than two white men also hired at this level of employment.[27] When Johnson complained about the pay disparity, he was fired. Johnson subsequently sued, and his superiors argued that he had not filed a timely Title VII claim and therefore the suit should be dismissed. However, in light of the Ledbetter Act, a federal district court ruled that Johnson could proceed with his lawsuit. By early 2010, the parties settled out of court with a mutually agreeable resolution, which was not disclosed.[28]

Additional policy feedback can be seen in Obama's issuance of Executive Order 13506 creating the White House Council on Women and Girls, which, on the heels of the Ledbetter Act, sought to push even further the contributions that women make to the U.S. economy. The council consists of every cabinet official as well as other public- and private-sector leaders, and its purpose is to "establish a coordinated Federal response to issues that particularly impact the lives of women and girls and to ensure that Federal programs and policies address and take into account the distinctive concerns of women and girls, including women of color and those with disabilities."[29]

President Obama also signed Executive Order 13665 on April 8, 2014, which prevents federal contractors from retaliating against employees for comparing salaries.[30] On that same day he also issued his presidential memorandum "Advancing Pay Equality through Compensation Data Collection," which requires contractors to report compensation data to the government by gender and race. Obama's actions here were intended to leverage support for pay equality between women and men.

In addition, bolstered by passage of the Ledbetter Act, more groups are joining the cause to pass the Paycheck Fairness Act, which would lower legal standards that protect employers from complaints of discrimination. Although this act has failed to muster support in the U.S. Senate, women's rights advocates, public health specialists, and some state GOPs are pushing for stronger pay equity laws.[31] In California, for example, Republicans in both the Assembly and Senate have worked with Democrats to pass a state law that virtually mirrors the Paycheck Fairness Act.[32]

The social framing of women in society also affects the durability of policy drifts on pay equity. Yet the social construction of women did not detrimentally affect, at least overtly, the passage of and durability of the last iteration of policy drifts, the Ledbetter Act. Gender may have been an implicit or covert concern among opponents to the act, but any elected official would be hard pressed to state explicitly today that women do not deserve to be paid equitably in comparison to men. Historically it was commonplace for organizations to blatantly treat women differently from men and not conceal their views that they deserved less pay than their male counterparts. These were institutionalized practices and sometimes mandated by law. For example, the 1935 National Recovery Act required women holding federal government jobs to be paid 25 percent less than men in the same jobs. When it was no longer socially or legally acceptable to tell women that they deserved less pay than men, subtle forms of disparate treatment emerged.

With respect to the Ledbetter Act, opponents strategically framed their concerns not in the context of women's rights, but rather in terms of the economic ramifications for businesses or private enterprise. As discussed in chapter 3, gender was referred to only once, in a remarkably offensive, patronizing statement by Representative Ric Keller (R-FL), who argued that "there is an old saying, hard cases make bad law. That applies here. Do we throw out the statute of limitations in employment cases because *a nice lady* waited 19 years to file a lawsuit? Common sense tells you the answer is no."[33]

In a broader sense, however, social construction may speak to the persistent inequalities between women and men in pay as well as other aspects of employment. For example, despite passage of the Lilly Ledbetter Fair Pay Act, pay inequities persist. As discussed in chapter 3, the pay gap between women and men may be narrowing, but today women earn only eighty cents for every dollar earned by men.[34] Moreover, there is continued resistance in Congress to passing the Paycheck Fairness Act, which would prevent unequal pay in the first place by strengthening the Equal Pay Act of 1963. Could a perception of women as less deserving be driving congressional inaction here?[35] Or is it really an economic issue? And if so, why not raise the starting pay of women coming into organizations and at the same time, lower the starting pay of men? Women continue to be treated differently from men in the workplace, and hence, may still be viewed, perhaps unconsciously, as less deserving than men vis-á-vis their pay as well as other facets of employment.[36] Again, the social construction of women can ultimately impact policy durability.

Civil Rights: LGBT Employment Rights

While the policy drift seen in the Ledbetter Act is marked by durability, the employment of LGBT persons continues to suffer from instability. As noted in chapter 3, in 2015 the U.S. Supreme Court upheld the constitutionality of same-sex marriages in *Obergefell v. Hodges*. Yet there is no federal law to protect LGBT persons in the workplace. Instead, a patchwork of state laws exists, some protecting them from employment discrimination while others do not. To date, efforts to pass a federal law, the Employment Non-Discrimination Act (ENDA), first introduced in 1994, have failed because the U.S. Congress has been unable to mobilize enough support to pass the bill. In addition, efforts to pass the 2015 Equality Act, which would amend Title VII of the Civil Rights Act of 1964 to include sexual orientation and gender identity, have also failed to move through Congress. Certainly, a number of stakeholders have supported passage of ENDA as well as the Equality Act. LGBT and human rights groups certainly lead the cause, which many others have joined, including mostly Democrats in Congress as well as a number of business interests that acknowledge the importance of diversity in their workplaces. The lack of a federal law is one explanation for the lack of stability in policy reform or drifts on the issue of LGBT employment rights.

President Obama, in the absence of federal law, took a number of executive actions to address LGBT employment rights, thereby creating a significant policy drift in this area of civil rights. In 2014, for example, he signed Executive Order 13672, which prohibits federal contractors and subcontractors from discriminating on the basis of sexual orientation or gender identity.[37] This executive order also adds gender identity as a protected class to E.O. 13087, signed by President Clinton in 1998 to prohibit discrimination based on sexual orientation in federal civilian employment. In addition, the Equal Employment Opportunity Commission (EEOC), an independent federal agency, issued rulings that made discrimination in the workplace based on sexual orientation and gender identity illegal under Title VII. Obama's Justice Department under the direction of Attorney General Eric Holder also began to interpret Title VII's prohibition against sex discrimination to cover gender identity and transgender status. These, too, were critical policy drifts supporting the employment rights of LGBT workers.

But these drifts do not promote policy stability because they are not based in federal statutory law or common law. That is to say, some executive actions (e.g., executive orders) do not have the same force or staying power as does federal legislation. Thus, to the extent that policy drifts are driven by presidential actions, they may be more susceptible to change when a new president is elected into office, particularly when there is a party change. We saw this with respect to LGBT employment policies when the Democrat Obama assumed the presidency after the Republican Bush. Importantly, however, administrative law can be just as powerful as statutes enacted by Congress. Although the courts have not issued rulings on whether Title VII of the Civil Rights Act covers discrimination based on sexual orientation or gender identity,[38] the EEOC has interpreted Title VII to cover both, as discussed in chapter 3.[39] These EEOC rulings have the force of law and establish important precedents for administrative law in the area of LGBT employment.

Perhaps the primary, underlying reason for the instability in policy drifts on LGBT employment has to do with the social construction of LGBT persons. Although some progress has been made in terms of how society frames and depicts them, they are still very marginalized in this nation; this is especially the case for transgender persons, who continue to be harassed and victimized. Indeed, some research has found that the public judges transgender persons more harshly than they do gays and lesbians. The research further shows that the public is less supportive of policies to support trans persons as compared to gays and lesbians.[40] As addressed in chapter 3, homosexuality was considered a mental disorder by the American Psychiatric Association until 1973, and, as Celia Kitzinger points out, even in the 1980s lesbianism was viewed as a pathology by psychoanalysts.[41] As of 2016, there were ten countries across the world where homosexuality is punishable by death: Yemen, Iran, Nigeria, Mauritania, Qatar, Saudi Arabia, Afghanistan, Somalia, Sudan, and United Arab Emirates.[42] Close to seventy additional countries make homosexuality illegal, punishable by varying penalties other than death, including prison sentences and fines.[43]

In addition, LGBT persons are more likely to be the target of hate crimes than any other group of people in the United States.[44] LGBT individuals surpassed Jewish people, Muslims, and African Americans in the amount of hate crimes reported per one million. As Joe Solmonese, president of the Human Rights Campaign Foundation, has stated, "There is plenty of evidence that violent, bias-motivated crimes are a serious, widespread problem across the United States. It's not the frequency or number of these crimes, however, that set them apart from other types of crime. It's the impact these crimes have on the victims, their families, their communities and, in some instances, the entire country."[45]

Societal views toward LGBT individuals have been captured in a host of venues, including in congressional committee hearings on efforts to pass employment discrimination laws to protect LGBT workers. For example, in hearings before the House on the 2007 ENDA, the American Association of Christian Schools offered this statement in opposition to the bill:

> This legislation would have a deleterious effect on the ability of religious Americans to follow the dictates of their respective faiths while still in accordance with the law. The issue of homosexuality is a contentious one in American society. The Bible, the Torah, and the Qu'ran all explicitly condemn homosexual behavior, and millions of Americans recognize these religious texts as the foundation for their beliefs regarding human conduct. . . . If the Non-Employment Discrimination Act of 2007 (H.R. 2015) is passed by Congress and signed into law, religious organizations and religious people would be compelled to act in conflict with their deeply-held religious beliefs.[46]

Similarly, Diane Gramley, president of the American Family Association of Pennsylvania, provided this statement: "Americans expect to feel safe within their work places. The passage of the Employment Non-Discrimination Act could present certain safety issues and employee relations problems to small and large businesses alike." Even though the provision on gender identity had been stricken from the bill, she nonetheless went on to argue that passage of the bill would provide transgender persons with a "foot in the door" as "radical transgender activists will still cry 'discrimination' and demand full 'inclusion'" in employment discrimination law.[47]

And Wendy Wright, president of Concerned Women for America, explicitly discussed LGBT persons in the context of morality:

> ENDA will force employers and employees with moral or religious beliefs regarding homosexuality or bisexuality to disavow these convictions, a violation of the right to conscience. . . . This legislation will be used as a tool to punish businesses that have moral standards. . . . Groups such as Christian schools, Christian camps, faith-based soup kitchens and Bible book stores would be forced to adopt a view of human sexuality which

directly conflicts with fundamental tenets of their faith. If H.R. 2015 is passed by Congress and signed into law, the U.S. government will, in effect, become an adversary to moral sexuality and religious conviction. Please do not punish Americans who believe that it is important to apply their moral convictions in the workplace.[48]

In short, negative social constructions of LGBT persons greatly impact policy durability.

LGBT workers continue to file EEOC claims for disparate treatment, harassment, and the use of degrading sex-based epithets such as "faggot" or "tranny."[49] And bullying, harassment, and violence against LGBT students in schools is on the rise, which affects young adults academically, emotionally, mentally, and physically. Fear of persecution and lack of acceptance lead many LGBT youth to drop out of school. LGBT youth are also at increased risk for suicide, suicide attempts, and suicidal thoughts and behaviors.[50] Unless the behaviors of the perpetrators of homophobic offenses are addressed, the next generation of society's workforce will continue to victimize LGBT persons, even if laws are in place by then.

Although societal attitudes toward LGBT individuals have improved in recent years, there continues to be disapproval of their lifestyles. Despite the U.S. Supreme Court's ruling in *Obergefell*, 44 percent of adults nationwide oppose same-sex marriage, and religious beliefs are a major factor: about 45 percent believe that engaging in homosexual behavior is a sin. And "coming out" to parents continues to be a major challenge; almost 60 percent of all LGBT adults who told their mother said that the experience was difficult, and 65 percent who told their father reported the same.[51] The struggle of LGBT persons to find universal acceptance and recognition continues, making the passage of federal employment discrimination law a distant reality.

In sum, policy drifts in the area of LGBT employment rights lack durability. We have not yet reached a point where the government is willing to lend broad support for a national law to protect the employment rights of LGBT workers. Republicans in Congress in particular have blocked efforts to pass a national law, and unless the federal courts step up to the plate to provide some protections, LGBT policy drifts in the area of employment will not be sustainable.

Climate Control

When Bill Clinton ran against President George H. W. Bush in the 1992 presidential campaign, Bush mockingly referred to Clinton's running mate, Al Gore, as the "ozone man." "This guy," Bush said, "is so far out in the environmental extreme we'll be up to our necks in owls and outta work for every American."[52] Clinton defeated Bush in the presidential race, and Vice President Gore led the way in efforts to combat global warming. As discussed in chapter 4, the Kyoto Protocol was one of the first serious efforts to curb global warming. Gore negotiated that treaty on behalf of the United States and was successful in forging its adoption in December 1997. But the protocol was never ratified because not only did the U.S. Congress refuse to take part in the treaty, but the Senate preempted further movement on it by overwhelmingly passing the Byrd-Hagel Resolution, 95–0, before the conference even took place. Recall from chapter 4 that this resolution is the measure that stipulates that developing countries must make binding commitments to limit the emission of greenhouse gases; in the case of the Kyoto Protocol, they did not. Even though such resolutions are not binding legally, they signal the Senate's intention to support or oppose presidential action. With a 95–0, bipartisan vote opposing the Kyoto Protocol, Clinton and Gore stood no chance of ratifying the treaty.

The melee resulting from efforts to curb global warming via the Kyoto Protocol provides one explanation why policy drifts in the area of global warming lack durability: the U.S. Congress simply has not been willing to legislate climate policy in any broad sense. The last major law passed by Congress was the Clean Air Act of 1970 as amended, which does not explicitly address climate concerns. Even when environmentally minded Democrats have occupied the White House and Congress was controlled by the Democrats, lawmakers have simply been unwilling to take action.

However, in terms of stakeholder structure, the shift in office from the Clinton to the Bush administration led to one of the most significant policy drifts on global warming. The lack of support from President Bush on environmental policy in general and the disinclination of his EPA director to regulate the greenhouse gases that cause global warming prompted a group of stakeholders, including state and local governments and environmental groups, to sue the EPA. The U.S. Supreme Court's 2007 ruling in that case, *Massachusetts v. EPA*, not only acknowledged the EPA's authority to regulate such gases, but forced the agency to use those regulatory powers.[53] This in turn led a different set of stakeholders—states and industry groups—to sue the EPA for issuing greenhouse gas regulations. The EPA once again prevailed, which suggests that at least the policy drift legitimizing the EPA's administrative authority under *Massachusetts* to issue rules and regulations pursuant to the Clean Air Act is and will remain sustainable, unless of course a different set of Supreme Court justices overturn that decision at some later date.[54] However, it is the specific rules that the EPA issues, especially on global warming, that lack sustainability, and changes in stakeholder structure and ideologies play a large role.

In accordance with President Obama's efforts to address climate change and in the absence of congressional action, the EPA developed the Clean Power Plan (CPP), generally referred to as the global warming rule, aimed at reducing the primary driver of global warming, carbon dioxide emissions. A coalition of state governments backed by industry groups sued the EPA over the rule, seeking to abolish it.[55] The U.S. Court of Appeals for the D.C. Circuit denied the request, but agreed to review the merits of the case at a later date. On appeal, before the D.C. Circuit even rendered a decision on the merits of the case, the U.S. Supreme Court in a 5–4 decision stayed the global warming rule until a decision on its merits could be issued. In a surprising move, Justice Kennedy, who voted with the majority in *Massachusetts*, which supported the scientific evidence of global warming, voted to block implementation of the global warming rule in *West Virginia*. In the oral arguments in *Massachusetts*, Kennedy was clearly annoyed when the attorney for the states, James Milkey, made the statement that it wasn't necessary for the Court to pass judgment on the science of climate change. Kennedy immediately challenged him, asking, "But don't we have to do that in order to decide the standing argument, because there's no injury if there's not global warming?"[56]

Ultimately, Kennedy joined the majority opinion in *Massachusetts*, which recognized the science behind global warming:

> The harms associated with climate change are serious and well recognized. The [EPA's] own objective assessment of the relevant science and

a strong consensus among qualified experts indicate that global warming threatens . . . a precipitate rise in sea levels, severe and irreversible changes to natural ecosystems, a significant reduction in winter snowpack with direct and important economic consequences, and increases in the spread of disease and the ferocity of weather events.[57]

Given his position on *Massachusetts*, it is unknown why Justice Kennedy signed on to Justice Roberts's briefly worded 5–4 order to stay the CPP global warming rule. As discussed in chapter 4, Kennedy is the swing vote on the Court, and he has been known to vacillate on a number of issues. It is possible that he switched his position on global warming, but unless the High Court issues a full ruling on the merits of *West Virginia*, the EPA's CPP will remain in legal limbo. The ambiguity and opacity here again speak to the lack of sustainability of global warming policy drifts.

Another interesting development regarding stakeholders is the willingness of some states, even those participating in the lawsuit against the EPA (*West Virginia v. EPA*), to begin complying with the EPA's global warming rule. For example, the Republican governor of Wyoming, a leading coal-producing state, instructed his environmental agency to begin preparations to comply with the CPP. Wyoming is one of twenty states moving in this direction. Even in those Republican-led states that have ordered environmental officials to ignore the CPP, regulators are beginning to develop strategies for complying with the CPP. Nonetheless, if the High Court ultimately strikes down the CPP policy drift, it is unlikely that those states opposing efforts to combat global warming (especially coal-producing states) will develop their own climate control rules.[58]

Another explanation for the lack of durability on global warming policy drifts is the lack of stability in the broader policy area of climate control. As noted, there is no federal law that is designed to regulate climate change. The Clean Air Act regulates air emissions to control air pollution. And as seen in chapter 4, the politics of global warming as played out on not just the national stage but globally as well has precluded any meaningful effort to enact a law regulating greenhouse gas emissions.[59]

In addition, climate and more specifically global warming represents a public or general interest policy drift, which tends to face greater challenges in terms of sustainability because it lacks viable special interests, and may represent a cost or loss to those narrower, more privileged interests. Moreover, the benefits to the overall public are generally widely diffused and are not very apparent from a political perspective.[60] In addition, the immediate effect of the climate change policy may be costly even to the public in the form of, for example, increased monthly electricity expenditures. The U.S. Energy Information Administration (EIA), a unit in the U.S. Department of Energy, released data showing that the CPP will lead to a spike in electricity costs. It estimates that between 2020 and 2025, prices will be around 3 to 7 percent higher as a result of the CPP, though the EIA does predict that prices in most parts of the country will drop by 2030.[61]

Another example of policy feedback can be seen in the form of investments toward maintaining the EPA's global warming rule. Jay Faison, a conservative from North Carolina, promised to spend $5 million through his CleanPath Action Fund to back five Republican members of Congress if they supported actions to curb the greenhouse gases responsible for global warming.[62]

Faison is obviously committed to curbing climate change, and he hopes that his financial backing in key congressional elections will encourage Republicans to support such efforts as well. He explains that "what we are trying to do is to prove to the party, through these races, that clean energy wins races, to build a political safe space for the Republican Party to talk about this. . . . It is difficult for a politician to consistently act in an area with no reward. We have their back."[63] The policy feedback as represented in Faison's investment in these five Republican congressional races is important, but unless other members of Congress come on board, it is unlikely that his efforts will lead to sustainability in the EPA's climate policy drifts.

Society's perception of environmentalists has changed considerably over the past few decades. President George H. W. Bush's mocking reference to Al Gore as the "ozone man" is not only anachronistic but would not be tolerated today. Once viewed as hippies, flaky and uber-eccentric, environmentalists are now seen in more positive ways, especially in light of the visible ecological deterioration that environmental groups have helped to address. Today, they are sometimes seen as elitist members of special interests who work to preserve nature often at the expense of rural communities.[64] As the environmental movement has become more of a cultural norm, however, society tends to perceive environmentalists as much more acceptable.

On the other hand, there continues to be a more radical environmental movement that has a very negative public image. This movement emerged in the 1980s in response to a perception that mainstream environmentalists failed to achieve meaningful, significant changes in environmental policy. John Cianchi suggests that the

> radical environmental activist lifestyle can be dangerous, uncomfortable and frightening. . . . Such activists are willing to undertake what for most of us would be an unacceptable level of discomfort, disobedience and confrontation. Their tactics include forms of law-breaking such as trespassing on facilities to record breaches of environmental laws and conditions, blockading entrances to logging coupes, locking themselves on to industrial equipment and placing themselves in small inflatable boats between whalers and their prey.[65]

These, however, are generally fringe groups that tend to lack any coordinated or organized power. In any case, the social construction of environmentalists may not be consequential in terms of the durability of policy drifts.

Unless there is some cataclysmic event that triggers greater support for efforts to combat global warming, efforts to address climate control in this country and perhaps globally will not be sustainable. Even then, there will be naysayers and skeptics, especially within fossil fuel–producing industries and states that will work to gut global warming policy drifts. When elected officials who are responsible for enacting laws in this country refer to global warming as a "conspiracy" and a "hoax," there is a low probability that positive action on climate change will be taken.[66]

Looking Ahead

Policy drifts and their derivative processes are integral to democratic governance. As seen in the cases presented in this book, democratic rule is promoted through the shared powers model; it is at the heart of American democracy. But it further shows that governance unfolds over time, as policies drift. Moreover, adoption or implementation of a policy is not a fixed end point. The process may appear incoherent, but it is a rational part of the public policy-making process as it has evolved in this nation. Even when challenges to democratic governance seem insurmountable, any stakeholder or coalition of stakeholders can push for policy drifts.

For example, over the past several decades there has been a slow accretion of power to the U.S. Supreme Court. And the Court has welcomed its role as arbiter of important constitutional matters, even if this meant tying the hands of the other branches of the federal government as well as the states. For ideological matters such as climate control, pay equity, and same-sex marriage, the Supreme Court has rendered 5–4 decisions, where an unelected official, such as a Justice Anthony Kennedy, who accepts his role as the swing vote on the Court, has been the sole decision maker or policy maker on issues involving constitutional law. But as argued here, the states as well as Congress have the power—indeed, the responsibility—to break political logjams to engage in the policy process especially over ideological matters. In the case of climate control, Congress has been reluctant to take on judicial activism, thus abandoning its obligation to participate in policy making over this critical, contentious policy domain. Yet Congress did defy the High Court in the case of pay equity, where it eventually passed a law to counteract a regressive policy drift.

Some have argued that executive actions by the president or administrative actions by the bureaucracy pervert democracy and accountability. Has the executive branch sidestepped the formal rulemaking process, bypassing the constraints of the Administrative Procedure Act of 1946, which allows for public participation in the policy conversation? First, as seen in this book, the president has the authority to issue executive orders under the U.S. Constitution, which gives the president "executive power." Article II, Section 3 of the Constitution provides that the president shall "take Care that the Laws be faithfully executed," which has been understood to include the issuance of formal executive orders or directives. Terry Moe and William Howell point out that the "fact is, presidents have always acted unilaterally to make law. The Louisiana Purchase, the freeing of the slaves, the internment of the Japanese, the desegregation of the military, the initiation of affirmative action, the imposition of regulatory review—these are but a few of the most notable examples."[67] Thus, executive actions are part of the constitutionally prescribed democratic framework. Similarly, while the Constitution grants Congress power to make laws, federal agencies are responsible for making administrative law, which fosters democratic values especially in terms of transparency and accountability. Notice-and-comment rulemaking, for instance, requires agencies to publish notices of proposed actions and allows interested persons or groups to participate in rulemaking proceedings. Congress, the president, and the courts can ultimately reverse administrative actions.

In certain areas of public policy, as we have seen in this book, it may be that Congress has become weaker as vast discretion has shifted to the executive branch. Rather than empowering the career bureaucracy, however, it has elevated the importance of the administrative presidency. To some degree, the courts and federalism do more checking than Congress.

In regard to the three particular cases addressed in this book, we see that no one size fits all, and we cannot conclude that certain policy frameworks (e.g., advocacy coalition) will always apply to a particular policy domain. Pigeonholing is imprudent, and as we have seen, the models, strategies, and frameworks overlap to a certain degree. Moreover, the policy type or area may be inconsequential. For example, one cannot claim that regulatory policy is marked by durability. In the area of civil rights policy, for example, pay equity has been relatively stable. However, employment protections for LGBT workers are marked by instability. In any case, when stasis is thrown into political turmoil, policy drifts will ensue, which seems inevitable.

ACKNOWLEDGMENTS

I would like to thank Tony Bertelli and Dean Sherry Glied of the Wagner School, New York University, for providing me with a visiting professorship during my sabbatical year to work on this book. The experience, time, and ability to knock around ideas with Tony were invaluable. I would also like to thank several individuals who read and commented on draft chapters, including Frank Thompson, Beryl Radin, David Rosenbloom, and the anonymous reviewers for New York University Press. I also extend my deepest gratitude to my editor, Caelyn Cobb, for her support, encouragement, and remarkable editing. Thanks also to NYU's Ilene Kalish and Dorothea Stillman Halliday for all their assistance and diligence in getting this book into press. Last but not least, I would like to thank Rosalie Morales Kearns for her outstanding copyediting of this book.

NOTES

CHAPTER 1. THE MAKING OF LAW, POLICY, AND POLICY DRIFTS

1 See Jacob S. Hacker, "Policy Drift: The Hidden Politics of U.S. Welfare State Retrenchment," in *Beyond Continuity: Institutional Change in Advanced Political Economies*, ed. Wolfgang Streeck and Kathleen Thelen (Oxford: Oxford University Press, 2005), 40–82; and Guenther Kress, Gustav Koehier, and J. Fred Springer, "Policy Drift: An Evaluation of the California Business Enterprise Program," *Policy Studies Journal* 8 (1980): 1101–8.

2 Haynes Johnson, *The Age of Anxiety: McCarthyism to Terrorism* (Orlando: Harcourt, 2006).

3 *West Virginia v. EPA*, No. 15A773, 2016 U.S. LEXIS 981, bbreaction02.bakerbotts.com, accessed February 17, 2016.

4 Hacker, "Policy Drift"; Jacob S. Hacker, "Privatizing Risk without Privatizing the Welfare State: The Hidden Politics of Social Policy Retrenchment in the United States," *American Political Science Review* 98 (2004): 243–60.

5 Hacker, "Privatizing Risk," 243.

6 Also see David H. Rosenbloom, *Building a Legislative-Centered Public Administration* (Tuscaloosa: University of Alabama Press, 2000); and David H. Rosenbloom, "Public Administration Theory and the Separation of Powers," *Public Administration Review* 43 (1983): 219–27.

7 Beryl A. Radin and Willis D. Hawley, *The Politics of Federal Reorganization: Creating the U.S. Department of Education* (Elmsford, NY: Pergamon, 1988), 3.

8 See Theodore J. Lowi, "Distribution, Regulation and Redistribution: The Functions of Government," in *Public Policies and Their Politics*, ed. Randall B. Ripley (New York: Norton, 1966), 27–40. Regulatory policies seek to limit the actions or behaviors of groups or institutions; distributive policies distribute benefits to certain populations from government expenditures; redistributive policies redistribute revenues acquired from one group to benefit others.

9 Richard P. Nathan, *The Administrative Presidency* (New York: Wiley, 1983); William G. Resh, *Rethinking the Administrative Presidency* (Baltimore: Johns Hopkins University Press, 2015); Robert F. Durant and William G. Resh, "'Presidentializing' the Bureaucracy," in *The Oxford Handbook of American Bureaucracy*, ed. Robert F. Durant (New York: Oxford University Press, 2010), 545–68.

10 See, for example, Timothy J. Conlan, Paul L. Posner, and David R. Beam, *Pathways of Power: The Dynamics of National Policymaking* (Washington, D.C.:

Georgetown University Press, 2014); Eric A. Posner and Adrian Vermeule, *The Executive Unbound: After the Madisonian Republic* (New York: Oxford University Press, 2011); and Kenneth J. Meier and John Bohte, *Politics and the Bureaucracy: Policymaking in the Fourth Branch of Government*, 5th ed. (Belmont, CA: Wadsworth Cengage Learning, 2007).

11 See Beryl A. Radin and Paul Posner, "Policy Tools, Mandates, and Intergovernmental Relations," in Durant, *The Oxford Handbook of American Bureaucracy*, 447–71; and Daniel J. Elazar, *Exploring Federalism* (Tuscaloosa: University of Alabama Press, 1987).

12 See Louis Fisher, *The Politics of Shared Power: Congress and the Executive*, 4th ed. (College Station: Texas A&M University Press, 1998); Paul A. Sabatier, "Fostering the Development of Political Theory," in *Theories of the Policy Process*, 2nd ed., ed. Paul A. Sabatier (Boulder: Westview, 1999), 261–75; Barbara C. Crosby and John M. Bryson, *Leadership for the Common Good: Tackling Public Problems in a Shared-Power World*, 2nd ed. (San Francisco: Jossey-Bass/John Wiley, 2005); John W. Kingdon, *Agendas, Alternatives, and Public Policies*, 2nd ed. (New York: Longman, 2010); Thomas A. Birkland, *An Introduction to the Policy Process: Theories, Concepts, and Models of Public Policy Making*, 4th ed. (New York: Routledge, 2015); and Thomas A. Birkland, *An Introduction to the Policy Process: Theories, Concepts, and Models of Public Policy Making*, 3rd ed. (Armonk, NY: M. E. Sharpe, 2011). Also see the immense amount of literature on intergovernmental relations.

13 The terms "theories" and "frameworks" are used interchangeably for the purposes of this book. But see, for example, Sabatier, "Fostering the Development of Political Theory," who addresses the differences between the two.

14 Lowi, "Distribution, Regulation and Redistribution"; Kenneth J. Meier, *Politics and the Bureaucracy: Policymaking in the Fourth Branch of Government*, 2nd ed. (Monterey, CA: Brooks/Cole, 1987); Randall Ripley and Grace Franklin, *Congress, the Bureaucracy, and Public Policy* (Homewood, IL: Dorsey, 1980).

15 For example, a number of states filed suit against the federal government when the U.S. Department of Homeland Security issued directives in 2014 granting certain protections to immigrants.

16 See, for example, David H. Rosenbloom, Robert Kravchuk, and Richard Clerkin, *Public Administration: Understanding Management, Politics, and Law in the Public Sector*, 8th ed. (New York: McGraw-Hill, 2015); and Rosenbloom, "Public Administration Theory."

17 James Madison, "The Particular Structure of the New Government and the Distribution of Power among Its Different Parts," *Federalist Paper* No. 47 (February 1, 1788). Also see Madison's *Federalist Papers* Nos. 10 and 51, which provided the core framework of American politics. Here, Madison set forth the basic tenets of American constitutionalism: separated institutions and checks and balances. The separation of powers ensured that power would be shared by the three branches of government, and powers would be checked by each to ensure that no single branch dominated. James Madison, "The Structure of the Government Must

Furnish the Proper Checks and Balances between the Different Departments,"
Federalist Paper No. 51 (February 6, 1788), www.constitution.org, accessed September 9, 2015; James Madison, "The Utility of the Union as a Safeguard against
Domestic Faction and Insurrection," *Federalist Paper* No. 10 (November 22, 1787),
www.constitution.org, accessed September 9, 2015. Also see Gerald M. Pomper
and Marc D. Weiner, eds., *The Future of American Democratic Politics: Principles
and Practices* (New Brunswick: Rutgers University Press, 2003).

18 John Locke, *Two Treatises of Government* (Minneapolis: Filiquarian, 2007; first
published 1689); Montesquieu, *The Spirit of the Laws* (Berkeley: University of
California Press, 1977; first published 1748).

19 Anthony M. Bertelli and Laurence E. Lynn Jr., *Madison's Managers: Public Administration and the Constitution* (Baltimore: Johns Hopkins University Press, 2006).
Others have argued that each branch of government has a discrete role in the policy
process. See, for example, Gerald Rosenberg, "Judicial Independence and the Reality of Political Power," *Review of Politics* 54 (1992): 369–98; and Lon L. Fuller, "The
Forms and Limits of Adjudication," *Harvard Law Review* 92 (1978): 353–409.

20 *NFIB (National Federation of Independent Business) v. Sebelius*, 567 U.S. 519, 132
S.Ct. 2566 (2012); *King v. Burwell*, 576 U.S. ___, 135 S. Ct. 2480 (2015).

21 In September 2015 a federal district court ruled that the House had the right to
sue the Obama administration in this matter. See *House of Representatives v. Burwell, 130 F. Supp. 3d 53* (2015). The court also ruled that the House would in fact be
injured if the administration was spending money without an appropriation.

22 James Q. Wilson, John DiIulio Jr., and Meena Bose, *American Government* (Boston: Wadsworth Cengage, 2014), 24, emphasis in original.

23 See, for example, Paul A. Sabatier and Christopher Weible, eds., *Theories of the
Policy Process*, 3rd ed. (Boulder: Westview, 2014); B. Guy Peters, *American Public
Policy: Promise and Performance*, 9th ed. (Thousand Oaks, CA: CQ Press, 2013);
Birkland, *An Introduction to the Policy Process, 3rd and 4th eds.*; Deborah Stone,
Policy Paradox: The Art of Political Decision Making, 3rd ed. (New York: Norton,
2011); Kingdon, *Agendas, Alternatives, and Public Policies*; Edella Schlager and
William Blomquist, "A Comparison of Three Emerging Theories of the Policy
Process," *Political Research Quarterly* 49 (1996): 651–72; Frank Baumgartner and
Bryan Jones, "Agenda Dynamics and Policy Subsystems," *Journal of Politics* 53
(1991): 1044–74; Radin and Hawley, *The Politics of Federal Reorganization*; Charles
E. Lindblom, *The Policy-Making Process* (Englewood Cliffs, NJ: Prentice-Hall,
1968); and Charles E. Lindblom, "The Science of 'Muddling Through,'" *Public
Administration Review* 19 (1959): 79–88.

24 Harold D. Lasswell, *Politics: Who Gets What, When, How* (New York: McGraw-
Hill, 1936).

25 See Sabatier, "Fostering the Development of Political Theory"; Gary Brewer and
Peter deLeon, *Foundations of Policy Analysis* (Homewood, IL: Dorsey, 1983); and
Charles Jones, *An Introduction to the Study of Public Policy* (Belmont, CA: Wad-
sworth, 1970).

26 On the open-systems framework, see, for example, Richard Hofferbert, *The Study of Public Policy* (Indianapolis: Bobbs-Merrill, 1974); on institutional rational choice, see Elinor Ostrom, "Rational Choice Theory and Institutional Analysis: Toward Complementarity," *American Political Science Review* 85 (1991): 237–43; and Elinor Ostrom, "An Agenda for the Study of Institution," *Public Choice* 48 (1986): 3–25; on the "policy streams" framework, see Kingdon, *Agendas, Alternatives, and Public Policies.*

27 For an excellent review of these policy-making models, see Birkland, *An Introduction to the Policy Process,* 3rd *and* 4th *eds.*

28 Clarke E. Cochran, Lawrence C. Mayer, T. R. Carr, N. Joseph Cayer, Mark J. McKenzie, and Laura R. Peck, *American Public Policy: An Introduction,* 11th ed. (Boston: Cengage Learning, 2016), 8. Also see Michael E. Kraft and Scott R. Furlong, *Public Policy: Politics, Analysis, and Alternatives* (Washington, D.C.: CQ Press, 2015); B. Guy Peters, *Institutional Theory in Political Science: The New Institutionalism,* 3rd ed. (New York: Continuum, 2012); and W. Richard Scott, *Institutions and Organizations: Ideas, Interests, and Identities,* 4th ed. (Thousand Oaks, CA: Sage, 2014).

29 B. Guy Peters, "Institutional Theory: Problems and Prospects," Political Science Series, Institute for Advanced Studies, Vienna, 69 (2000), www.ihs.ac.at, accessed January 6, 2016.

30 See, for example, Peters, *Institutional Theory in Political Science.*

31 Kraft and Furlong, *Public Policy,* 82.

32 Paul Pierson, "Increasing Returns, Path Dependence, and the Study of Politics," *American Political Science Review* 94 (2000): 251–67.

33 See, for example, Jacob S. Hacker, "The Historical Logic of National Health Insurance: Structure and Sequence in the Development of British, Canadian, and U.S. Medical Policy," *Studies in American Political Development* 12 (1998): 57–130; and William Sewell, "Three Temporalities: Toward an Eventful Sociology," in *The Historic Turn in the Human Sciences,* ed. Terrance McDonald (Ann Arbor: University of Michigan Press, 1996), 245–80.

34 Pierson, "Increasing Returns," 251.

35 See, for example, Birkland, *An Introduction to the Policy Process*; Conlan, Posner, and Beam, *Pathways of Power,* 3rd *and* 4th *eds.*; and Stone, *Policy Paradox.*

36 Robert Alan Dahl, *Pluralist Democracy in the United States: Conflict and Consent* (Chicago: Rand McNally, 1967).

37 Elmer E. Schattschneider, *The Semi-Sovereign People* (New York: Holt, Rinehart and Winston, 1960); C. Wright Mills, *The Power Elite* (reprint, New York: Oxford University Press, 2000).

38 Martin Gilens and Benjamin I. Page, "Testing Theories of American Politics: Elites, Interest Groups, and Average Citizens," *Perspectives on Politics* 12 (2014): 564–81.

39 Paul A. Sabatier, "Toward Better Theories of the Policy Process," *PS: Political Science and Politics* 24 (1991): 147–56, 147.

40 Paul A. Sabatier and Hank C. Jenkins-Smith, "The Advocacy Coalition Framework: An Assessment," in Sabatier, *Theories of the Policy Process*, 2nd ed., 117–66; Schlager and Blomquist, "A Comparison of Three Emerging Theories."

41 Christopher M. Weible and Paul A. Sabatier, "A Guide to the Advocacy Coalition Framework," in *Handbook of Public Policy Analysis: Theory, Politics, and Methods*, ed. Frank Fischer, Gerald J. Miller, and Mara S. Sidney (New York: CRC Press, 2006): 123–36, 124–25.

42 Lucie Cerna, "The Nature of Policy Change and Implementation: A Review of Different Theoretical Approaches," OECD, 2013, www.oecd.org, accessed January 6, 2016.

43 Baumgartner and Jones, "Agenda Dynamics and Policy Subsystems"; Frank Baumgartner and Bryan Jones, *Agendas and Instability in American Politics*, 2nd ed. (Chicago: University of Chicago Press, 2009); James L. True, Bryan D. Jones, and Frank R. Baumgartner, "Punctuated-Equilibrium Theory: Explaining Stability and Change in Public Policymaking," in Sabatier, *Theories of the Policy Process*, 2nd ed., 97–116; Bryan D. Jones and Frank R. Baumgartner, "From There to Here: Punctuated Equilibrium to the General Punctuation Thesis to a Theory of Government Information Processing," *Policy Studies Journal* 40 (2012): 1–19.

44 Baumgartner and Jones, *Agendas and Instability in American Politics*, xvii.

45 Birkland, *An Introduction to the Policy Process*, 3rd ed., 300. Also see Thomas A. Birkland, "Disasters, Lessons Learned, and Fantasy Documents," *Journal of Contingencies and Crisis Management* 17 (2009): 146–56.

46 Gerard W. Boychuk, *National Health Insurance in the United States and Canada* (Washington, D.C.: Georgetown University Press, 2008).

47 Juliet E. Carlisle, Jessica T. Feezell, Kristy E. H. Michaud, and Eric R. A. N. Smith, *The Politics of Energy Crises* (New York: Oxford University Press, 2017).

48 Streeck and Thelen, *Beyond Continuity*; Kathleen Thelen, *How Institutions Evolve: The Political Economy of Skills in Germany, Britain, the United States, and Japan* (Cambridge, UK: Cambridge University Press, 2004); Kathleen Thelen, "How Institutions Evolve: Insights from Comparative Historical Analysis," in *Comparative Historical Analysis in the Social Sciences*, ed. James Mahoney and Dietrich Rueschemeyer (Cambridge, UK: Cambridge University Press, 2003), 208–40.

49 Thelen, *How Institutions Evolve*, 35.

50 See Thelen, "How Institutions Evolve."

51 Also see Lindblom, "The Science of 'Muddling Through'"; and Lindblom, *The Policy-Making Process*. Lindblom argues that the policy process is incremental, piecemeal, or "muddled through," and that policy making is "an extremely complex analytical and political process to which there is no beginning and no end, and the boundaries of which are most uncertain." *The Policy-Making Process*, 4.

52 Thelen, "How Institutions Evolve," 229.

53 Hacker, "Privatizing Risk."

54 Kress, Koehier, and Springer, "Policy Drift."

55 Ibid., 1101.

56 Ibid.

57 Hacker, "Privatizing Risk," 243.

58 Ibid., 246.

59 Paul A. Sabatier, "An Advocacy Coalition Framework of Policy Change and the Role of Policy-Oriented Learning Therein," *Policy Sciences* 21 (1988): 129–68, 130.

60 Daniel Béland, "Ideas and Institutional Change in Social Security: Conversion, Layering, and Policy Drift," *Social Science Quarterly* 88 (March 2007): 20–38, 20.

61 Beryl A. Radin, *Challenging the Performance Movement: Accountability, Complexity, and Democratic Values* (Washington, D.C.: Georgetown University Press, 2006).

62 There is a plethora of literature on the bureaucracy and its historical underpinnings. For example, the public administration literature examines bureaucracy from a variety of perspectives, from an apolitical, neutral entity (see Woodrow Wilson, "The Study of Administration," *Political Science Quarterly* 2 [1887]: 197–222) to the fourth branch of government (see Meier and Bohte, *Politics and the Bureaucracy*; and David Nachmias and David H. Rosenbloom, *Bureaucratic Government, USA* [New York: St. Martin's, 1980]).

63 See Richard Neustadt, *Presidential Powers and the Modern Presidents* (New York: Free Press, 1991).

64 Nathan, *The Administrative Presidency*.

65 Frank J. Thompson, "The Administrative Presidency and Fractious Federalism: Lessons from Obamacare," presentation at annual conference of the American Society for Public Administration, Washington, D.C., 2014, www.aspanet.org, accessed January 6, 2016.

66 David H. Rosenbloom, "President George W. Bush's Theory of a Unitary Executive Branch and the Rule of Law in the United States," *Journal of Political and Parliamentary Law* 1 (2008): 227–54; Steven G. Calabresi and Christopher S. Yoo, *The Unitary Executive: Presidential Power from Washington to Bush* (New Haven: Yale University Press, 2008); Ryan J. Barilleaux and Christopher S. Kelley, eds., *The Unitary Executive and the Modern Presidency* (College Station: Texas A&M University Press, 2010).

67 See Richard J. Ellis, *The Development of the American Presidency*, 2nd ed. (New York: Routledge, 2015); and Richard W. Waterman, "The Administrative Presidency, Unilateral Power, and the Unitary Executive Theory," *Presidential Studies Quarterly* 39 (2009): 5–9.

68 See Kirti Datla and Richard L. Revesz, "Deconstructing Independent Agencies (and Executive Agencies)," *Cornell Law Review* 98 (2013): 769–843.

69 William F. West, "Administrative Rulemaking: An Old and Emerging Literature," *Public Administration Review* 65 (2005): 655–68; William F. West, "The Politics of Administrative Rulemaking," *Public Administration Review* 42 (1982): 420–26. Also see Susan Webb Yackee, "Sweet-Talking the Fourth Branch: The Influence of Interest Group Comments on Federal Agency Rulemaking," *Journal of Public Administration Research and Theory* 16 (2006): 103–24, who illustrates how interest

groups are able to impact bureaucratic rulemaking. Career bureaucrats can also obstruct policy efforts by, for example, leaking information to the press, threatening to resign, or simply dragging their feet.

70 See, for example, David S. Rubenstein, "Administrative Federalism as Separation of Powers," *Washington and Lee Law Review* 72 (2015): 171–255.

71 See, for example, Frederick C. Mosher, *Democracy and the Public Service*, rev. ed. (New York: Oxford University Press, 1982), who illustrates how the bureaucracy, as a democratic institution, promotes the interests of the people.

72 Meier and Bohte, *Politics and the Bureaucracy*; H. George Frederickson, Kevin B. Smith, Christopher W. Larimer, and Michael Licari, *The Public Administration Theory Primer*, 3rd ed. (Boulder: Westview, 2016). Some, however, have argued that the media are the fourth branch of government. See, for example, Timothy E. Cook, *Governing with the News: The News Media as a Political Institution* (Chicago: University of Chicago Press, 1998); and Rachel Luberda, "The Fourth Branch of the Government: Evaluating the Media's Role in Overseeing the Independent Judiciary," *Notre Dame Journal of Law, Ethics and Public Policy* 22 (2008): 507–32.

73 B. Guy Peters, *The Politics of Bureaucracy: An Introduction to Comparative Public Administration*, 6th ed. (New York: Routledge, 2010), 15–16.

74 Gordon Adams, *The Iron Triangle: The Politics of Defense Contracting* (New York: Council on Economic Priorities, 1981), 207. Also see Graham T. Allison and Philip Zelikow, *Essence of Decision: Explaining the Cuban Missile Crisis*, 2nd ed. (New York: Longman, 1999).

75 See Theodore J. Lowi, *The End of Liberalism: The Second Republic of the United States* (New York: Norton, 2009), who argues that interest groups have become so powerful in this nation that democracy has been severely compromised.

76 The terms "issue networks" and "policy networks" are used interchangeably here. For different treatments, see, for example, Wilson, DiIulio, and Bose, *American Government*. See also Sabatier and Weible, *Theories of the Policy Process*, 3rd ed.; and Hugh Heclo and Aaron Wildavsky, *The Private Government of Public Money* (London: Macmillan, 1974). Also, a good deal of this literature has been advanced in the European context. See R. A. W. Rhodes, "Policy Networks: A British Perspective," *Journal of Theoretical Politics* 2 (1990): 293–317; and R. A. W. Rhodes and David Marsh, "New Directions in the Study of Policy Networks," *European Journal of Political Research* 21 (1992): 181–205.

77 Hugh Heclo, "Issue Networks and the Executive Establishment," in *The New American Political System*, ed. Anthony King (Washington, D.C.: AEI, 1978), 87–124, 102.

78 Mark C. Miller and Jeb Barnes, eds., *Making Policy, Making Law: An Interbranch Perspective* (Washington, D.C.: Georgetown University Press, 2004).

79 Birkland, *An Introduction to the Policy Process*, 3rd ed., 130.

80 To the extent that the citizenry is excluded from the shared powers model, democracy can be compromised. However, as many have argued, the professional

cadre of civil service in the executive branch of government will work to promote the best interests of the public. See, for example, Mosher, *Democracy and the Public Service*; and Lowi, *The End of Liberalism*.

81 Larry N. Gerston, *Public Policymaking in a Democratic Society: A Guide to Civic Engagement*, 2nd ed. (New York: Routledge, 2008).

82 Eric M. Patashnik, *Reforms at Risk: What Happens after Major Policy Changes Are Enacted?* (Princeton: Princeton University Press, 2008), 3.

83 See, for example, ibid; Eric M. Patashnik, "After the Public Interest Prevails: The Political Sustainability of Policy Reform," *Governance* 16 (2003): 203–34; Frank J. Thompson, *Medicaid Politics: Federalism, Policy Durability, and Health Reform* (Washington, D.C.: Georgetown University Press, 2012); and Matthew Lockwood, "The Political Sustainability of Climate Policy: The Case of the UK Climate Change Act," *Global Environmental Change* 23 (2013): 1339–48. This issue of policy durability will be further addressed in chapter 5.

CHAPTER 2. PRIVACY RIGHTS AND U.S. SURVEILLANCE POLICY DRIFTS

1 Papers of Benjamin Franklin, Pennsylvania Assembly: Reply to the Governor, November 11, 1755, www.franklinpapers.org, accessed October 12, 2015.

2 Although the framework of policy drifts is relied upon in this chapter, the punctuated equilibrium theory, or PET, is also relevant, as the drifts were very significant. But, as discussed in chapter 1, there are similarities between PET and policy drifts. And the policy drift framework, like PET, can certainly describe the magnitude, scale, and pace of the policy change. It is also worth noting that the framework of "focusing events" could also be applied. See Thomas A. Birkland, *Lessons of Disaster: Policy Change after Catastrophic Events* (Washington D.C.: Georgetown University Press, 2006); and Thomas A. Birkland, *After Disaster: Agenda Setting, Public Policy, and Focusing Events* (Washington, D.C.: Georgetown University Press, 1997).

3 *Boyd v. United States*, 116 U.S. 616 (1886). Also see Samuel Warren and Louis Brandeis, "The Right to Privacy," *Harvard Law Review* 4 (1890): 193–220, who advocated for the right to privacy as an individual freedom. There was a Fifth Amendment claim as well. This decision was later modified by, for example, *Fisher v. United States*, 425 U.S. 391 (1976).

4 *Boyd*, 1866, 616.

5 Certainly, since the beginning of civilization, those in power have established surveillance networks to track the actions and behaviors of citizens and formal or informal configurations of presumed adversaries or rivals competing for power. See, for example, Edward Luttwak, *The Grand Strategy of the Roman Empire: From the First Century A.D. to the Third* (Baltimore: Johns Hopkins University Press, 1976).

6 *Olmstead v. United States*, 277 U.S. 438 (1928). Congress did pass a federal wiretapping law as a temporary measure to prevent the disclosure of government secrets during World War I. But it was the *Olmstead* case that provided the first legal

precedent to the reach of Fourth Amendment privacy rights. See Priscilla M. Regan, *Legislating Privacy* (Chapel Hill: University of North Carolina Press, 1995).

7 Neil Richards, *Intellectual Privacy: Rethinking Civil Liberties in the Digital Age* (New York: Oxford University Press, 2015).

8 *Olmstead*, 1928, 438, lawyer's edition.

9 Ibid., 442–43. See Richards, *Intellectual Privacy* for his compelling discussion of Justice Louis Brandeis's dissent in *Olmstead*.

10 See Richard F. Hamm, *Shaping the Eighteenth Amendment: Temperance Reform, Legal Culture, and the Polity, 1880–1920* (Chapel Hill: University of North Carolina Press, 1995).

11 Obviously, since the rights of blacks had not yet been established, the first ten amendments to the Constitution ignored the rights of black slaves.

12 Morton H. Halperin, Jerry J. Berman, Robert L. Borosage, and Christine M. Marwick, *The Lawless State: The Crimes of the U.S. Intelligence Agencies* (New York: Penguin, 1976).

13 *Katz v. United States*, 389 U.S. 347 (1967).

14 Also see the U.S. Supreme Court's 1967 decision in *Berger v. New York*, 388 U.S. 41 (1967), which invalidated a New York state law under the Fourth Amendment; the law authorized electronic surveillance without required procedural safeguards.

15 Gallup, "Civil Liberties," 2015, www.gallup.com, accessed October 6, 2015.

16 Public Law 107–56, Uniting and Strengthening America by Providing Appropriate Tools Required to Intercept and Obstruct Terrorism (October 26, 2001), www.gpo.gov, accessed September 16, 2015.

17 FISA, 50 U.S. Code Chapter 36.

18 In an interview with David Frost about the legality of his actions, Nixon replied, "Well, when the president does it, that means that it is not illegal." Interview by David Frost with Richard Nixon, May 19, 1977, www.landmarkcases.org, accessed January 9, 2017.

19 The CIA, for example, has relied historically on illegal intelligence operations in its efforts to destabilize governments across the globe, specifically those that the agency viewed as possible threats to American democracy—socialist or communist countries across Europe and Central and South America.

20 See Stephen J. Schulhofer, *More Essential Than Ever: The Fourth Amendment in the Twenty-First Century* (New York: Oxford University Press, 2012).

21 50 U.S. Code § 1802, emphasis added.

22 50 U.S. Code § 1801(h)(4). See Cedric Logan, "The FISA Wall and Federal Investigations," *New York University Journal of Law and Liberty* 4 (2009): 209–51.

23 The Patriot Act also made changes to the ECPA, which amended Title III of the Omnibus Crime Control and Safe Streets Act of 1968 (see table 2.1). The ECPA resulted from two 1967 Supreme Court cases—*Katz v. United States* and *Berger v. New York*—as well as the Church Committee findings on the FBI's Counter Intelligence Program, or COINTELPRO, which was an illegal, covert operation aimed at surveilling and discrediting domestic political groups or organizations.

24 This was a proposed amendment to the bill H.R. 2500, to increase appropriations for the Departments of Commerce, Justice, and State, the Judiciary, and related agencies to fight terrorism.

25 See Combating Terrorism Act of 2001, www.cdt.org, accessed September 22, 2015. This act was passed by the Senate. Also see 2001 Combating Terrorism Act, S. 1562, www.cdt.org, accessed July 5, 2017.

26 See Intelligence to Prevent Terrorism Act of 2001, S. 1448, www.congress.gov, accessed September 21, 2015. This bill was not acted upon.

27 Neil A. Lewis and Robert Pear, "Terror Laws Near Votes in House and Senate," *New York Times*, October 5, 2001, www.nytimes.com, accessed January 9, 2017.

28 *Congressional Record*, House, October 12, 2001, H6706, www.congress.gov, accessed September 22, 2015.

29 Michael Moore, *The Official Fahrenheit 9–11 Reader* (New York: Penguin, 2004).

30 *Congressional Record*, House, October 12, 2001, H6707.

31 Ibid.

32 Ibid., H6713.

33 Ibid., H6767.

34 Ibid., H6768–69.

35 Ibid., H6768.

36 Ibid., H6707.

37 Library of Congress, n.d., www.congress.gov, accessed September 22, 2015.

38 U.S. House of Representatives roll call, October 24, 2001, USA Patriot Act, clerk. house.gov, accessed September 21, 2015.

39 Dafna Linzer, "Secret Surveillance May Have Occurred before Authorization," *Washington Post*, January 4, 2006, www.washingtonpost.com, accessed September 23, 2015. These facts came to light only after the *New York Times* exposed Bush's authorization of warrantless wiretapping of domestic communications in December 2015. See James Risen and Eric Lichtblau, "Bush Lets U.S. Spy on Callers without Courts," *New York Times*, December 16, 2005, www.nytimes.com, accessed September 29, 2015. This is addressed more extensively later in the chapter.

40 On June 6, 2001, Senator Jim Jeffords of Vermont, previously a Republican, declared himself an independent and announced that he would join the Democratic caucus, giving the Democrats majority control. Tom Daschle (D-SD) became Senate majority leader.

41 *Congressional Record*, Senate, October 25, 2001, S10991–92, www.congress.gov, accessed September 22, 2015.

42 Ibid., S10993.

43 Ibid., S11015, emphasis added.

44 Ibid., S11019–20.

45 Ibid., S11022.

46 U.S. Senate roll call, October 25, 2001, USA Patriot Act, www.senate.gov, accessed September 21, 2015.

47 See Section 224 of the act. The House's version of the bill originally called for a five-year sunset provision, while the Senate version had none; the Bush administration sought no sunset but later argued for a ten-year provision. See *Congressional Record*, Senate, October 25, 2001, S11007.

48 The Patriot Act also changed the Electronic Communications Privacy Act of 1986, the Money Laundering Control Act of 1986, the Bank Secrecy Act of 1970, and the Immigration and Nationality Act of 1952.

49 See Section 218 of the Patriot Act, Public Law 107–56.

50 Risen and Lichtblau, "Bush Lets U.S. Spy on Callers."

51 See "Bush Says He Signed NSA Wiretap Order," CNN, December 17, 2005, www.cnn.com, accessed September 23, 2015. The Bush administration also defended its NSA warrantless spying program under Congress's September 14, 2001, Authorization to Use Military Force (AUMF), which mandates war against the perpetrators of 9/11 and those who harbor them. David Cole, "Reviving the Nixon Doctrine: NSA Spying, the Commander-in-Chief, and Executive Power in the War on Terror," *Washington and Lee Journal of Civil Rights and Social Justice* 13 (2006): 17–40.

52 Sunya Kashan, "The USA Patriot Act: Impact on Freedoms and Civil Liberties," *ESSAI* 7 (2009): 86–90.

53 In 2002 President Bush issued the secret executive order; the program was initially so secret it was simply referred to as "the Program." Later it would be called the Terrorist Surveillance Program or the President's Surveillance Program (PSP). The code name for information collected was Stellarwind. See Risen and Lichtblau, "Bush Lets U.S. Spy on Callers."

54 On March 6, 2002, Attorney General John Ashcroft issued a memorandum on intelligence sharing procedures that increased the exchange of information between intelligence and law enforcement officials in the "initiation, operation, continuation, or expansion of FISA searches or surveillance." John Ashcroft, "Intelligence Sharing Procedures for Foreign Intelligence and Foreign Counterintelligence Investigations Conducted by the FBI," memorandum, March 6, 2002, www.fas.org, accessed September 28, 2015.

55 The three-member appeals court, the U.S. Foreign Intelligence Surveillance Court of Review, ruled in November 2002 that the Justice Department had broad powers to use wiretaps obtained for intelligence operations to prosecute terrorists. See www.justice.gov, accessed September 28, 2015.

56 It should be noted that Executive Order 12333, issued by President Reagan in 1981, was intended to restrict intelligence collection activities engaged in by executive branch agencies, including the NSA. It operated in conjunction with the Foreign Intelligence Surveillance Act of 1978. However it was viewed by the intelligence community as authorizing the expansion of data collection activities that targeted foreigners abroad, and where collection occurs outside the United States. President George W. Bush amended E.O. 12333 in 2004 with E.O. 13355 and again in

2008, with E.O. 13470, to strengthen the role of the director of national intelligence in surveillance gathering.

57 The Department of Homeland Security was created as a cabinet-level department on November 25, 2002, to develop and coordinate a national strategy to safeguard the country against terrorism. Its first director was Tom Ridge.

58 Parenthetically, Nacchio was indicted by federal prosecutors not long afterwards for insider trading and served almost five years in prison after a federal district court found him guilty on all charges; Nacchio maintains that his prosecution was retaliation for his refusal to grant the NSA permission to surveil its customers. Dionne Searcey, "Former Qwest CEO Joseph Nacchio: Tales from a White-Collar Prison Sentence," *Wall Street Journal*, September 30, 2013, www.wsj.com, accessed September 23, 2015.

59 Robert D. Novak, "FBI Surprise?," *Washington Post*, September 27, 2001, www.washingtonpost.com, accessed September 23, 2015.

60 Shane Harris, *The Watchers: The Rise of America's Surveillance State* (New York: Penguin, 2010), emphasis in original.

61 Amy B. Zegart, *Spying Blind: The CIA, the FBI, and the Origins of 9/11* (Princeton: Princeton University Press, 2007).

62 Ibid., 4.

63 The Gulf War, sometimes referred to as Operation Desert Storm, was a war waged by the United States, under the presidency of George H. W. Bush, along with coalition forces from thirty-four nations, against Iraq in response to its invasion and annexation of Kuwait. Bush was criticized by some for not removing Saddam Hussein from power; his secretary of defense as the time, Dick Cheney, was more inclined to topple Hussein's regime. By the time his son, George W. Bush, became president, some groups claimed that he along with his vice president, Dick Cheney, manufactured the weapons of mass destruction claim in an effort to finally overthrow Hussein. Richard Clarke, a counterterrorism advisor on the National Security Council, later told a reporter that on the night of 9/11 in a meeting with the president and his advisors, Bush's secretary of defense, Donald Rumsfeld, said,

> "You know, we've got to do Iraq," and everyone looked at him—at least I looked at him and Powell looked at him—like, What the hell are you talking about? And he said—I'll never forget this—"There just aren't enough targets in Afghanistan. We need to bomb something else to prove that we're, you know, big and strong and not going to be pushed around by these kind of attacks."

Cullen Murphy and Todd S. Purdum, "Farewell to All That: An Oral History of the Bush White House," *Vanity Fair*, February 2009, www.vanityfair.com, accessed September 24, 2015.

64 See, for example, Michael R. Gordon and Judith Miller, "U.S. Says Hussein Intensifies Quest for A-Bomb Parts," *New York Times*, September 8, 2002, www.nytimes.com, accessed September 24, 2015. It should be noted that the *New York*

Times later ran a story stating that there were some aging chemical weapons in Iraq that American service members were exposed to, but they were not part of an active arsenal; instead, they were the remains of Iraq's arms programs from the Iran-Iraq war in the 1980s. C. J. Chivers, "The Secret Casualties of Iraq's Abandoned Chemical Weapons," *New York Times*, October 14, 2014, www.nytimes.com, accessed September 24, 2015.

65 Gallup, "Seventy-Two Percent of Americans Support War against Iraq," March 24, 2003, www.gallup.com, accessed September 23, 2015.

66 Joseph C. Wilson, "What I Didn't Find in Africa," *New York Times*, July 6, 2003, www.nytimes.com, accessed September 24, 2015.

67 Joseph C. Wilson, *The Politics of Truth: Inside the Lies That Led to War and Betrayed My Wife's CIA Identity; A Diplomat's Memoir* (New York: Carroll and Graf, 2004).

68 See, for example, William J. Broad and Judith Miller, "A Nation Challenged," *New York Times*, October 18, 2001, www.nytimes.com, accessed September 24, 2015; and Gordon and Miller, "U.S. Says Hussein Intensifies Quest."

69 Warren P. Strobel, "Analyst for Military Portrays Discord among War Planners before Invasion," *Seattle Times*, May 21, 2005, www.seattletimes.com, accessed September 24, 2015.

70 *Muslim Community Association of Ann Arbor v. Ashcroft*, 459 F. Supp. 2d 592 (E.D.M.I. 2006). In another case, *Ziglar v. Abbasi* (2017 WL 2621317, June 19, 2017), Muslim immigrants who were detained in a Brooklyn facility after the 9/11 attacks filed a suit against high-ranking Bush administration officials, seeking monetary damages pursuant to the 1971 Supreme Court decision in *Bivens v. Six Unknown Named Agents* (403 U.S. 388), which allowed for monetary damages against officials creating unconstitutional policies. The U.S. Supreme Court ruled that the government officials were not liable for any damages, even though the immigrants may have been mistreated.

71 *ACLU v. Department of Justice*, 321 F. Supp. 2d 24 (D.D.C. 2004). The ACLU filed additional cases against the Department of Defense under the Freedom of Information Act, for example, seeking photographs depicting the abuse of prisoners in Iraq's Abu Ghraib prison and in Afghanistan. See, for example, *ACLU v. Department of Defense*, 543 F.3d 59 (2d Cir. 2008).

72 *Doe v. Ashcroft*, 334 F. Supp. 2d 471 (S.D.N.Y. 2004). However, the district court ordered a temporary stay to provide the government with time to appeal. The U.S. Court of Appeals for the Second Circuit extended the stay, and U.S. Supreme Court Justice Ruth Bader Ginsburg, sitting as circuit justice, affirmed the extension. *Doe v. Gonzales*, 126 S. Ct. 1, 5 (2005), ordered unsealed by and superseded by *Doe v. Gonzales*, 127 S. Ct. 1 (2005). Circuit justices are members of the U.S. Supreme Court who are each assigned to supervise a certain circuit. They are responsible for addressing various appeals or applications—for example, emergency stays (including stays of execution in death penalty cases) and routine requests for extensions of time. The U.S. Court of Appeals later vacated and remanded the

decision; see *Doe v. Gonzales*, 449 F.3d 415 (2d Cir. 2006), in light of the provisions of the Patriot Improvement and Reauthorization Act discussed later in this chapter. The district court once again ruled in favor of the plaintiffs; see *Doe v. Gonzales*, 500 F. Supp. 2d 386 (S.D.N.Y. 2007). These cases have sometimes been referred to as *Doe I, Doe II*, and *Doe III*. See Andrew E. Nieland, "National Security Letters and the Amended Patriot Act," *Cornell Law Review* 92 (2007): 1201–37; Christopher P. Banks, "National Security Letters and Diminishing Privacy Rights," in *The Impact of 9/11 and the New Legal Landscape: The Day That Changed Everything?*, ed. Matthew J. Morgan (New York: Palgrave MacMillan, 2009), 91–102; and Joshua A. Altman, "A Schrödinger's Onion Approach to the Problem of Secure Internet Communications," *Washington University Global Studies Law Review* 7 (2008): 103–35. Also see discussion of national security letters (NSLs) later in the chapter.

73 Beth DeFalco, "Cities Pass Resolutions Saying Terrorism Fight Must Not Destroy Civil Liberties," Associated Press, January 10, 2003, www.theintelligencer.com, accessed September 30, 2015.

74 *Mayfield v. United States*, 504 F. Supp. 2d 1023 (D. Ore. 2007).

75 *Mayfield v. United States*, rev'd, 588 F.3d 1252 (9th Cir. 2009); *cert. denied*, 562 U.S. 1002 (2010).

76 *Humanitarian Law Project v. Gonzales*, 380 F. Supp. 2d 1134 (C.D. Cal. 2005). The case initially began in 1998 with constitutional challenges to key provisions of the Antiterrorism and Effective Death Penalty Act of 1996, Public Law 104–132, 110 Stat. 1214, which aids America in its fight against terrorism.

77 Two of the judges were appointed by President Bill Clinton and the other by President Jimmy Carter.

78 *Humanitarian Law Project v. Mukasey*, 552 F.3d 916 (9th Cir. 2007), www.lexis-nexis.com, accessed September 30, 2015.

79 *Holder v. Humanitarian Law Project*, 561 U.S. 1 (2010). The six justices in the majority were Chief Justice Roberts and Justices Stevens, Scalia, Kennedy, Thomas, and Alito. Justices Ginsburg, Breyer, and Sotomayor dissented.

80 Jennifer C. Evans, "Hijacking Civil Liberties: The USA Patriot Act of 2001," *Loyola University Chicago Law Journal* 33 (2002): 933–90; Lisa Finnegan Abdolian and Harold Takooshian, "The USA Patriot Act: Civil Liberties, the Media, and Public Opinion," *Fordham Urban Law Journal* 30 (2002): 1429–53.

81 "A Travesty of Justice," editorial, *New York Times*, November 16, 2001, www.nytimes.com, accessed September 23, 2015.

82 Jennifer Lee, "Kucinich, Declaring for President, Takes Populist Stance," *New York Times*, October 14, 2003, www.nytimes.com, accessed September 28, 2015.

83 Joel Roberts, "Kerry's Top Ten Flip-Flops," CBS News, September 29, 2004, www.cbsnews.com, accessed September 28, 2015.

84 Bill Brubaker, "Bush Signs New Version of Patriot Act," *Washington Post*, March 9, 2006, www.washingtonpost.com, accessed September 28, 2015.

85 For comparison of the bills, see www.govtrack.us, accessed September 28, 2015.

86 George W. Bush, "President Thanks Attorney General Gonzales at Swearing-In Ceremony," February 14, 2005, georgewbush-whitehouse.archives.gov, accessed September 29, 2015.

87 *Congressional Record*, Senate, July 29, 2005, S9560, www.congress.gov, accessed September 29, 2015.

88 *Congressional Record*, Senate, March 1, 2006, S1558, www.congress.gov, accessed September 29, 2015.

89 Ibid.

90 House and Senate roll call, March 2, 2006, www.educate-yourself.org, accessed September 29, 2015.

91 The House bill was introduced by Representative Sensenbrenner (R-WI).

92 *Congressional Record*, House, July 21, 2005, H6212, www.congress.gov, accessed September 28, 2015.

93 Ibid.

94 *Congressional Record*, House, February 1, 2006, H65, www.gpo.gov, accessed September 28, 2015.

95 House and Senate roll call, March 2, 2006, www.educate-yourself.org, accessed September 29, 2015.

96 Larry Abramson and Maria Godoy, "The Patriot Act: Key Controversies," NPR News, February 14, 2006, www.npr.org, accessed September 30, 2015.

97 This provision is part of the 2004 Intelligence Reform and Terrorism Prevention Act (IRTPA), Section 6001(a).

98 See discussion of *Doe* cases, earlier in the chapter.

99 Brian T. Yeh and Charles Doyle, *USA Patriot Improvement and Reauthorization Act of 2005: A Legal Analysis* (Washington, D.C.: Congressional Research Service, 2006), www.fas.org, accessed September 29, 2015.

100 Ibid.

101 For example, with the FISA Amendments in 2008, as discussed later in the chapter.

102 Risen and Lichtblau, "Bush Lets U.S. Spy on Callers."

103 The *New York Times* report also exposed the fact that four librarians from Connecticut were issued a "gag order," an order by the FBI not to discuss its demand for patrons' records. Such orders were issued under a national security letter (NSL), which, as discussed earlier in this chapter, are administrative subpoenas for records that the FBI can issue without prior court approval. Also see discussion of *Doe* cases presented earlier. These four librarians eventually publicly identified themselves as the collective John Doe.

104 It is not known whether these officials were political appointees or career bureaucrats. Some, however, suggest that one was William Binney, a high-level NSA career official, who resigned on October 31, 2001, because of his growing dissatisfaction with the NSA's spying program. Binney is considered to be the "original NSA whistleblower."

105 Risen and Lichtblau, "Bush Lets U.S. Spy on Callers."

106 Ibid.

107 Calabresi and Yoo, *The Unitary Executive*; Rosenbloom, "President George W. Bush's Theory of a Unitary Executive Branch."

108 Michael Nelson, ed., *Guide to the Presidency and the Executive Branch*, 5th ed. (Thousand Oaks, CA: CQ Press, 2013); Ryan J. Barilleaux and Christopher S. Kelley, "Going Forward: The Unitary Executive, Presidential Power, and the Twenty-First Century Presidency," in Barilleaux and Kelley, *The Unitary Executive and the Modern Presidency*, 219–30; Waterman, "The Administrative Presidency"; Peter M. Shane, *Madison's Nightmare: How Executive Power Threatens American Democracy* (Chicago: University of Chicago Press, 2009).

109 Carol D. Leonnig and Dafna Linzer, "Surveillance-Court Judge Quits in Protest," *Seattle Times*, December 21, 2005, www.seattletimes.com, accessed September 30, 2015.

110 One FISA court judge, Colleen Kollar-Kotelly, had been briefed on the spying program by the administration, and did raise the same concern in 2004.

111 Leonnig and Linzer, "Surveillance-Court Judge Quits."

112 Public Law 110–55, 121 Stat. 552 (2007).

113 George W. Bush, "The President's Radio Address," *Public Papers of the President*, July 28, 2007, www.presidency.ucsb.edu, accessed October 1, 2015.

114 House roll call, August 3, 2007, www.govtrack.us, accessed October 1, 2015.

115 The Democrats held fewer than fifty seats in the Senate at this time, but they had an operational majority because the two independent senators generally caucused with the Democrats for organizational purposes.

116 Senate roll call, August 3, 2007, www.govtrack.us, accessed October 1, 2015.

117 Edward C. Liu, *Reauthorization of the FISA Amendments Act* (Washington D.C.: Congressional Research Service, 2013), www.fas.org, accessed October 8, 2015.

118 Ellen Nakashima and Joby Warrick, "House Approves Wiretap Measure," *Washington Post*, August 5, 2007, www.washingtonpost.com, accessed October 1, 2015; Shahab Mossavar-Rahmani, "The Protect America Act: One Nation under Surveillance," *Loyola of Los Angeles Entertainment Law Review* 29 (2008): 133–62.

119 Laura K. Donohue, "Section 702 and the Collection of International Telephone and Internet Content," *Harvard Journal of Law and Public Policy* 38 (2015): 117–265.

120 Liu, *Reauthorization of the FISA Amendments Act*.

121 House roll call, June 20, 2008, clerk.house.gov, accessed October 1, 2015.

122 Senate roll call, July 9, 2008, www.senate.gov, accessed October 1, 2015. Three senators did not vote: Kennedy (D-MA), McCain (R-AZ), and Sessions (R-AL).

123 Eric Rosenbach and Aki J. Peritz, "Confrontation or Collaboration? Congress and the Intelligence Community," Belfer Center, Harvard University, 2009, belfer-center.ksg.harvard.edu, accessed October 8, 2015.

124 *Amnesty v. McConnell*, 646 F. Supp. 2d 633 (S.D.N.Y. 2009).

125 *Amnesty v. Blair*, 09–4112 (2d Cir. 2011).

126 *Amnesty v. Clapper*, 568 U.S. ___, 133 S. Ct. 1138 (2013). James Clapper was now director of national intelligence.

127 Also known as the Islamic State of Iraq and the Levant (ISIL).

128 See Kevin Whitelaw, "Obama Gambles on Afghan Escalation," NPR, December 1, 2009, www.npr.org, accessed October 1, 2015. While President Obama did not fulfill his campaign promise made in 2012 to end the war in Afghanistan by December 2014, he did reduce the American military presence there. However, by the end of 2015 there was still an American force of close to ten thousand troops charged with carrying on the hunt for Al Qaeda and Islamic State militants. President Obama said that the soldiers would stay at least until 2017.

129 Richard Wolffe, "The Incremental Revolutionary," *Newsweek*, January 12, 2008, www.newsweek.com, accessed October 12, 2015.

130 Eric Lichtblau and James Risen, "Officials Say U.S. Wiretaps Exceeded Law," *New York Times*, April 15, 2009, www.nytimes.com, accessed October 1, 2015.

131 "Obama Signs Patriot Act Extension," *Washington Times*, February 27, 2010, www.washingtontimes.com, accessed October 1, 2015.

132 House roll call, February 25, 2010, Medicare Physician Payment Reform Act, clerk.house.gov, accessed October 1, 2015.

133 Patriot Act Extension, Legislative Bulletin, February 15, 2011, www.dpc.senate.gov, accessed October 1, 2015.

134 It became known later that the person Manning was communicating with was Assange.

135 Apparently, Manning contacted the *Washington Post* and the *New York Times* to learn whether they would be interested in the secret materials, but to no avail.

136 Rosemary O'Leary, *The Ethics of Dissent: Managing Guerrilla Government* (Thousand Oaks, CA: CQ Press, 2014); David Leigh and Luke Harding, *WikiLeaks: Inside Julian Assange's War on Secrecy* (London: Guardian Books, 2011).

137 O'Leary, *The Ethics of Dissent*; Leigh and Harding, *WikiLeaks*.

138 See Leigh and Harding, *WikiLeaks*.

139 See Julie Tate and Ernesto Londoño, "Judge Finds Manning Not Guilty of Aiding the Enemy, Guilty of Espionage," *Washington Post*, July 30, 2013, www.washingtonpost.com, accessed October 7, 2015; Charlie Savage, "Obama Commutes Manning's Term in U.S. Leak Case," *New York Times*, January 18, 2017, A1; and Charlie Savage, "Chelsea Manning Leaves Prison, Closing an Extraordinary Leak Case," *New York Times*, May 16, 2017, www.nytimes.com, accessed May 18, 2017. Assange became a target of U.S. investigation for his role in releasing Manning's classified documents. In 2010 Sweden opened an investigation of alleged sexual offenses Assange committed in that country; he has since been protected by political asylum at the Ecuadorian embassy in London.

140 Sofia Ranchordá, "Sunset Clauses and Experimental Regulations: Blessing or Curse for Legal Certainty?," *Statute Law Review* 36 (2014): 28–45, slr.oxfordjournals.org, accessed October 8, 2015.

141 Ibid., 5.

142 David A. Fahrenthold, "In Congress, Sunset Clauses Are Commonly Passed but Rarely Followed Through," *Washington Post*, December 15, 2012, www.washingtonpost.com, accessed October 7, 2015.

143 *Congressional Record*, House, May 26, 2011, H3742, www.congress.gov, accessed October 9, 2015.

144 *Congressional Record*, Senate, May 23, 2011, S3217, www.congress.gov, accessed October 9, 2015.

145 Ibid.

146 House roll call, May 26, 2011, politics.nytimes.com, accessed October 8, 2015. Twenty-nine House members did not vote.

147 Senate roll call, May 26, 2011, politics.nytimes.com, accessed October 8, 2015. Five senators, including Chuck Schumer (D-NY), did not vote.

148 The House voted on September 12, 2012 to pass the act, 301–118; 74 Democrats voted in favor, while 111 voted against; see House roll call, www.govtrack.us, accessed October 12, 2015. In the Senate, on December 28, 2012, it passed 73–23; 30 Democrats voted in favor, 19 against; see Senate roll call, www.govtrack.us, accessed October 12, 2015.

149 Peter Baker, Helene Cooper, and Mark Mazzettimay, "Bin Laden Is Dead, Obama Says," *New York Times*, May 1, 2011, www.nytimes.com, accessed October 19, 2015.

150 Glenn Greenwald, "NSA Collecting Phone Records of Millions of Verizon Customers Daily," *Guardian*, June 6, 2013, www.theguardian.com, accessed October 14, 2015.

151 Ibid. This statement is apparently based on the Supreme Court's 1979 decision in *Smith v. Maryland*, discussed later in the chapter, which ruled that the installation and use of a pen register—which traces all phone numbers from a designated telephone line—was not a "search" within the meaning of the Fourth Amendment, and hence no warrant was required.

152 Snowden also revealed that the British spy agency, the Government Communications Headquarters, intercepted Internet data, including email messages, Internet histories and calls, and Facebook posts, and shared them with the NSA.

153 Luke Harding, *The Snowden Files: The Inside Story of the World's Most Wanted Man* (New York: Vintage, 2014).

154 Ibid.

155 *Citizenfour*, movie script (2014), www.springfieldspringfield.co.uk, accessed October 19, 2015.

156 "President Obama's Dragnet," editorial, *New York Times*, June 6, 2013, www.nytimes.com, accessed October 19, 2015.

157 Steven Nelson, "NSA Phone Record Program Illegal, Appeals Court Finds," *U.S. News and World Report*, May 7, 2015, www.usnews.com, accessed October 19, 2015.

158 *Klayman v. Obama*, 957 F. Supp. 2d 1 (D.D.C. 2013), at 11. *Klayman II* was filed on June 12, 2013, where the plaintiffs sued the same government defendants and also Facebook, Yahoo, Google, Microsoft, YouTube, AOL, PalTalk, Skype, Sprint, AT&T, and Apple.

159 The court did not issue a ruling on the First and Fifth Amendment claims.

160 *Klayman v. Obama*, 42.

161 Ibid., 40.

162 *Smith v. Maryland*, 442 U.S. 735 (1979). For a discussion of the third-party doctrine, see Alexander Galicki, "The End of *Smith v. Maryland*?," Georgetown University Law Center, 2014.

163 *Smith v. Maryland*, 735. Justice Powell did not participate in the discussion or decision.

164 *Klayman v. Obama*, 31.

165 Ibid., 32.

166 Ibid., 33.

167 The three D.C. Circuit judges produced four opaque opinions.

168 *Klayman v. Obama*, 800 F.3d 559 (2015) at 563–64. Of the three-member panel, two were appointed by President Reagan, and one by President George W. Bush.

169 *Paul v. Obama*, docket://gov.uscourts.dcd.1-14-cv-00262 (D.D.C. 2014), www.amlaw.com, accessed October 19, 2015. Also see the case on www.docketalarm.com for the convoluted case history; accessed October 29, 2015.

170 *ACLU v. Clapper*, 959 F. Supp. 2d 724 (S.D.N.Y. 2013).

171 Ibid., 747.

172 Of the three judges issuing this unanimous ruling, two are Obama appointees and one is a Clinton appointee.

173 *ACLU v. Clapper*, 785 F.3d 787 (2nd Cir. 2015), at 812–13. It should further be noted that the U.S. Court of Appeals for the Second Circuit ordered that, in light of passage of the USA Freedom Act on June 2, 2015, the parties could submit supplemental briefs on their behalf; see 2015 U.S. App. LEXIS 12244 (2015).

174 *ACLU v. Clapper*, 785 F.3d 787 (2nd Cir. 2015), at 818, emphasis added.

175 Also see Nelson, "NSA Phone Record Program Illegal."

176 Also see *ACLU v. Clapper*, 804 F.3d 617 (2nd Cir. 2015).

177 *Smith v. Obama*, 24 F. Supp. 3d 1005 (D. Idaho 2014). Also see, for example, *Jewel v. NSA*, 810 F.3d 622 (9th Cir. 2015).

178 *Smith v. Obama*, 2014, at 1007.

179 Ibid., 1010.

180 Timothy Geverd, "Bulk Telephony Metadata Collection and the Fourth Amendment," *John Marshall Journal of Information Technology and Privacy Law* 31 (2014): 191–235.

181 *Smith v. Obama*, 816 F.3d 1239 (9th Cir. 2016).

182 *ACLU v. Clapper*, 785 F.3d 787 (2nd Cir. 2015).

183 Charlie Savage and Jonathan Weisman, "NSA Collection of Bulk Call Data Is Ruled Illegal," *New York Times*, May 8, 2015.

184 An earlier version of this bill was introduced on September 25, 2013, in a previous session of Congress, but was not acted upon.

185 *Congressional Record*, House, May 22, 2014, H4794, www.congress.gov, accessed October 26, 2015.

186 Ibid.

187 House roll call, May 13, 2015, clerk.house.gov, accessed October 26, 2015. Six members did not cast a vote.

188 Savage and Weisman, "NSA Collection of Bulk Call Data."

189 *Congressional Record*, Senate, May 31, 2015, S3331–40, www.congress.gov, accessed October 26, 2015.

190 *Congressional Record*, Senate, May 11, 2015, S2751–53, www.congress.gov, accessed October 26, 2015.

191 *Congressional Record*, Senate, May 19, 2015, S3009–10, www.congress.gov, accessed October 26, 2015.

192 Senate roll call, June 2, 2015, www.opencongress.org, accessed October 26, 2015. One senator did not cast a vote.

193 Steven Nelson, "NSA Whistleblowers Oppose Freedom Act, Endorse Long-Shot Bill," *U.S. News and World Report*, April 27, 2015, www.usnews.com, accessed October 29, 2015.

194 Evan Perez, "New Conservative Legal Challenge to NSA Phone Data Program," CNN, June 5, 2015, www.cnn.com, accessed October 29, 2015.

195 Foreign Intelligence Surveillance Court, "In Re Motion in Opposition to Government's Request to Resume Bulk Data Collection under Patriot Act Section 2015," June 29, 2015, 14–15, www.fisc.uscourts.gov, accessed October 27, 2015.

196 Ibid.

197 *ACLU v. Clapper*, 804 F.3d 617 (2nd Cir. 2015), at 618.

198 *Klayman v. Obama*, 142 F. Supp. 3d 172 (D.D.C. 2015), at 197–98.

199 Also, as discussed earlier in this chapter, provisions of the FISA Amendments Act Reauthorization Act of 2012, which allows the NSA to continue wiretapping Americans without a warrant, is set to expire in December 2017. Congress will then need to decide whether to renew these provisions. Given its history, however, it seems unlikely that our lawmakers will curtail or end the government's spying on Americans. See Jennifer Stisa Granick, *American Spies: Modern Surveillance, Why You Should Care, and What to Do about It* (Cambridge: Cambridge University Press, 2017).

200 Public Law 114–23 (June 2, 2015).

201 Jennifer Steinhauer and Jonathan Weisman, "U.S. Surveillance in Place since 9/11 Is Sharply Limited," *New York Times*, June 3, 2015, A1, A17.

202 See "Do NSA's Bulk Surveillance Programs Stop Terrorists?," New America Foundation report, January 13, 2014, www.newamerica.org; and "NSA Phone Record Collection Does Little to Prevent Terrorist Attacks, Group Says," *Washington Post*, January 12, 2014, www.washingtonpost.com, both accessed November 16, 2015.

203 Office of Inspector General, U.S. Department of Justice, *A Review of the FBI's Use of Section 215 Orders: Assessment of Progress in Implementing Recommendations and Examination of Use in 2007 through 2009* (May 2015), 44, oig.justice.gov, accessed November 30, 2015.

204 Ibid., 66.

205 Ibid., 45.

206 "Mass Surveillance Isn't the Answer," editorial, *New York Times*, November 17, 2015, www.nytimes.com, accessed November 30, 2015.

207 U.S. Government Accountability Office, *Gun Control and Terrorism: FBI Could Better Manage Firearm-Related Background Checks Involving Terrorist Watch List Records* (January 19, 2005), www.gao.gov, accessed June 21, 2016.

208 Amitai Etzioni, *How Patriotic Is the Patriot Act? Freedom versus Security in the Age of Terrorism* (New York: Routledge, 2005), 1, emphasis added.

209 Gallup, "Civil Liberties."

210 Nathan, *The Administrative Presidency*; Calabresi and Yoo, *The Unitary Executive*.

211 As Birkland would maintain, the three branches were operating a "policy monopoly," a "concentrated, closed system of the most important actors in policy making." Birkland, *An Introduction to the Policy Process*, 3rd ed., 300.

212 Scott Shane, "After Paris Attacks, CIA Director Rekindles Debate over Surveillance," *New York Times*, November 16, 2015, www.nytimes.com, accessed November 16, 2015.

213 "France's Diminished Liberties," editorial, *New York Times*, January 4, 2016, A18.

214 Early indications point to the federal government's persistence in surveilling citizens, as seen in the Obama administration's efforts to force Apple to help the FBI unlock the iPhone of one of the San Bernardino terrorists who was killed in the attack. Apple insists that the breach of privacy would create a universal backdoor software program that would enable the FBI to potentially unlock any iPhone and could also create opportunities for North Korean, Chinese, or Iranian hackers.

215 John Zorabedian, "Where Do U.S. Presidential Candidates Stand on Privacy and Surveillance?," Naked Security, February 2, 2016, nakedsecurity.sophos.com, accessed January 4, 2017.

216 Ibid.

217 Scott Shane, "Visceral Fear, Dubious Cure," *New York Times*, January 29, 2017, A1, A17.

218 Peter Baker, "Trump Modifies Ban on Migrants as Outcry Grows," *New York Times*, January 30, 2017, A1, A11.

CHAPTER 3. CIVIL RIGHTS LAW AND POLICY DRIFTS

1 In terms of education, gender was not a protected class until 1972 with passage of Title IX of the Education Amendments.

2 Affirmative action has also remained controversial, but it is not legislated. Policies have evolved and drifted as a result of judicial proceedings. Affirmative action is not addressed here.

3 The 1972 Equal Employment Opportunity Act extended Title VII coverage to public sector employees.

4 *Ledbetter v. Goodyear Tire & Rubber Co.*, 550 U.S. 618 (2007).

5 Because the laws and policies addressed in this chapter apply to LGBTs, the acronym LGBTQ, where the Q represents those who identify as queer or questioning, is not adopted here.

6 *Griggs v. Duke Power Co.*, 401 U.S. 424 (1971). Also see *Phillips v. Marietta Corporation*, 400 U.S. 542 (1971), where the U.S. Supreme Court held that Title VII prohibits employers from refusing to hire women with preschool-age children while hiring men with such children.

7 *Griggs*, 431.

8 Ibid.

9 Norma M. Riccucci, *Managing Diversity in Public Sector Workforces* (Boulder: Westview, 2002).

10 *Ledbetter*, 628.

11 *Lorance v. AT&T Technologies*, 490 U.S. 900 (1989).

12 *Ledbetter*, 645, emphasis in original.

13 Ibid., 646.

14 Ibid., 661.

15 Simon Lazarus, "Courting Big Business," *American Prospect*, May 30, 2007, www.prospect.org, accessed November 5, 2015.

16 *Bazemore v. Friday*, 478 U.S. 385 (1986).

17 Julia M. Fox, "An Interpretation and Application of the Lilly Ledbetter Fair Pay Act of 2009," *Boston University Public Interest Law Journal* 24 (2015): 143; Katie Putnam, "On Lilly Ledbetter's Liberty: Why Equal Pay for Equal Work Remains an Elusive Reality," *William and Mary Journal of Women and the Law* 15 (2009): 685; Jeremy A. Weinberg, "Blameless Ignorance? The Ledbetter Act and Limitation Periods for Title VII Pay Discrimination Claims," *New York University Law Review* 84 (2009): 1756.

18 *Bazemore*, 397.

19 Ibid., 395.

20 The 1986 Court consisted of Chief Justice Burger (a Nixon appointee), along with Justices Marshall (appointed by President Johnson), Blackmun, Powell (both appointed by President Nixon), Brennan (appointed by President Eisenhower), White (appointed by President Kennedy), O'Connor, Rehnquist (both appointed by President Reagan), and Stevens (appointed by President Ford). See discussion in this chapter for the composition in *Ledbetter*.

21 See EEOC Compliance Manual, Section 2-IV-C(1)(a), www.eeoc.gov, accessed January 14, 2016.

22 Ibid., Section 2-IV-C(4).

23 U.S. Department of Justice, Brief for the United States, *Ledbetter v. Goodyear* (2006), www.justice.gov, accessed November 5, 2015.

24 *Congressional Record*, House, July 30, 2007, H8942, www.congress.gov, accessed November 5, 2015.

25 Ibid., H8942–43.

26 Ibid., H8943.

27 *Congressional Record*, House, August 4, 2007, H1746, www.congress.gov, accessed November 5, 2015.

28 *Congressional Record*, House, July 30, 2007, H8944.

29 *Congressional Record*, House, August 4, 2007, H1774.

30 *Congressional Record*, House, July 30, 2007, H8943.

31 *Hearing before the Committee on Education and Labor*, 110th Congress, June 12, 2007, Statement by Lily Ledbetter, www.gpo.gov, accessed November 5, 2015.

32 Ibid.

33 *Congressional Record*, House, July 30, 2007, H8945, emphasis added.

34 Supporting organizations included, for example, the American Civil Liberties Union, AFL-CIO, American Federation of Teachers, National Education Association, American Library Association, Leadership Conference on Civil Rights, National Employment Lawyers Association, Hadassah, National Women's Law Center, American Association of University Women, Alliance for Justice, National Partnership for Women and Families, Coalition of Labor Union Women, Moms Rising, National Organization for Women, American Association of Retired Persons, 9to5, National Association of Working Women, Service Employees International Union, and Religious Action Center of Reform Judaism.

35 House roll call, July 31, 2007, www.govtrack.us, accessed November 9, 2015. Nine did not cast a vote: two Democrats and seven Republicans.

36 Libby Quaid, "McCain Opposes Equal Pay Bill in Senate," *Huffington Post*, May 1, 2008, www.huffingtonpost.com, accessed November 5, 2015.

37 Ibid.

38 Gail Collins, "McCain's Compassion Tour," *New York Times*, April 26, 2008, www.nytimes.com, accessed November 9, 2015.

39 Hillary Clinton was also a major supporter of the Ledbetter Act, but by this point she had lost the primary to Obama.

40 "The Democrats' Secret Weapon: Lilly Ledbetter," editorial, *New York Times*, August 28, 2008, campaignstops.blogs.nytimes.com, accessed November 9, 2015.

41 Cloture is invoked to stop debate or end a filibuster.

42 See *Congressional Record*, Senate, April 23, 2008, www.congress.gov, accessed November 9, 2015.

43 Ibid., S3288.

44 Ibid., S3274.

45 See Congressional Budget Office, "Lilly Ledbetter Fair Pay Act of 2007," July 18, 2007, www.congress.gov, accessed November 9, 2015.

46 There was one vacant seat in the House when Representative Kirsten Gillibrand (D-NY) resigned her House seat to replace Hillary Clinton's vacant seat in the Senate.

47 Some argue that true control of the Senate requires sixty members of the same party, since the number of votes required for cloture is three-fifths, or sixty of the current one hundred senators.

48 Paycheck Fairness Act, H.R. 12, January 6, 2009, www.congress.gov, accessed November 10, 2015.

49 House roll call, January 9, 2009, H.R. 12, www.govtrack.us, accessed July 7, 2017.

50 House roll call, January 9, 2009, H.R. 11, www.govtrack.us, accessed November 10, 2015.

51 See "Crazy/Stupid Republican of the Day," n.d., republicinsanity.tumblr.com, accessed November 10, 2015.

52 "Whitfield Crosses Party Lines to Support Wage Discrimination Bill," Bluegrass Politics, January 27, 2009.

53 See Democratic Policy Committee, "S. 181, The Lilly Ledbetter Fair Pay Act of 2009," Legislative Bulletin, January 15, 2009, www.dpc.senate.gov, accessed November 10, 2015.

54 See Title VII Fairness Act, S. 166, 111th Congress (2009), www.govtrack.us, accessed November 10, 2015.

55 See *Congressional Record*, Senate, January 22, 2009, www.congress.gov, accessed November 10, 2015.

56 Ibid., S760.

57 Ibid., S761, emphasis added.

58 Senate roll call, January 22, 2009, S. 181, www.govtrack.us, accessed November 10, 2015.

59 See "New Jersey's 7th Congressional District," Wikiwand, www.wikiwand.com, accessed November 10, 2015.

60 House roll call, January 27, 2009, clerk.house.gov, accessed November 10, 2015.

61 In 2015 women Republicans in the Senate introduced a watered-down version of the act: the Workplace Advancement Act, sponsored by Senators Deb Fischer (NE), Kelly Ayotte (NH), Susan Collins (ME), and Shelley Moore Capito (WV). This act would essentially make it illegal for employers to retaliate against employees for conferring with others about their pay. This provision is but one of many in the Democrats' Paycheck Fairness Act.

62 This Executive Order amends E.O. 11246.

63 See Lilly Ledbetter and Cecilia Muñoz, 'Taking Action in Honor of National Equal Pay Day," White House Blog, April 8, 2014, obamawhitehouse.archives.gov, accessed November 11, 2015.

64 See "Advancing Pay Equality through Compensation Data Collection," presidential memorandum, April 8, 2014, obamawhitehouse.archives.gov, accessed December 3, 2015.

65 See "Fact Sheet: New Steps to Advance Equal Pay on the Seventh Anniversary of the Lilly Ledbetter Fair Pay Act," White House, January 29, 2016, obamawhitehouse.archives.gov, accessed February 1, 2016.

66 On April 4, 2017, Senator Patty Murray (D-WA) introduced the bill, S. 819, Paycheck Fairness Act, www.congress.gov, accessed July 7, 2017.

67 In 2015 a pay equity law was passed in California, making it the toughest in the country. The California Fair Pay Act requires employers to pay women and men

the same wages for "substantially similar work," even at different work sites or if their titles are different. See Patrick McGreevy and Chris Megerian, "California Now Has One of the Toughest Equal Pay Laws in the Country," *Los Angeles Times*, October 6, 2015, www.latimes.com, accessed January 19, 2016.

68 Equal Pay Day was established in 1996 by the National Committee on Pay Equity; this origination, founded in 1979, is a coalition of women's and civil rights organizations, labor unions, professional, legal, and educational associations, and a number of other groups working to eliminate wage discrimination based on gender and race.

69 Latifa Lyles, "It's Time for Equal Pay Now," *Huffington Post*, April 14, 2015, www.huffingtonpost.com, November 10, 2015.

70 Organization for Economic Co-operation and Development, "Gender Wage Gap," 2014, www.oecd.org, accessed December 21, 2015; Beryl A. Radin and Joan Price Boase, "Federalism, Political Structure, and Public Policy in the United States and Canada," *Journal of Comparative Policy Analysis: Research and Practice* 2 (2000): 65–89.

71 *United States v. Windsor*, 570 U.S. ___, 133 S. Ct. 2675 (2013).

72 *Obergefell v. Hodges*, 576 U.S. ___, 135 S. Ct. 2584 (2015). There was some resistance initially to the Supreme Court's *Obergefell* ruling. Three states—Texas, Louisiana, and Mississippi—attempted to set up roadblocks by instructing county clerks not to issue marriage licenses to gay or lesbian couples. Where such orders were rescinded, one county clerk took it upon herself to rebuff the Supreme Court and not issue licenses because of her religious beliefs. Kim Davis, the clerk in Rowan County, Kentucky, said that her Christian faith bars her from authorizing same-sex marriages. She defied a direct order from Governor Steven Beshear to issue the licenses. Davis was eventually jailed for her refusal to issue licenses, and upon her release she altered the licenses, replacing her name and office with the phrase "pursuant to federal court order." See, for example, Matthew Diebel, "Kentucky Governor Rips Kim Davis Lawsuit as 'Forlorn,'" *USA Today*, October 1, 2015, www.usatoday.com, accessed December 15, 2015; Jason Hanna, Ed Payne, and Catherine E. Shoichet, "Kim Davis Released, but Judge Bars Her from Withholding Marriage Licenses," CNN, September 8, 2015, www.cnn.com, accessed December 15, 2015.

73 Even members of the Mormon Church have been willing to support same-sex relationships, in opposition to church leadership. In July 2015 the Church of Jesus Christ of Latter-day Saints updated its doctrine after the *Obergefell* decision to treat Mormons in same-sex relationships as apostates. Children raised in such relationships would be banished from the church until they became adults and were willing to renounce their parents' union. This led to a mass exodus of Mormons from the church, arguing that gay and lesbian unions have become more socially acceptable, not to mention legal. In response to this outcry, Mormon leaders made a minor concession, allowing children of gay or lesbian unions to receive baptismal rights only if their "primary residence" is not with their same-sex

parents. See Laurie Goodstein, "New Policy on Gay Couples and Their Children Roils Mormon Church," *New York Times*, November 13, 2015, www.nytimes.com, accessed December 15, 2015.

74 Also see Phillip J. Cooper, *Civil Rights in Public Service* (New York: Routledge, 2017); Charles W. Gossett, "Lesbian, Gay, Bisexual, and Transgendered Employees in the Public Sector Workforce," in *Public Personnel Management: Current Concerns, Future Challenges*, 5th ed., ed. Norma M. Riccucci (New York: Longman, 2012), 60–76; Roddrick A. Colvin, *Gay and Lesbian Cops: Diversity and Effective Policing* (Boulder: Lynne Rienner, 2012); Roddrick A. Colvin, "Innovations in Antidiscrimination Laws: Research on Transgender-Inclusive Cities," *Journal of Public Management and Social Policy* 14 (2008): 19–34; Roddrick A. Colvin, "The Rise of Transgender-Inclusive Laws: How Well Are Municipalities Implementing Supportive Nondiscrimination Public Employment Policies?," *Review of Public Personnel Administration* 27 (2007): 336–60; Roddrick A. Colvin, "Innovation of State-Level Gay Rights Laws: The Role of Fortune 500 Corporations," *Business and Society Review* 111 (2006): 363–86; Gregory B. Lewis, "Lifting the Ban on Gays in the Civil Service: Federal Policy towards Gay and Lesbian Employees since the Cold War," *Public Administration Review* 57 (1997): 387–95; Gregory B. Lewis and Reynold S. Galope, "Support for Gay and Lesbian Rights: How and Why the South Differs from the Rest of the Country," *American Review of Politics* 34 (2013–2014): 271–97.

75 See, for example, Gil Seinfeld, "Reflections on Comity in the Law of American Federalism," *Notre Dame Law Review* 90 (2015): 1309.

76 Kevin Stainback and Donald Tomaskovic-Devey, *Documenting Desegregation: Racial and Gender Segregation in Private Sector Employment since the Civil Rights Act* (New York: Russell Sage Foundation, 2012).

77 See Radin and Posner, "Policy Tools, Mandates, and Intergovernmental Relations"; Radin and Boase, "Federalism, Political Structure, and Public Policy"; Daniel J. Elazar, *American Federalism: A View from the States* (New York: Harper and Row, 1984); and Kenneth C. Wheare, *Federal Government*, 4th ed. (Oxford: Oxford University Press, 1964).

78 Scott Barclay, Mary Bernstein, and Anna-Maria Marshall, eds., *Queer Mobilizations: LGBT Activists Confront the Law* (New York: New York University Press, 2009).

79 Pew Research Center, *A Survey of LGBT Americans*, June 13, 2013, www.pewsocialtrends.org, accessed November 16, 2015.

80 Human Rights Campaign, "The Cost of the Closet and the Rewards of Inclusion," 2014, www.hrc.org.

81 Human Rights Campaign, "New HRC Study Shows That American Public Strongly Supports Federal Non-Discrimination Protections," June 16, 2014, www.hrc.org, accessed November 16, 2015.

82 Representatives Bella Abzug (D-NY) and Ed Koch (D-NY) introduced the Equality Act of 1974, the first national law proposed in Congress that would end

discrimination against lesbians and gays in the United States by adding sexual orientation to Title VII. It did not include transgender people. It was not passed. There were other similar bills, but 1994 marked the first time ENDA was introduced to Congress.

83 David F. Burrelli, "An Overview of the Debate on Homosexuals in the U.S. Military," in *Gays and Lesbians in the Military: Issues, Concerns, and Contrasts*, ed. Wilbur J. Scott and Sandra Carson Stanley (New York: Aldine de Gruyter, 1994), 19. Congress had enacted laws covering the military much earlier making sodomy with anyone "of the same or opposite sex or with an animal" a crime. See Uniform Code of Military Justice, 925, Article 125, "Sodomy," www.ucmj.us, accessed November 16, 2015.

84 Some states in the early 1990s were just beginning to enact antidiscrimination legislation to protect at least lesbians and gays in the workplace.

85 *Meinhold v. U.S. Department of Defense*, 808 F. Supp. 1455 (C.D. Cal. 1993).

86 Ibid., 1456.

87 Ibid., 1455.

88 One judge was appointed by President Carter, one by President Reagan, and the other by President George H. W. Bush.

89 *Meinhold v. U.S. Department of Defense*, 34 F.3d 1469 (9th Cir. 1994), at 1477.

90 Ibid. For additional cases, see, for example, *Walmer v. U.S. Department of Defense*, 835 F. Supp. 1307 (D. Kan. 1993); and *Pruitt v. Weinberger*, 659 F. Supp. 625 (C.D. Cal. 1987).

91 Tracy Baim, *Obama and the Gays: A Political Marriage* (Chicago: Prairie Avenue, 2010).

92 Eric Schmitt, "Military Cites Wide Range of Reasons for Its Gay Ban," *New York Times*, January 27, 1993, www.nytimes.com, accessed November 18, 2015.

93 U.S. Department of Justice, "Assessment of Our Litigating Position in the Military Homosexual Cases," memorandum, December 9, 1993, www.clintonlibrary.gov, accessed December 3, 2015. On October 10, 2014, a number of White House papers from the Clinton Library were released. See "Gays in the Military," Parts 1, 2, and 3, www.clintonlibrary.gov, accessed December 3, 2015.

94 "Pres. Mtg w/JCS—1/25/93," handwritten notes, January 25, 1993, 26, Clinton Library. See starred entry by recorder of minutes, www.clintonlibrary.gov, accessed December 3, 2015.

95 Schmitt, "Military Cites Wide Range of Reasons."

96 Eric Schmitt, "Compromise on Military Gay Ban Gaining Support among Senators," *New York Times*, May 12,1993, www.nytimes.com, accessed November 18, 2015.

97 Ibid. For hearings on gays in the military, see, for example, *Congressional Record*, Senate, February 4, 1993, S1334; and *Hearings before the House Committee on Armed Services*, May 4 and 5, 1993, congressional.proquest.com.

98 In June 2016 the Pentagon announced that it was lifting its ban on transgender persons from serving openly in the military.

99 Republicans included Michael Huffington (CA), Ronald K. Machtley (RI), Constance Morella (MD), and Christopher H. Shays (CT). The independent was Bernie Sanders (VT).

100 See *Congressional Record*, House, July 19, 1994, www.congress.gov, accessed November 17, 2015. Given the lack of documentation (e.g., published hearings), it is unclear whether the subcommittee voted not to report the legislation to the full committee, or if a quorum was even present to vote. If a quorum is not present, action on the bill cannot be taken, and the bill effectively dies. Members of the subcommittee were all men: Chairperson Major Owens (D-NY), Donald Payne (D-NJ), Robert Scott (D-VA), Thomas Sawyer (D-OH), Cass Ballenger (R-NC), Bill Barrett (R-NE), and Harris Fawell (R-IL).

101 See *Congressional Record*, Senate, June 23, 1994, www.congress.gov, accessed November 17, 2015. All but two of the co-sponsors were Democrats. The Republican co-sponsors were John Chafee of Rhode Island and Jim Jeffords of Vermont, who in 2001 left the party to become an independent. Five senators were women. See congressional.proquest.com, accessed January 19, 2016.

102 *Hearings before the Committee on Labor and Human Resources on S. 2238, Employment Non-Discrimination Act of 1994*, 103rd Congress, July 29, 1994, 1–2, us.archive.org, accessed November 17, 2015.

103 Ibid., 3.

104 Ibid., 12.

105 Ibid., 59.

106 Ibid., 4–6.

107 Ibid., 7.

108 Ibid., 11.

109 Ibid., 9.

110 Ibid., 10.

111 Ibid., 90.

112 Senators Pell and Bingaman provided written statements to the committee.

113 U.S. Senate, "Hearing of the Committee," 1994, at 106–7. It should be noted that the United States lags behind at least European countries in terms of LGBT employment protections. In the European Union, for example, discrimination on the basis of sexual orientation is prohibited by the Employment Equality Directive and the Gender Equality Directive. See Directive 2000/78/EC and Directive 2006/54/EC, eur-lex.europa.eu, both accessed January 9, 2017.

114 See *Congressional Record*, Senate, September 10, 1996, S10129, www.congress.gov, accessed November 17, 2015.

115 See Employment Nondiscrimination Act of 1996, S.2056, 104th Congress (1995–1996), www.congress.gov, accessed November 17, 2015.

116 See Senate roll call, September 10, 1996, S. 2056, www.senate.gov, accessed November 17, 2015. One senator, Mark Pryor (D-AR), did not vote.

117 So, too, did Senator Donald Nickles (R-OK). See *Congressional Record*, Senate, September 10, 1996, www.congress.gov, accessed January 20, 2016.

118 U.S. Senate, "Senate Report 142, No. 123, The Employment Non-Discrimination Act of 1996," (1996), babel.hathitrust.org, accessed January 20, 2016.

119 Jerome Hunt, "A History of the Employment Non-Discrimination Act," Center for American Progress, July 19, 2011, www.americanprogress.org, accessed July 7, 2017. It was introduced by Representative Studds on June 15, 1995. See *Congressional Record*, House, June 15, 1995, www.congress.gov, accessed January 20, 2016.

120 But see *Hearings before the House Subcommittee on Government Programs*, July 17, 1996, www.archive.org, accessed January 20, 2016.

121 See Employment Non-Discrimination Act of 2007, H.R. 2015, 110th Congress (2007–2008), www.congress.gov, accessed November 17, 2015.

122 See *Hearings before the House Subcommittee on Health, Employment, Labor and Pensions*, September 5, 2007, www.gpo.gov, accessed November 17, 2015.

123 See House roll call, November 7, 2007, www.govtrack.us, accessed November 17, 2015.

124 See Employment Non-Discrimination Act of 2007, H.R. 3685, 110th Congress (2007–2008), www.congress.gov, accessed November 17, 2015.

125 Timothy J. Burger, "Inside George W. Bush's Closet," *Politico*, July–August 2014, www.politico.com, accessed November 18, 2015.

126 See *Congressional Record*, House, April 25, 2013, H.R. 1755, www.congress.gov, accessed November 18, 2015.

127 See *Congressional Record*, House, April 25, 2013, www.congress.gov, accessed November 18, 2015.

128 See *Congressional Record*, Senate, April 25, 2013, S. 815, www.congress.gov, accessed November 17, 2015.

129 U.S. Senate, "Senate Report 113–105, The Employment Non-Discrimination Act of 2013," (September 12, 2013), www.congress.gov, accessed November 18, 2015.

130 Ibid.

131 Ibid.

132 The religious organizations include, for example, Affirmation—Gay and Lesbian Mormons, African-American Ministers in Action, American Jewish Committee, Anti-Defamation League, Association of Welcoming & Affirming Baptists, Bend the Arc Jewish Action, B'nai B'rith International, Brethren Mennonite Council for Lesbian, Gay, Bisexual and Transgender Interests, Call To Action, Central Conference of American Rabbis, the Catholic offshoot Dignity USA, Disciples Home Missions, Episcopal Church, Lutherans for Full Participation, United Church of Christ, Wider Church Ministries, United Methodist General Board of Church and Society, and United Synagogue of Conservative Judaism.

133 U.S. Senate, "Senate Report 113–105," 2013.

134 Executive Office of the President, "Statement of Administration Policy," November 4, 2013, congressional.proquest.com, accessed November 23, 2015.

135 U.S. Senate, "Senate Report 113–105," 2013.

136 See Senate roll call, November 4, 2013, www.senate.gov, accessed November 18, 2015.

137 See *Congressional Record*, House, September 17, 2014, www.congress.gov, accessed November 18, 2015. In 2014 Representative Jared Polis (D-CO), who introduced ENDA to the House in 2013, filed a discharge petition, which sought to move ENDA out of committee and to the floor for consideration without a report from the committee. It failed. In addition, six House Republicans who had previously co-sponsored ENDA wrote a letter to House Speaker John Boehner (R-OH) in December 2014, urging him to allow for a vote on the bill before the end of the 113th Congress. They even encouraged him to attach ENDA to any legislative vehicle, including the National Defense Authorization Act, to ensure a positive vote. Their efforts failed. The six House Republicans were Ileana Ros-Lehtinen (FL), Richard Hanna (NY), Charles Dent (PA), Frank LoBiondo (NJ), Chris Gibson (NY), and Jon Runyan (NJ). See Michael Key, "Republican ENDA Supporters Beseech Boehner to Allow Vote," *Washington Blade*, December 3, 2014, www.washingtonblade.com, accessed January 21, 2016.

138 Baim, *Obama and the Gays*, 94–95.

139 White House, "Presidential Memorandum on Federal Benefits and Non-Discrimination, and Support of the Lieberman-Baldwin Benefits Legislation," June 17, 2009, www.whitehouse.gov, accessed November 23, 2015.

140 Ibid. Although President Obama worked to repeal the Defense of Marriage Act (DOMA), it was the U.S. Supreme Court's 2013 decision in *United States v. Windsor* that found DOMA to be unconstitutional. However, in *Smelt v. United States*, 447 F.3d 673 (9th Cir. 2006), the U.S. Department of Justice (DOJ) issued a brief defending the constitutionality of DOMA. Justice Department attorneys argued that the DOJ must stand by the laws of the land, even if it doesn't agree with them. In a reversal, by 2011, Attorney General Eric Holder released a statement that the DOJ would no longer defend DOMA. Some speculated that the reversal came after Vice President Joe Biden let it slip in an interview that President Obama supported gay marriage.

141 White House, "Extension of Benefits to Same-Sex Domestic Partners of Federal Employees," presidential memorandum, June 2, 2010, www.whitehouse.gov, accessed November 23, 2015.

142 See House roll call, December 15, 2010, clerk.house.gov, accessed November 23, 2015; and Senate roll call, December 18, 2010, politics.nytimes.com, accessed November 23, 2015.

143 The act did not take full effect until September 20, 2011, as the law provided for the Department of Defense to develop a plan for ending the policy.

144 Matthew Rosenberg, "Pentagon Moves to Allow Transgender People to Serve Openly in the Military," *New York Times*, July 13, 2015, www.nytimes.com, accessed December 14, 2015; Matthew Rosenberg, "Transgender People Will Be Allowed to Serve Openly in Military," *New York Times*, June 30, 2016, www.nytimes.com, accessed July 5, 2016.

145 Obama Administration Policy, "Human Rights Campaign," n.d., www.hrc.org, accessed December 7, 2015. The 2015 *Obergefell* ruling discussed in this chapter may supersede some of these efforts.

146 E.O. 11478 (1969) prohibits discrimination in the federal civilian workforce on the basis of race, color, religion, sex, national origin, handicap, and age; E.O. 13087, issued by President Bill Clinton in 1998, added sexual orientation as a protected class.

147 White House, "President Obama Signs a New Executive Order to Protect LGBT Workers," July 21, 2014, obamawhitehouse.archives.gov, accessed December 7, 2015.

148 Office of the Press Secretary, White House, "Fact Sheet: Taking Action to Support LGBT Workplace Equality Is Good For Business," July 21, 2014, obamawhitehouse. archives.gov, accessed December 7, 2015.

149 *Macy v. Holder*, EEOC Appeal No. 0120120821 (April 20, 2012), www.eeoc.gov, accessed December 7, 2015.

150 Sarah M. Stephens, "What Happens Next? Will Protection against Gender Identity and Sexual Orientation Workplace Discrimination Expand during President Obama's Second Term?," *Washington and Lee Journal of Civil Rights and Social Justice* 19 (2013): 365; Laura Anne Taylor, "A Win for Transgender Employees: Chevron Deference for the EEOC's Decision in *Macy v. Holder*," *Journal of Law and Family Studies* 15 (2013): 181.

151 *Price Waterhouse v. Hopkins*, 490 U.S. 228 (1989); *Macy v. Holder*, online, quoting *Price Waterhouse* at 239.

152 *Macy v. Holder*, online, emphasis added.

153 *Macy v. Holder*, online, quoting *Price Waterhouse* at 244. The EEOC consists of five members, appointed by the president and confirmed by the Senate. It is a bipartisan commission, mandating that no more than three persons from the same party serve on the commission. In 2012 there were three Democrats: Jacqueline Berrien (chair) and Chai Feldblum, both Obama appointees, and Stuart Ishimaru, a George W. Bush appointee, who was later reappointed by Obama. The two Republicans serving in 2012 were Victoria Lipnic, an Obama appointee, and Constance Barker, appointed first by George W. Bush and then reappointed by Obama in 2011.

154 *Schwenk v. Hartford*, 204 F.3d 1187 (9th Cir. 2000); *Smith v. City of Salem*, 378 F.3d 566 (6th Cir. 2004); *Glenn v. Brumby*, 663 F.3d 1312 (11th Cir. 2011).

155 Also see *Schroer v. Billington*, 577 F. Supp. 2d 293 (D.D.C. 2008).

156 David H. Rosenbloom, *Administrative Law for Public Managers*, 2nd ed. (Boulder: Westview, 2015); Rosenbloom, "Public Administration Theory"; West, "Administrative Rulemaking"; West, "The Politics of Administrative Rulemaking."

157 David Taffet, "Trans Professor Denied Tenure," *Dallas Voice*, May 5, 2011, www. dallasvoice.com, accessed December 10, 2015.

158 *United States and Rachel Tudor v. Southeastern Oklahoma State University and the Regional University System of Oklahoma*, Case No. CIV-15–324-C (W.D. Okla.

2015). A substantive ruling in this case has not yet been rendered. Also see a 2016 ruling in the case, where district court judge Robin J. Cauthron rejected the university's request for "all facts and records supporting" the claim that Tudor "is a male-to-female transgender." Judge Cauthron found that the university had "failed to demonstrate any relevance for those discovery requests." *United States and Rachel Tudor v. Southeastern Oklahoma State University*, 2016 WL 4250482, 2016 U.S. Dist. LEXIS 105492 (W.D. Okla., Aug. 10, 2016). See also Transgender Legal Defense and Education Fund, "Transgender Woman Asks Fifth Circuit Court of Appeals to Allow a Path Forward for Her Title VII Discrimination Case," January 4, 2017, transgenderlegal.org, accessed January 12, 2017.

159 U.S. Department of Justice, "Justice Department Files Lawsuit Alleging That Southeastern Oklahoma State University Discriminated against Transgender Woman," March 30, 2015, www.justice.gov, accessed December 10, 2015.

160 Ibid.

161 Ibid.

162 Resh, *Rethinking the Administrative Presidency*; Thompson, "The Administrative Presidency and Fractious Federalism"; Rosenbloom, "President George W. Bush's Theory of a Unitary Executive Branch"; Calabresi and Yoo, *The Unitary Executive*; Nathan, *The Administrative Presidency*. See chapter 1 for a further discussion of the administrative presidency and unitary executive theory, which hold that the president has exclusive control over the federal branch of government. Also see, for example, Waterman, "The Administrative Presidency"; and Barilleaux and Kelley, "Going Forward."

163 *EEOC v. Lakeland Eye Clinic*, M.D. Fla. Civ. No. 8:14-cv-2421-T35 AEP, filed Sept. 25, 2014.

164 EEOC, "Lakeland Eye Clinic Will Pay $150,000 to Resolve Transgender/Sex Discrimination Lawsuit," April 13, 2015, www.eeoc.gov, accessed December 14, 2015.

165 *EEOC v. R. G. & G. R. Harris Funeral Homes, Inc.*, 100 F. Supp. 3d 594 (E.D. Mich. 2015), www.lexisnexis.com, accessed December 10, 2015.

166 Ibid.

167 For additional cases filed by the EEOC, see www1.eeoc.gov, accessed April 10, 2016.

168 On remand, a district court judge in 1990 ordered Price Waterhouse to pay Hopkins close to $400,000 in back pay and also awarded Hopkins the partnership she was denied by Price Waterhouse; see *Hopkins v. Price Waterhouse*, 737 F. Supp. 1202 (D.D.C. 1990). But by this time, Hopkins had accepted a high-level post at the World Bank.

169 *Baldwin v. Foxx*, EEOC Appeal No. 0120133080 (July 15, 2015), www.eeoc.gov, accessed December 7, 2015. Three Democrats of the EEOC ruled for Baldwin: Jenny Yang, chair, an Obama appointee, and Chai Feldblum and Charlotte A. Burrows, both Obama appointees. The two Republicans, Lipnic and Barker, voted against. It is unclear why these two Republicans voted in favor of Macy, and inclusion of transgender employees under Title VII, and against Baldwin, where Title VII

would cover gay employees. It should further be noted that the Justice Department under the Trump administration has stated that it does not agree with the EEOC's ruling that Title VII protects employees from discrimination based on sexual orientation. See Alan Feuer, "Justice Department Claims Gay Workers Aren't Protected by Major Civil Rights Law," *New York Times*, July 28, 2017, A17.

170 *Baldwin v. Foxx*, online. For additional rulings by the EEOC, see www.eeoc.gov, accessed April 10, 2016.

171 *Baldwin v. Foxx*, online. In October 2014 the EEOC submitted a friend-of-the-court brief with the U.S. Circuit Court of Appeals for the Seventh Circuit in *Muhammad v. Caterpillar*, 767 F.3d 694 (7th Cir. 2014), advancing the interpretation of Title VII that it adopted in *Baldwin*. In *Muhammad*, the plaintiff was fired in retaliation for his complaint of harassment based on race and sexual orientation. The circuit court panel ruled that Title VII does not prohibit harassment based on sexual orientation. Muhammad petitioned for panel rehearing, which ultimately denied his petition. However, as the EEOC reports, "in a significant step, the panel issued an amended opinion removing its original rulings regarding the scope of Title VII coverage. The opinion no longer repeats or relies upon statements from prior Seventh Circuit decisions that Title VII does not prohibit sexual-orientation discrimination or retaliation for related opposition conduct." See EEOC reporting on litigation, www.eeoc.gov, accessed December 9, 2015. It should be noted that the federal courts have issued contradictory rulings on this matter. For example, a panel of the U.S. Court of Appeals for the Seventh Circuit ruled in 2016 in *Hively v. Ivy Tech Community College* (No. 15–1720, 7th Cir. April 4, 2017) that Title VII of the Civil Rights Act of 1964 did not protect gays and lesbians. But the full Seventh Circuit Court of Appeals ruled in April 2017 that Title VII *does* protect gays and lesbians. In March 2017 a panel of the U.S. Court of Appeals for the Eleventh Circuit ruled in *Evans v. Georgia Regional Hospital* (No. 15–15234, 11th Cir. March 10, 2017) that Title VII did not cover gays and lesbians. The full Eleventh Circuit denied a request for an *en banc* rehearing before all active judges, thus keeping the panel's decision in place.

172 *Federal Register*, "Spouse under the Family and Medical Leave Act," Final Rule (February 2, 2015), www.dol.gov, accessed December 14, 2015.

173 President Obama's reliance on the administrative presidency model, unlike that of Presidents Nixon and Reagan, was based more on cooperation with the bureaucracy rather than antagonism.

174 Rosenbloom, *Administrative Law for Public Managers*; Rosenbloom, *Building a Legislative-Centered Public Administration*; David H. Rosenbloom, Rosemary O'Leary, and Joshua Chanin, *Public Administration and Law*, 3rd ed. (New York: CRC Press, 2010); James Arnt Aune and Martin J. Medhurst, *The Prospect of Presidential Rhetoric* (College Station: Texas A&M University Press, 2008); Waterman, "The Administrative Presidency."

175 In 1952 the steel companies sued the federal government after President Truman nationalized the steel industry to avoid a strike by labor unions. See *Youngstown Sheet & Tube Co. v. Sawyer*, 343 U.S. 579 (1952).

176 *U.S. House of Representatives v. Burwell*, Civil Action No. 14–1967 (RMC), September 9, 2015, *SCOTUS Blog*, www.scotusblog.com, accessed November 18, 2015.

177 *U.S. House of Representatives v. Burwell*, Civil Action No. 14–1967 (RMC), May 12, 2016, *SCOTUS Blog*, www.scotusblog.com, accessed June 30, 2016.

178 Margot Sanger-Katz, "What Does Executive Order against the Health Law Actually Do?," *New York Times*, January 22, 2017, A11. The U.S. Congress has also been working aggressively to gut the Affordable Care Act, but as of July 2017 it has been unsuccessful in doing so.

179 The directives included the Deferred Action for Parents of Americans and Lawful Permanent Residents (DAPA), which would protect immigrants without documentation who lived in the United States since 2010 and whose children are American citizens or lawful permanent residents, and Deferred Action for Childhood Arrivals (DACA), which protects immigrants who entered the country before their sixteenth birthday.

180 See *Texas v. United States*, 86 F. Supp. 3d 591 (S.D. Tex. 2015); *aff'd*, 809 F.3d 134 (5th Cir. 2015).

181 *United States v. Texas*, 579 U.S. ___ (2016).

182 See *Congressional Record*, House, July 23, 2015, "Cosponsors: H.R.3185—114th Congress (2015–2016)," www.congress.gov.

183 See *Congressional Record*, Senate, July 23, 2015, S.1858, www.congress.gov.

184 Juliet Eilperin, "Obama Supports Altering Civil Rights Act to Ban LGBT Discrimination," *Washington Post*, November 10, 2015, www.washingtonpost.com, accessed December 15, 2015.

185 Matt Baume, "Debunking Right-Wing Opposition to the Equality Act," *Advocate*, July 24, 2015, www.advocate.com, accessed December 15, 2015.

186 Andrew T. Walker, "The Equality Act: Bad Policy That Poses Great Harms," *Public Discourse*, July 24, 2015, www.thepublicdiscourse.com, accessed December 15, 2015.

187 Laura Meckler, "New Gay-Rights Push Faces Uphill Climb in Congress," *Wall Street Journal*, July 7, 2015, www.wsj.com, accessed December 15, 2015.

188 Chris Johnson, "Some LGBT Advocates Not on Board with Equality Act," *Washington Blade*, July 21, 2015, www.washingtonblade.com, accessed December 15, 2015.

189 Alexa Ura, "Bathroom Fears Flush Houston Discrimination Ordinance," *Texas Tribune*, November 3, 2015, www.texastribune.org, accessed November 23, 2015.

190 Ibid.

191 See, for example, *Grimm v. Gloucester County School Board*, No. 15–2056 (4th Cir. 2016). Initially, the U.S. Supreme Court did not decide whether to hear an appeal to this case, but it did issue a temporary injunction preventing Gavin Grimm from using the boys' bathroom. See *Gloucester County School Board v. Grimm*, 136 S. Ct. 2442 (2016). However, when Trump rescinded Obama's directive protecting transgender students' right to use the bathroom corresponding with their gender identity, the Supreme Court decided not to hear an appeal to *Grimm*, but instead

returned the case to the Fourth Circuit Court of Appeals in light of that new development. See Adam Liptak, "Justices Step out of the Debate in a Transgender Rights Case," *New York Times*, March 7, 2017, A1, A11.

192 Matt Apuzzo and Alan Blinder, "North Carolina May Risk Aid with Bias Law," *New York Times*, April 1, 2016, A1, A3.

193 Alan Blinder, Richard Pérez-Peña, and Eric Lichtblau, "Countersuits over North Carolina's Bias Law," *New York Times*, May 9, 2016, www.nytimes.com, accessed May 16, 2016. In late December 2016 the repeal of HB2 failed in the North Carolina legislature, even after a Democrat, Roy Cooper, defeated McCrory in the gubernatorial election in November 2016. Governor-elect Cooper promised to lead the fight to repeal HB2. See Lynn Bonner, "Gov. Roy Cooper Promotes Consensus While Demanding a Repeal of HB2," *Raleigh (NC) News & Observer*, January 7, 2017, www.newsobserver.com, accessed January 11, 2017.

194 The states were Alabama, Arizona, Georgia, Louisiana, Maine, Oklahoma, Tennessee, Texas, Utah, West Virginia, and Wisconsin.

195 *Texas v. United States*, Civil Action No. 7:16-cv-00054-O (N.D. Tx. 2016), August 21, 2016, www.texasattorneygeneral.gov, accessed August 23, 2016.

196 *Carcaño v. McCrory*, 1:16cv236 (M.D. N.C. August 26, 2016), www.ncmd.uscourts. gov, accessed August 29, 2016.

197 Bryan Lowry, "Gov. Sam Brownback Rescinds Protected-Class Status for LGBT State Workers in Kansas," *Kansas City Star*, February 10, 2015, www.kansascity. com, accessed December 17, 2015.

198 Other states (e.g., Missouri) in a pure federalism move (i.e., where states seek to buck federal laws or policies), sought to pass legislation in response to *Obergefell* that would provide legal protections to opponents of same-sex marriage, such as religious groups.

199 Rich Sugg, "As Gov. Sam Brownback Signals Intolerance with Gay Marriage Directive, Gov. Jay Nixon Promotes Equality," *Kansas City Star*, July 8, 2015, www. kansascity.com, accessed December 17, 2015.

200 Jan Diehm, "Employment Non-Discrimination Act 2013: The 'T' in LGBT Protections," *Huffington Post*, February 2, 2016, www.huffingtonpost.com, accessed August 11, 2016. Also, some research has found that public attitudes toward transgender persons and policies applying to them are significantly more negative than they are toward gays and lesbians. See Daniel C. Lewis, Andrew R. Flores, Donald P. Haider-Markel, Patrick R. Miller, Barry L. Tadlock, and Jami K. Taylor, "Degrees of Acceptance: Variation in Public Attitudes toward Segments of the LGBT Community," *Political Research Quarterly*, forthcoming, DOI: 10.1177/1065912917717352.

201 Birkland, *An Introduction to the Policy Process*, 4th ed.; Baumgartner and Jones, *Agendas and Instability in American Politics*.

202 See, for example, Dana D. Nelson, *Bad for Democracy: How the Presidency Undermines the Power of the People* (Minneapolis: University of Minnesota Press, 2008); Shane, *Madison's Nightmare*; and Marshall J. Breger and Gary J. Edles, *Indepen-*

dent Agencies in the United States: Law, Structure, and Politics (New York: Oxford University Press, 2015).

203 Shane, *Madison's Nightmare*, 175–76.

204 Richard Gonzales, "LGBT Rights Activists Fear Trump Will Undo Protections Created under Obama," NPR, November 10, 2016, www.npr.org, accessed January 9, 2017.

205 Glenn Thrush and Maggie Haberman, "Ivanka Trump and Her Husband Help to Thwart Rollback of Gay Rights," *New York Times*, February 4, 2017, A10.

206 Jeremy W. Peters, "Trump Keeps 2014 Order Protecting Gay Workers," *New York Times*, January 31, 2017, A17.

207 Jeremy W. Peters, Jo Becker, and Julie Hirschfeld Davis, "Trump Rescinds Obama Directive on Bathroom Use," *New York Times*, February 23, 2017, A1, A16.

208 The Pentagon stated, however, that transgender persons could continue to serve until Trump's announcement was clarified. See Helene Cooper, "Transgender People Can Still Serve in Military for Now, Pentagon Says," *New York Times*, July 28, 2017, A17.

209 Kenneth J. Meier and Laurence J. O'Toole, *Bureaucracy in a Democratic State: A Governance Perspective* (Baltimore: Johns Hopkins University Press, 2006); Frederick C. Mosher, *Democracy and the Public Service* (New York: Oxford University Press, 1968); Paul H. Appleby, *Policy and Administration* (Tuscaloosa: University of Alabama Press, 1949); Norton E. Long, "Power and Administration," *Public Administration Review* 9 (1949): 257–64.

210 Mosher, *Democracy and the Public Service*; Appleby, *Policy and Administration*.

211 Mosher, *Democracy and the Public Service*, 3.

212 See the literature on representative bureaucracy, which empirically demonstrates how women and people of color in the bureaucracy push for the needs and interests of their counterparts in the general population. See, for example, Kenneth J. Meier, "Latinos and Representative Bureaucracy: Testing the Thompson and Henderson Hypotheses," *Journal of Public Administration Research and Theory* 3 (1993): 393–414; Kenneth J. Meier, "Representative Bureaucracy: A Theoretical and Empirical Exposition," *Research in Public Administration* 2 (1993): 1–35; Kenneth J. Meier, "Representative Bureaucracy: An Empirical Analysis," *American Political Science Review* 69 (1975): 526–42; Sally C. Selden, *The Promise of Representative Bureaucracy: Diversity and Responsiveness in a Government Agency* (Armonk, NY: Sharpe, 1997); Jessica E. Sowa and Sally C. Selden, "Administrative Discretion and Active Representation: An Expansion of the Theory of Representative Bureaucracy," *Public Administration Review* 63 (2003): 700–710; Norma M. Riccucci and Marcia Meyers, "Linking Passive and Active Representation: The Case of Front-Line Workers in Welfare Agencies," *Journal of Public Administration Research and Theory* 14 (2004): 585–97; Norma M. Riccucci, Gregg G. Van Ryzin, and Cecilia F. Lavena, "Representative Bureaucracy in Policing: Does It Increase Perceived Legitimacy?," *Journal of Public Administration Research and Theory* 24 (2014):

537–51; and Vicky M. Wilkins, "Exploring the Causal Story: Gender, Active Representation, and Bureaucratic Priorities," *Journal of Public Administration Research and Theory* 17 (2007): 77–94.

213 Meier and O'Toole, *Bureaucracy in a Democratic State*, 7.

CHAPTER 4. THE POLITICS OF CLIMATE CONTROL POLICY DRIFTS

1 U.S. NOAA, "2010 Tied for Warmest Year on Record," January 12, 2011, www.noaanews.noaa.gov, accessed February 2, 2016. And 2016 was the second-warmest year. See Justin Gillis, "2016 Was Second-Warmest Year on Record," *New York Times*, January 10, 2017, A9.

2 James Inhofe, *The Greatest Hoax: How the Global Warming Conspiracy Threatens Your Future* (Washington, D.C.: WND Books, 2012).

3 Michael W. Chapman, "Ted Cruz: 'Climate Change Is Not Science—It's Religion,'" CNS News, October 30, 2015, www.cnsnews.com, accessed April 20, 2016.

4 Pew Research Center, "As U.S. Energy Production Grows, Public Policy Views Show Little Change," 2014, www.people-press.org, accessed February 12, 2016.

5 *Massachusetts v. EPA*, 549 U.S. 497 (2007); Richard L. Revesz, *Environmental Law and Policy*, 3rd ed. (New York: Foundation, 2015); Barry G. Rabe, "Introduction: The Challenges of U.S. Climate Governance," in *Greenhouse Governance: Addressing Climate Change in America*, ed. Barry G. Rabe (Washington, D.C.: Brookings Institution Press, 2010), 3–23.

6 Nicholas Stern, *The Economics of Climate Change: The Stern Review* (Cambridge: Cambridge University Press, 2007).

7 Dianne Rahm, *Climate Change Policy in the United States: The Science, the Politics and the Prospects for Change* (Jefferson, NC: McFarland, 2010), 9.

8 Barry G. Rabe, "A New Era in States' Climate Policies?," in *Changing Climate Politics: U.S. Policies and Civic Action*, ed. Yael Wolinsky-Nahmias (Thousand Oaks, CA: CQ Press, 2015), 55–81; Barry G. Rabe, *Statehouse and Greenhouse: The Emerging Politics of American Climate Change Policy* (Washington, D.C.: Brookings Institution, 2004). The Energy Independence and Security Act of 2007 was aimed at greater energy independence and increasing the production of clean renewable fuels. It also sought to promote research on greenhouse gases, including efforts to capture and store those gases.

9 The Clean Air Act was first passed in 1963, but significant amendments were added in 1970 and 1990. As amended, the act identified six pollutants to be regulated by the EPA: carbon monoxide, lead, nitrogen dioxide, sulfur dioxide, ground-level ozone, and soot. See Robert E. Krebs, *The Basics of Earth Science* (Westport, CT: Greenwood, 2003).

10 William Antholis and Strobe Talbott, *Fast Forward: Ethics and Politics in the Age of Global Warming*, rev. ed. (Washington, D.C.: Brookings Institution, 2010); Lisa Heinzerling, "Climate Change and the Clean Air Act," *University of San Francisco Law Review* 42 (2007): 111–53.

11 For a review of the laws at the state level, see "Climate Change Laws of the United States of America," Columbia Law School, n.d., web.law.columbia.edu, accessed February 3, 2016.

12 Rabe, "A New Era," 55.

13 See, for example, G. Thomas Farmer and John Cook, *Climate Change Science: A Modern Synthesis* (New York: Springer, 2013); John Houghton, *Global Warming: The Complete Briefing*, 5th ed. (Cambridge: Cambridge University Press, 2015); and David Archer, *Global Warming: Understanding the Forecast*, 2nd ed. (Hoboken, NJ: Wiley, 2012).

14 U.S. Global Change Research Program, *The Impacts of Climate Change on Human Health in the United States: A Scientific Assessment*, health2016.globalchange.gov, accessed January 12, 2017. The study was produced by the U.S. Global Change Research Program (USGCRP), which is a coalition of researchers from thirteen federal agencies responsible for research and development that support the nation's response to global change: the Departments of Agriculture, Commerce, Defense, Energy, Health and Human Services, Interior, State, and Transportation, the EPA, NASA, the National Science Foundation, USAID, and the Smithsonian Institution. The study, reported on April 7, 2015, can be found at s3.amazonaws.com, accessed April 5, 2016.

15 The term "climategate" was coined by the *Telegraph* journalist James Delingpole. See Christopher Booker, "Climate Change: This Is the Worst Scientific Scandal of Our Generation," *Telegraph*, November 28, 2009, www.telegraph.co.uk, accessed July 10, 2017.

16 Andrew Revkin, "Hacked E-Mail Is New Fodder for Climate Dispute," *New York Times*, November 20, 2009, www.nytimes.com, accessed February 3, 2016.

17 As discussed later in the chapter, this was but one of the many international summits on climate change.

18 The Koch brothers (Charles and David H.), two of the wealthiest and most influential persons in U.S. politics, funded a web of conservative organizations that seized the opportunity to promote the smear campaign against the scientists and discredit the climate change movement. In the end, the climate scientists were exonerated by independent inquiries. For a more comprehensive review, see Jane Mayer, *Dark Money: The Hidden History of the Billionaires behind the Rise of the Radical Right* (New York: Doubleday, 2016).

19 United Nations Framework Convention on Climate Change (UNFCCC), Copenhagen Climate Change Conference, December 2009, www.unfccc.int, accessed February 3, 2016.

20 Richard J. Lazarus, "Climate Change Law in and over Time," *Harvard Law Review* 2 (2010): 32.

21 David Freestone and Ellen Hey, eds., *The Precautionary Principle and International Law: The Challenge of Implementation* (The Hague: Kluwer Law International, 1996); Per Sandin, "Dimensions of the Precautionary Principle," *Human and Ecological Risk Assessment: An International Journal* 5 (1999): 889–907.

22 Nicholas Askounes Ashford and Charles C. Caldart, *Environmental Law, Policy, and Economics: Reclaiming the Environmental Agenda* (Cambridge: MIT Press, 2008).

23 Ibid., 176.

24 See "Rio Declaration on Environment and Development," United Nations Conference on Environment and Development, Rio de Janeiro, June 3–14, 1992, www.unep.org, accessed February 3, 2016.

25 Richard Revesz and Jack Lienke, *Struggling for Air: Power Plants and the "War on Coal"* (New York: Oxford University Press, 2016); Michelle C. Pautz, "Regulating Greenhouse Gas Emissions: The Supreme Court, the Environmental Protection Agency, Madison's 'Auxiliary Precautions,' and Rohr's 'Balance Wheel,'" *Public Integrity* 18 (2016): 149–66.

26 Hari M. Osofsky and Jacqueline Peel, "The Grass Is Not Always Greener: Congressional Dysfunction, Executive Action, and Climate Change in Comparative Perspective," *Chicago-Kent Law Review* 91 (2016), www.lexisnexis.com, accessed February 11, 2016.

27 Cary Funk and Lee Rainie, "Climate Change and Energy Issues," chap. 2 of "Americans, Politics, and Science Issues," Pew Research Center, July 1, 2015, www.pewinternet.org, accessed February 3, 2016.

28 See "Fossil Fuel Funding to Congress: Industry Influence in the U.S.," Oil Change International, n.d., www.priceofoil.org, accessed February 3, 2016.

29 Andrew E. Dessler, *Introduction to Modern Climate Change*, 2nd ed. (New York: Cambridge University Press, 2011); Stern, *The Economics of Climate Change*; William D. Nordhaus, "A Review of the *Stern Review on the Economics of Climate Change*," *Journal of Economic Literature* 46 (2007): 686–702.

30 See, for example, Youba Sokona and Fatma Denton, "Climate Change Impacts: Can Africa Cope with the Challenges?," *Climate Policy* 1 (2001): 117–23; and Dessler, *Introduction to Modern Climate Change*. It should also be noted that efforts to slow or stop the effects of global warming are especially important to low-income and racial and ethnic minority Americans as they are disproportionately impacted by the effects of climate change. Manifestations of climate change such as storms, floods, and climate variability have a much more serious impact on African Americans and other racial and ethnic minorities economically and socially and in terms of health and well-being. Hurricane Katrina, along with its aftermath, is but one example of how the results of climate change can have a disparate and often tragic impact on communities of color.

31 "A Bad Climate for Development," *Economist*, September 17, 2009, www.economist.com, accessed February 4, 2016.

32 Dennis R. Parker, "Policy Prescriptions from the Oil Industry," in *Global Climate Change*, ed. Andrew J. Hoffman (San Francisco: New Lexington, 1998), 73.

33 Ibid.

34 For a listing of global summits and conferences, see, for example, Dana Fisher, *National Governance and the Global Climate Change Regime* (Lanham, MD: Row-

man and Littlefield, 2004); and "A Brief History of Climate Change," BBC News, September 20, 2013, www.bbc.com, accessed February 4, 2016.

35 Jeffrey A. Frankel, "Greenhouse Gas Emissions," Brookings Policy Brief Series, No. 50, Brookings Institution, 1999, www.brookings.edu, accessed February 4, 2016.

36 See Wilson, DiIulio, and Bose, *American Government*; Richard A. Arenberg and Robert B. Dove, *Defending the Filibuster: The Soul of the Senate* (Bloomington: Indiana University Press, 2012); and John C. Roberts, "Majority Voting in Congress: Further Notes on the Constitutionality of the Senate Cloture Rule," *Journal of Law and Politics* 20 (2004): 505–47. The U.S. House of Representatives has a Rules Committee, which places limits on debates when a bill goes to the floor. The Senate has no such counterpart.

37 Tora Skodvin and Steinar Andresen, "An Agenda for Change in U.S. Climate Policies? Presidential Ambitions and Congressional Powers," *International Environmental Agreements: Politics, Law and Economics* 9 (2009): 263–80, 274.

38 This first conference followed a series of meetings held by the United Nations in the 1970s. See John W. Zillman, "A History of Climate Activities," *World Meteorological Association Bulletin* 58, no. 3 (2009), https://public.wmo.int, accessed February 8, 2016.

39 Colin P. Summerhayes, *Earth's Climate Evolution* (Hoboken, NJ: Wiley-Blackwell, 2015). It should be noted that the Montreal Protocol, agreed to on September 16, 1987, aimed at phasing out chemicals that damage the ozone layer, was ratified by the U.S. Senate in 1988; the United States has joined its four subsequent amendments. It went into force in 1989. Its purpose was not aimed at climate change, but it has had a greater impact on the elimination of greenhouse gases than the Kyoto Protocol. See "A Brief History of Climate Change," BBC, September 20, 2013, www.bbc.com, accessed February 8, 2016. For details on how EPA bureaucrats influenced the signing of the Montreal Protocol, see Norma M. Riccucci, *Unsung Heroes: Federal Execucrats Making a Difference* (Washington, D.C.: Georgetown University Press, 1995).

40 The IPCC is open to all member countries of the United Nations and the WMO. See www.ipcc.ch, accessed February 8, 2016.

41 See "Toward a Climate Agreement," UN and Climate Change webpage, www.un.org, accessed February 8, 2016. The UNFCCC was negotiated at the Earth Summit in Rio de Janeiro in 1992.

42 See UN Climate Change Newsroom, newsroom.unfccc.int, accessed February 8, 2016.

43 The Marrakesh Accord (2001), the Bali Action Plan (2007), and the Durban Platform (2011) were also agreements adopted to continue action through the UNFCCC. Luke Tomlinson, *Procedural Justice in the United Nations Framework Convention on Climate Change* (New York: Springer, 2015).

44 David G. Victor, *The Collapse of the Kyoto Protocol and the Struggle to Slow Global Warming* (Princeton: Princeton University Press, 2001), viii.

45 It should be noted that there is some uncertainty about compliance with future targets for emissions, since, first, it is difficult to predict future emission levels, and second, limiting emissions might prove more costly than anticipated. To address this concern, however, the protocol has called for "emissions trading," which, as set out in Article 17 of the protocol,

> allows countries that have emission units to spare—emissions permitted them but not "used"—to sell this excess capacity to countries that are over their targets. Thus, a new commodity was created in the form of emission reductions or removals. Since carbon dioxide is the principal greenhouse gas, people speak simply of trading in carbon. Carbon is now tracked and traded like any other commodity. This is known as the "carbon market."

UNFCCC (United Nations Framework Convention on Climate Change), "International Emissions Trading," February 9, 2016, unfccc.int, accessed March 1, 2016.

46 See Senate Resolution 98, July 25, 1997, www.congress.gov, accessed February 8, 2016.

47 While the insistence by the United States was most extreme, other nations also expressed concerned that developing countries had no binding commitments. The European Union, for example, also strongly pushed for the inclusion of developing countries. See Joanna Depledge, "Against the Grain: The United States and the Global Climate Change Regime," *Global Change, Peace and Security* 17 (2005): 11–27.

48 See Senate roll call, July 25, 1997, www.senate.gov, accessed February 8, 2016. Five senators did not vote.

49 *Hearings before the Subcommittee on International Economic Policy, Export and Trade Promotion on Senate Resolution 98*, June 19, 1997, www.gpo.gov, accessed March 9, 2016.

50 Ibid.

51 Ibid.

52 Ibid.

53 Ibid., June 26, 1997.

54 It should be noted that France, Russia, Japan, and Canada would later pull out of the Kyoto Protocol. See "Kyoto Protocol Fast Facts," CNN, March 31, 2015, www.cnn.com, accessed February 10, 2016.

55 See, for example, Duncan Clark, "Has the Kyoto Protocol Made Any Difference to Carbon Emissions?," *Guardian*, November 26, 2012, www.theguardian.com, accessed February 11, 2016.

56 During the Bush administration, the United States continued to attend the annual COP conferences, but it did not participate in any negotiations related to the Kyoto Protocol.

57 Eric Pianin, "U.S. Aims to Pull Out of Warming Treaty," *Washington Post*, March 28, 2001, www.globalpolicy.org, accessed February 10, 2016.

58 The UNFCCC requires its parties to provide periodic national reviews of their climate policies. The United States provides those reports and Congress holds

hearings here as well. See, for example, *Global Climate Change and the U.S. Climate Action Report: Hearings before the Committee on Commerce, Science, and Transportation*, July 11, 2002.

59 See, for example, Colin Provost, Brian J. Gerber, and Mark Pickup, "Flying under the Radar? Political Control and Bureaucratic Resistance in the Bush Environmental Protection Agency," in *President George W. Bush's Influence over Bureaucracy and Policy*, ed. Colin Provost and Paul Teske (New York: Palgrave MacMillan, 2009), 169–86; and Sara R. Rinfret and Michelle C. Pautz, *U.S. Environmental Policy in Action: Practice and Implementation* (New York: Palgrave MacMillan, 2014).

60 Walter A. Rosenbaum, "Improving Environmental Regulation at the EPA: The Challenge in Balancing Politics, Policy, and Science," in *Environmental Policy: New Directions for the Twenty-First Century*, 4th ed., ed. Norman J. Vig and Michael Craft (Washington, D.C.: CQ Press, 2006), 169–92; Norman J. Vig, "Presidential Leadership and the Environment," in *Environmental Policy: New Directions for the Twenty-First Century*, 8th ed., ed. Norman J. Vig and Michael Craft (Washington, D.C.: CQ Press, 2013), 84–108.

61 "Groups Blast Bush for Reversing Position on Emissions Reductions," CNN, March 15, 2001, www.cnn.com, accessed February 25, 2016.

62 Provost, Gerber, and Pickup, "Flying under the Radar?"

63 Joe Romm, "George Bush's EPA Chief: Clean Power Plan Is 'Most Flexible Thing' the Agency Has Done," *ClimateProgress*, October 16, 2015, thinkprogress.org, accessed February 25, 2016. It should be noted that career bureaucrats also wield a good deal of influence over environmental policy. And bureaucrats have become particularly agitated when presidents and their political appointees to head the EPA have worked to gut environmental policy or law. In such cases, they will work against the EPA administrator and work with interest groups and Congress to exert their influence over environmental policy. Career bureaucrats can drag their feet, leak information to the press, and employ other strategies to exercise their power. A good example here is during the Reagan administration, when the EPA was headed by Anne Gorsuch (later Burford), who was openly hostile to environmental interests. See, for example, Charles T. Goodsell, *The Case for Bureaucracy: A Public Administration Polemic*, 4th ed. (Washington D.C.: CQ Press, 2004); Marissa Martino Golden, *What Motivates Bureaucrats? Politics and Administration during the Reagan Years* (New York: Columbia University Press, 2000); Rosemary O'Leary, *Environmental Change: Federal Courts and the EPA* (Philadelphia: Temple University Press, 1993); and Riccucci, *Unsung Heroes*.

64 Marianne Lamont Horinko served as acting administrator from July 14 to November 5, 2003. Michael Leavitt served as administrator from November 6, 2003, to January 26, 2005. Stephen Johnson served from January 26, 2005, to January 20, 2009.

65 The emissions to be regulated included carbon dioxide, methane, nitrous oxide, and hydrofluorocarbons See *International Center for Technology Assessment v. Browner*, October 20, 1999, www.ciel.org, accessed February 10, 2016. Also see

Charles de Saillan, "United States Supreme Court Rules EPA Must Take Action on Greenhouse Gas Emissions: *Massachusetts v. EPA*," *Natural Resources Journal* 47 (2007): 793–814; and Erkki Hollo, Kati Kulovesi, and Michael Mehling, eds., *Climate Change and the Law* (Dordrecht, Netherlands: Springer, 2013).

66 *International Center for Technology Assessment v. Browner.*

67 42 U.S. Code § 7521, Emission Standards for New Motor Vehicles or New Motor Vehicle Engines.

68 Global warming had not yet reached epic proportions at the time of the Clean Air Act's passage. It was not until 1970 that Congress passed a more comprehensive clean air act that would address air pollution.

69 *International Center for Technology Assessment v. Browner.*

70 *Federal Register*, "Control of Air Pollution from New Motor Vehicles," Final Rule 65 (2000), 6698, www.gpo.gov, accessed February 18, 2016.

71 *Federal Register*, "Control of Air Pollution from New Motor Vehicles," Final Rule 66 (2001), 5002, www.gpo.gov, accessed February 18, 2016; U.S. Government Accountability Office, "Environmental Justice: EPA Should Devote More Attention to Environmental Justice When Developing Clean Air Rules," July 2005, www.gao.gov.

72 See *Federal Register*, "Control of Emissions from New and In-Use Highway Vehicles and Engines," Request for Comment 66 (January 23, 2001), 7486, www.gpo.gov, accessed January 12, 2017.

73 de Saillan, "United States Supreme Court Rules EPA Must Take Action."

74 *Federal Register*, "Proposed Consent Decree, Clean Air Act Citizen Suit," Request for Public Comment 68 (2003), 52922, www.gpo.gov, accessed February 18, 2016. It is uncertain whether Whitman clashed with President Bush on this proposed rule. However, as Fonte points out, Whitman once admitted that the Bush administration pandered to what "the members of the Republican Party want—as little regulation as possible." Francesca Fonte, "The Threat of Global Warming and the Roles of the EPA: EPA as an Independent Agency and as Advocate for the Environment and the Public?," *Albany Law Environmental Outlook Journal* 11 (2007): 365–87, 375. Also see Andrews, who argues that Whitman resigned because she was continually undercut by the Bush administration when she sought to carry out efforts to protect the environment. Richard N. L. Andrews, "The EPA at 40: An Historical Perspective," *Duke Environmental Law and Policy Forum* 21 (2011): 223–58.

75 *Federal Register*, "Proposed Consent Decree, Clean Air Act Citizen Suit," 52929.

76 Ibid.

77 States in the coalition included California, Connecticut, Illinois, Maine, Massachusetts, New Jersey, New Mexico, New York, Oregon, Rhode Island, Vermont, and Washington; the cities were New York, Baltimore, and Washington, D.C., as well as the territory of American Samoa.

78 *Massachusetts v. EPA*, 415 F.3d 50 (D.C. Cir. 2005). The D.C. Circuit Court of Appeals is empowered to consider all lawsuits under the Clean Air Act.

79 *Massachusetts v. EPA*, 2007, 503. Stevens's opinion was joined by Justices Kennedy, Souter, Ginsburg, and Breyer. In the dissent were Chief Justice Roberts and Justices Scalia, Thomas, and Alito.

80 Ibid., 534.

81 Ibid., 503, emphasis added.

82 Ibid., 533.

83 *Chevron U.S.A. v. Natural Resources Defense Council*, 467 U.S. 837 (1984).

84 *Massachusetts v. EPA*, 2007, 527.

85 Ibid., 525.

86 Darren Samuelsohn and Robin Bravender, "EPA Releases Bush-Era Endangerment Document," *New York Times*, October 13, 2009, www.nytimes.com, accessed March 1, 2016; Union of Concerned Scientists, "The EPA's Elusive Climate Change Endangerment Report," n.d., www.ucsusa.org, accessed March 1, 2016.

87 *Federal Register*, "Proposed Endangerment and Cause or Contribute Findings for Greenhouse Gases," Proposed Rule 78 (2009), 18886, www.epa.gov, accessed March 1, 2016.

88 *Federal Register*, "Endangerment and Cause or Contribute Findings for Greenhouse Gases," Final Rule 74 (2009), 66496, www.epa.gov, accessed March 1, 2016. See Timothy J. Conlan and Paul L. Posner, "Inflection Point? Federalism and the Obama Administration," *Publius* 41 (2011): 421–46, 439, who point out that the EPA's rule on tailpipe standards was patterned after California's law, which had the strictest standards.

89 See *Federal Register*, "Part V—Environmental Protection Agency" (April 2, 2010), www.gpo.gov, accessed March 1, 2016.

90 For a timeline, see *Federal Register*, "Part II—Environmental Protection Agency, Department of Transportation" (May 7, 2010), www.gpo.gov, accessed March 1, 2016.

91 *Federal Register*, "Part II—Environmental Protection Agency" (June 3, 2010), www.gpo.gov, accessed March 1, 2016.

92 Environmental and Energy Study Institute, "Fact Sheet: Timeline of EPA Actions of Greenhouse Gases," 2014, www.eesi.org, accessed March 1, 2016.

93 Francis Choi, "*Coalition for Responsible Regulation v. EPA*: An Analysis of Judicial Deference and Regulatory Discretion," *Ecology Law Quarterly* 40 (2013): 525–32.

94 *Coalition for Responsible Regulation, Inc. v. EPA*, 684 F.3d 102 (D.C. Cir. 2012), www.epa.gov, accessed March 1, 2016.

95 Ibid., 117, quoting *Massachusetts v. EPA*, 2007, 532–33.

96 Ibid., 117–18, quoting *Massachusetts v. EPA*, 2007, 533.

97 See 134 S. Ct. 468 (2013).

98 *Utility Air Regulatory Group v. EPA*, 573 U.S. ___, 134 S. Ct. 2427 (2014).

99 Pautz, "Regulating Greenhouse Gas Emissions."

100 Ibid.; Ryan Matthews, "Congress and Chaos: Reexamining the Role of Congress in Combating Climate Change," *University of the Pacific Law Review* 47 (2015): 1–23; David Marshall Coover III, "Square Pegs and Round Holes," *Texas Environmental*

Law Journal 45 (2015): 1–30; William N. Eskridge, "Congressional Overrides of Supreme Court Statutory Interpretation Decisions, 1967–2011," Faculty Scholarship Series, Paper 4888 (2014), digitalcommons.law.yale.edu, accessed April 18, 2016; Jonathan H. Adler, "Further Thoughts on Today's Supreme Court Decision on Greenhouse Gas Regulation," *Washington Post*, June 23, 2014, www.washingtonpost.com, accessed April 18, 2016. Also see *American Electric Power Company v. Connecticut*, 564 U.S. 410 (2011), where several states sued out-of-state power companies for the damages caused by greenhouse gas emissions by those industries. The suit was not brought under the Clean Air Act but rather under common law: the federal common law of interstate nuisance and state tort law. The U.S. Supreme Court ruled 8–0 that corporations cannot be sued for greenhouse gas emissions under federal common law, because regulation of such gases falls within the scope of the EPA's powers under the Clean Air Act. Justice Sotomayor recused herself because she was originally on the Second Circuit Court, which issued the lower court decision.

101 See Julian Agyeman, *Sustainable Communities and the Challenge of Environmental Justice* (New York: New York University Press, 2005); Barry G. Rabe, "Environmental Policy and the Bush Era: The Collision between the Administrative Presidency and State Experimentation," *Publius* 27 (2007): 413–31; and Rabe, *Statehouse and Greenhouse*.

102 See EPA, "State CO2 Emissions from Fossil Fuel Combustion, 1990–2013," n.d., www.epa.gov, accessed March 2, 2016.

103 See U.S. Energy Information Administration, "Which States Produce the Most Coal," April 4, 2016, www.eia.gov, accessed March 2, 2016.

104 See Petition for a Writ of Certiorari, Supreme Court, *Texas v. EPA*, 2013, Beveridge & Diamond, PC, www.bdlaw.com, accessed March 2, 2016.

105 See Brief, *Utility Air Regulatory Group v. EPA*, www.americanbar.org; and Lyle Denniston, "Argument Preview: Curbing Greenhouse Gases," *SCOTUS Blog*, February 22, 2014, www.scotusblog.com, accessed March 2, 2016.

106 Linda Greenhouse, "Justices Say EPA Has Power to Act on Harmful Gases," *New York Times*, April 3, 2007, www.nytimes.com.

107 See Conlan and Posner, "Inflection Point?"

108 See American Clean Energy and Security Act, H.R. 2454, 111th Congress (June 26, 2009), www.congress.gov, accessed March 9, 2016.

109 See coverage of House Committee on Energy and Commerce hearings, C-SPAN, April 22, 2009, www.c-span.org, accessed March 9, 2016.

110 Ibid.

111 Ibid.

112 Ibid.

113 *Hearings before the House Committee on Agriculture*, June 11, 2009, purl.access.gpo.gov, accessed March 10, 2016.

114 Ibid.

115 Ibid.

116 Ibid.

117 C-SPAN coverage of House Committee on Energy and Commerce hearings, April 22, 2009.

118 Ibid.

119 See House roll call, June 26, 2009, clerk.house.gov, accessed March 9, 2016.

120 See American Clean Energy and Security Act of 2009, H.R. 2454, 111th Congress (2009), www.govtrack.us, accessed July 12, 2016.

121 Daniel J. Weiss, "Anatomy of a Senate Climate Bill Death," Center for American Progress, October 12, 2010, www.americanprogress.org, accessed July 12, 2016.

122 President Obama followed by issuing Executive Order 13653 in November 2013, which requires the nation to prepare for the impacts of climate change. See Executive Order 13653, "Preparing the United States for the Impacts of Climate Change," November 1, 2013, obamawhitehouse.archives.gov, accessed March 2, 2016.

123 For a comprehensive timeline on President Obama's efforts to effect climate control policy, see Environmental and Energy Study Institute, "Fact Sheet: Timeline of Progress Made in President Obama's Climate Action Plan," August 5, 2015, www.eesi.org, accessed March 2, 2016. For example, as part of Obama's Climate Action Plan, the EPA in July 2015 finalized its rule to reduce emissions of hydrofluorocarbon (HFC), a potent human-made greenhouse gas.

124 Federal Register, "Carbon Pollution Emission Guidelines for Existing Stationary Sources," Proposed Rule 79 (2014), 34830, www.gpo.gov, accessed March 2, 2016.

125 William S. Scherman and Jason J. Fleischer, "The Environmental Protection Agency and the Clean Power Plan: A Paradigm Shift in Energy Regulation Away from Energy Regulators," Energy Law Journal 36 (2015), www.felj.org, accessed March 8, 2016.

126 Barbara Hollingsworth, "U.S. Senate Votes to Block EPA's Clean Power Plan," CNS News, November 18, 2015, www.cnsnews.com, accessed July 12, 2016; Richard S. Beth, "Disapproval of Regulations by Congress: Procedure under the Congressional Review Act," Congressional Research Service, October 10, 2001, www.senate.gov, accessed July 13, 2016.

127 Timothy Cama, "Obama Vetoes GOP Push to Kill Climate Rules," The Hill, December 19, 2015, http://thehill.com, accessed December 20, 2015.

128 Matthew Daly, "As Obama Pushes Climate Deal in Paris, Congress Tries to Stop Carbon Limits on U.S. Power Plants," U.S. News and World Report, December 1, 2015, www.usnews.com, accessed July 12, 2016.

129 Oklahoma v. EPA, Case No. 15-CV-0369-CVE-FHM, 2015, www.lawandenvironment.com, accessed February 17, 2016. The states were West Virginia, Alabama, Indiana, Kansas, Kentucky, Louisiana, Nebraska, Ohio, Oklahoma, South Carolina, South Dakota, and Wyoming.

130 Ibid.

131 See Letter from Solicitor General of West Virginia to Gina McCarthy, EPA, Docket No. EPA-HQ-OAR-20 13–0602 (August 5, 2015), www.ago.wv.gov, accessed February 17, 2016.

132 *West Virginia v. EPA*, No. 15–1363 (D.C. Cir. 2015), www.eenews.net, accessed February 17, 2016. The states that joined West Virginia were Texas, Alabama, Arkansas, Colorado, Florida, Georgia, Indiana, Kansas, Louisiana, Missouri, Montana, Nebraska, New Jersey, Ohio, South Carolina, South Dakota, Utah, Wisconsin, Wyoming, Kentucky, Louisiana, North Carolina, and Michigan; also included was the Arizona Corporation Commission, the public utilities commission of the state. This was a consolidated case.

133 *West Virginia v. EPA*, 2016 USCA Case #15–1363 Document #1594951, www.chamberlitigation.com, accessed February 17, 2016.

134 See "The Obama Administration's Climate Change Rule Faces Significant Republican Opposition and an Uphill Legal Fight," *E&E News*, www.eenews.net, accessed February 17, 2016.

135 See *West Virginia v. EPA*, via *SCOTUS Blog*, January 26, 2016, www.scotusblog.com, accessed February 17, 2016.

136 *West Virginia v. EPA*, 136 S. Ct. 1000 (2016), www.bakerbotts.com, accessed February 17, 2016. Ruling for the stay were Chief Justice Roberts and Justices Scalia, Anthony, Thomas, and Alito. Justices dissenting were all four justices from the Court's liberal wing—Ruth Bader Ginsburg, Stephen Breyer, Sonia Sotomayor, and Elena Kagan.

137 That is, in *Massachusetts*, Justices Stevens, Kennedy, Breyer, Ginsburg, and Souter ruled for the EPA, and Chief Justice Roberts and Justices Scalia, Thomas, and Alito dissented. Justice Sotomayor replaced Souter in 2009 and Justice Kagan replaced Stevens in 2010. In *West Virginia*, Justice Scalia delivered the opinion of the Court, in which Chief Justice Roberts and Justices Kennedy, Thomas, and Alito joined. Justice Kagan filed a dissenting opinion, in which Justices Ginsburg, Breyer, and Sotomayor joined.

138 See, for example, Cristian Farias, "Justice Scalia Calls Out a Colleague for Flip-Flopping on Juvenile Justice," *Huffington Post*, January 28, 2016, www.huffingtonpost.com, accessed March 8, 2016; Charlotte Alter, "Here's What Justice Kennedy Thinks about Abortion," *Time*, March 2, 2016, www.time.com, accessed March 14, 2016; and Steven Harmon Wilson, ed., *The U.S. Justice System: Law and Constitution in Early America* (Santa Barbara, CA: ABC-CLIO, 2012).

139 Massimo Calabresi and David Von Drehle, "What Will Justice Kennedy Do?," *Time*, June 18, 2012, www.time.com.

140 See *Federal Register*, "Mercury and Air Toxics Standards (MATS)," Final Rule (February 16, 2012), 9325, www.gpo.gov, accessed February 11, 2016.

141 Previous decisions by the High Court have held that federal regulatory agencies do not always need to account for costs when regulating public health or environmental issues. See "*Michigan v. EPA*," *Harvard Law Review* 129 (2015): 311–20, www.harvardlawreview.org, accessed February 11, 2016.

142 The *Michigan* case was consolidated with other lawsuits against the EPA challenging its mercury rule. See *White Stallion Energy Center v. EPA*, 748 F.3d 1222 (D.C. Cir. 2014).

143 Justice Scalia delivered the opinion of the Court, in which Chief Justice Roberts and Justices Kennedy, Thomas, and Alito joined. Justice Kagan filed a dissenting opinion, in which Justices Ginsburg, Breyer, and Sotomayor joined.

144 *Michigan v. EPA*, U.S. 576 ___, 135 S. Ct. 2699 (2015), www.supremecourt.gov, accessed February 11, 2016.

145 Adam Liptak and Coral Davenport, "Effort to Block Rule Set by the EPA Is Rejected," *New York Times*, March 4, 2016, A1; Matt Ford, "A Legal Win for the EPA," *Atlantic*, March 3, 2016, www.theatlantic.com, accessed March 7, 2016.

146 See, for example, Liptak and Davenport, "Effort to Block Rule."

147 *Obergefell v. Hodges*, 576 U.S. ___, 135 S. Ct. 2584 (2015).

148 Coral Davenport, "Climate Policy's Advocates Take a Page from the Same-Sex Marriage Playbook," *New York Times*, March 30, 2016, A11.

149 Linda Tsang and Alexandra M. Wyatt, "Clean Power Plan: Legal Background and Pending Litigation in *West Virginia v. EPA*," March 8, 2017, Congressional Research Service, https://fas.org, accessed July 11, 2017. In March 2017 President Trump issued an executive order aimed at reversing or gutting some of President Obama's climate and clean energy initiatives, including the CPP. In part it directs the EPA to review the CPP. Executive Order 13783, "Promoting Energy Independence and Economic Growth," March 28, 2017, www.whitehouse.gov, accessed July 11, 2017. Consequently, the EPA filed a motion in *West Virginia v. EPA* to hold the case in abeyance while it conducts a review of the CPP rule. In April 2017 the D.C. Circuit Court granted the motion for abeyance. See Kaitlin C. Straker and J. Michael Showalter, "EPA Litigation Snapshot: Pivotal Cases See Continued Delays," *Energy & Environmental Law Adviser*, May 15, 2017, www.energyenvironmentallawadviser.com, accessed July 11, 2017.

150 John Schwartz, "'Liberal' Reputation Precedes Ninth Circuit Court," *New York Times*, April 24, 2010, www.nytimes.com, accessed July 19, 2016.

151 There have been other substantive environmental efforts by the EPA that are not directly aimed at curbing greenhouse gases. For example, in July 2011 the EPA finalized its Cross-State Air Pollution Rule, also known as the Transport Rule or the Good Neighbor Rule, which requires states to cut pollution from their coal plants that would otherwise spread across the country. In April 2014 the U.S. Supreme Court in a 6–2 ruling upheld the rule. Justices Scalia and Thomas dissented. See *EPA v. EME Homer City Generation*, 572 U.S. ___, 134 S. Ct. 1584 (2014).

152 See Executive Order 13693, "Federal Leadership on Climate Change and Environmental Sustainability," March 19, 2015, obamawhitehouse.archives.gov, accessed March 8, 2016.

153 "Today Is an Historic Day," UN News Centre, April 22, 2016, www.un.org, accessed April 23, 2016.

154 European Commission, "Climate Action: Paris Agreement," n.d., ec.europa.eu, accessed March 30, 2016.

155 Justin Worland, "What to Know about the Historic 'Paris Agreement' on Climate Change," *Time*, December 12, 2015, time.com, accessed March 31, 2016.

156 Importantly, however, while this book was in press, the Trump administration withdrew from the Paris accord; but actual withdrawal could be tied up in procedural actions for years.

157 Karoun Demirjian and Steven Mufson, "Trick or Treaty? The Legal Question Hanging over the Paris Climate Change Conference," *Washington Post*, November 30, 2015, www.washingtonpost.com, accessed March 31, 2016; Robert V. Percival, "Presidential Power to Address Climate Change in an Era of Legislative Gridlock," *Virginia Environmental Law Journal* 32 (2014): 134–56.

158 Kate Sheppard, "Can Obama Sign a Climate Treaty without Congress?," *Mother Jones*, December 18, 2009, www.motherjones.com, accessed March 31, 2016.

159 Daniel Bodansky, "Legal Options for U.S. Acceptance of a New Climate Change Agreement," Center for Climate and Energy Solutions, May 2015, www.c2es.org, accessed March 31, 2016. The U.S. Congress generally requires a sixty-day notification upon the entry of such an agreement. See Michael John Garcia, "International Law and Agreements: Their Effect upon U.S. Law," Congressional Research Service, 2015, www.fas.org, accessed April 5, 2016.

160 Some argue, however, that because NAFTA was eventually approved by Congress, it represents a congressional-executive agreement. Bruce Ackerman and David Golove, "Is NAFTA Constitutional?," *Harvard Law Review* 108 (1995): 799–929; Glen S. Krutz and Jeffrey S. Peake, *Treaty Politics and the Rise of Executive Agreements: International Commitments in a System of International Powers* (Ann Arbor: University of Michigan Press, 2009).

161 See the speech by Senator Mike Lee (R-UT) before the Heritage Foundation condemning executive agreements and President Obama's use of them; November 4, 2015, www.lee.senate.gov, accessed March 31, 2016.

162 Krutz and Peake, *Treaty Politics*; Matthew A. Crenson and Benjamin Ginsberg, *Presidential Power: Unchecked and Unbalanced* (New York: Norton, 2007); Lisa L. Martin, *Democratic Commitments: Legislatures and International Cooperation* (Princeton: Princeton University Press, 2000); James A. Nathan and James K. Oliver, *Foreign Policy Making and the American Political System* (Baltimore: Johns Hopkins University Press, 1994).

163 Gary King and Lyn Ragsdale, *The Elusive Executive: Discovering Statistical Patterns in the Presidency* (Washington, D.C.: Congressional Quarterly Press, 1988), 112.

164 See, for example, *United States v. Belmont*, 301 U.S. 324 (1937); *United States v. Pink*, 315 U.S. 203 (1942); and *American Insurance Association v. Garamendi*, 539 U.S. 396 (2003). See also Bodansky, "Legal Options for U.S. Acceptance"; John H. Knox, "The United States, Environmental Agreements, and the Political Question Doctrine," *North Carolina Journal of International Law and Commercial Regulation* 40 (2015): 933–76; Curtis A. Bradley, *International Law in the U.S. Legal System* (Oxford: Oxford University Press, 2013); Hannah Chang, "International Executive Agreements on Climate Change," *Columbia Journal of Environmental Law* 35 (2010): 337–72; Louis Henkin, *Foreign Affairs and the United States Con-*

stitution, 2nd ed. (Oxford: Clarendon, 1996); and Sharon G. Hyman, "Executive Agreements: Beyond Constitutional Limits?," *Hofstra Law Review* 11 (1983): 805–44.

165 Henkin, *Foreign Affairs and the United States*, 222.

166 Bodansky, "Legal Options for U.S. Acceptance," v.

167 Adoption of the Paris Agreement, December 12, 2015, www.unfccc.int, accessed March 31, 2016.

168 Ibid.

169 David Doniger, "Paris Climate Agreement Explained: Does Congress Need to Sign Off?," National Resources Defense Council, December 12, 2015, www.nrdc.org, accessed March 31, 2016.

170 Ibid.

171 Although it was not directly related to the Paris Agreement, a summit meeting in Vienna in July 2016 negotiated an amendment to the Montreal Protocol that would ban the use of hydrofluorocarbons, chemicals used in refrigerators and air conditioners, which contribute to global warming.

172 See "An Enemy of the EPA to Head It," editorial, *New York Times*, December 8, 2016, A30.

173 Somini Sengupta, Melissa Eddy, and Chris Buckley, "Defiant Other Countries Reaffirm Fight against Climate Change," *New York Times*, June 2, 2017, A11; Brad Plumer, "The Climate Deal, and What the U.S. Departure Would Mean," *New York Times*, June 1, 2017, A9.

174 Robert D. Newton, "Administrative Federalism," *Public Administration Review* 38 (1978): 252–55; Robert Schwager, "The Theory of Administrative Federalism: An Alternative to Fiscal Centralization and Decentralization," *Public Finance Review* 27 (1999): 282–309; Beryl A. Radin, "Bureaucracies as Instruments of Federalism: Administrative Experience from India," in *Federalism: Comparative Perspectives from India and Australia*, ed. Ian Copland and John Richard (New Delhi: Manohar, 1999), 85–112; James E. Fleming and Jacob T. Levy, eds., *Federalism and Subsidiarity* (New York: New York University Press, 2014). For additional alternative theories of federalism (e.g., cooperative and coercive federalism), see Conlan and Posner, "Inflection Point?"; Charles M. Lamb and Eric M. Wilk, "Civil Rights, Federalism, and the Administrative Process," *Public Administration Review* 70 (2010): 412–21; Robert Schütze, *From Dual to Cooperative Federalism* (Oxford: Oxford University Press, 2009); Robert A. Schapiro, *Polyphonic Federalism: Toward the Protection of Fundamental Rights* (Chicago: University of Chicago Press, 2009); and Daphne A. Kenyon and John Kincaid, eds., *Competition among States and Local Governments* (Washington, D.C.: Urban Institute Press, 1991).

175 James Madison, "The Influence of the State and Federal Governments Compared," *Federalist Paper* No. 46 (January 29, 1788), www.congress.gov, accessed April 5, 2016.

176 Conlan, Posner, and Beam, *Pathways of Power*; John J. DiIulio Jr. and Donald F. Kettl, *Fine Print: The Contract with America, Devolution, and the Administrative Realities of American Federalism* (Washington, D.C.: Brookings Institution, 1995).

177 Frank J. Thompson and Michael K. Gusmanoy, "The Administrative Presidency and Fractious Federalism: The Case of Obamacare," *Publius* 44 (2014): 426–50.

178 Thompson, "The Administrative Presidency and Fractious Federalism."

179 Rubenstein, "Administrative Federalism as Separation of Powers," 171.

180 But see Conlan and Posner, "Inflection Point?," who argue that the strategy of coercive federalism was employed by the EPA in the area of climate change.

181 Meier, *Politics and the Bureaucracy*; Meier and Bohte, *Politics and the Bureaucracy*.

182 See, for example, Rosenbloom, O'Leary, and Chanin, *Public Administration and Law*; Rosenbloom, "Public Administration Theory"; John A. Rohr, *Civil Servants and Their Constitution* (Lawrence: University Press of Kansas, 2002); and Phillip J. Cooper, *Public Law and Public Administration*, 4th ed. (Independence, KY: Cengage Learning, 2007).

183 Lisa Schultz Bressman, "Beyond Accountability: Arbitrariness and Legitimacy in the Administrative State," *New York University Law Review* 78 (2003): 462.

184 Dwight Waldo, *The Administrative State: The Study of the Political Theory of American Public Administration* (New York: Ronald Press, 1948).

185 Richard J. Stillman II, "Review Article: Dwight Waldo's The Administrative State: A Neglected American Administrative State Theory for our Times," *Public Administration* 86 (2008): 581–90; Richard J. Stillman II, *Creating the American State: The Moral Reformers and the Modern Administrative World They Made* (Tuscaloosa: University of Alabama Press, 2002). There is also a considerable body of work addressing the tensions between bureaucracy and democracy. See, for example, William T. Gormley Jr. and Steven J. Balla, *Bureaucracy and Democracy: Accountability and Performance*, 3rd ed. (Thousand Oaks, CA: CQ Press, 2013); B. Guy Peters, "Bureaucracy and Democracy," *Public Organization Review* 10 (2010): 209–22; Meier and O'Toole, *Bureaucracy in a Democratic State*; and Appleby, *Policy and Administration*.

186 Edward L. Rubin, *Beyond Camelot: Rethinking Politics and Law for the Modern State* (Princeton: Princeton University Press, 2005), 2.

187 John A. Rohr, *To Run a Constitution: The Legitimacy of the Administrative State* (Lawrence: University Press of Kansas, 1986). Also see *Chevron U.S.A. v. Natural Resources Defense Council* (1984), as discussed earlier.

188 David H. Rosenbloom, "Reflections on 'Public Administrative Theory and the Separation of Powers,'" *American Review of Public Administration* 43 (2013): 381–96; Rosenbloom, "Public Administration Theory."

189 Rosenbloom, "Public Administration Theory," 225.

190 Rohr, *Civil Servants and Their Constitution*, 141.

191 Gillian E. Metzger, "Administrative Law as the New Federalism," *Duke Law Journal* 57 (2008): 2023. Also see Stuart Minor Benjamin and Ernest A. Young, "Tennis with the Net Down: Administrative Federalism without Congress," *Duke Law Journal* 57 (2008): 2111–55.

192 Metzger, "Administrative Law," 2091.

193 Ibid., 2023.

194 Pautz, "Regulating Greenhouse Gas Emissions."

195 Brian Galle and Mark Seidenfeld, "Administrative Law's Federalism: Preemption, Delegation, and Agencies at the Edge of Federal Power," *Duke Law Journal* 57 (2008): 1948–49. Galle and Seidenfeld also discuss how administrative rulemaking is more transparent than congressional law making.

196 Ibid., 1949.

197 Candace H. Beckett, "Separation of Powers and Federalism: Their Impact on Individual Liberty and the Functioning of Our Government," *William and Mary Law Review* 29 (1988): 635–51.

198 But see Erin Ryan, *Federalism and the Tug of War Within* (New York: Oxford University Press, 2011), who argues that the ANPR does not always provide for adequate participation.

199 Cary Coglianese, "Assessing Consensus: The Promise and Performance of Negotiated Rulemaking," *Duke Law Journal* 46 (1997): 1255–1349. Also see Dennis H. Esposito and Kristen W. Ulbrich, "Negotiated Rulemaking in Environmental Law," *Rhode Island Bar Journal* 46 (1998): 5–30, who point out that the Negotiated Rulemaking Act was passed in an effort to improve traditional rulemaking under the Administrative Procedures Act of 1946.

200 Coglianese, "Assessing Consensus."

201 Executive Order 13783, "Promoting Energy Independence and Economic Growth."

202 Tatiana Schlossberg, "What to Know about Trump's Order to Dismantle the Clean Power Plan," *New York Times*, March 27, 2017, www.nytimes.com, accessed June 5, 2017.

203 In addition, Trump changed the Obama administration's position on the environment by reviving two major oil pipelines blocked by President Obama. See Peter Baker and Coral Davenport, "President Revives Two Oil Pipelines Thwarted under Obama," *New York Times*, January 25, 2017, A1, A13.

204 See, for example, *Oklahoma v. EPA*, Case No. 15-CV-0369-CVE-FHM, 2015.

205 "An Enemy of the EPA to Head It."

206 Coral Davenport, "EPA Nominee Criticizes Rules to Protect Climate," *New York Times*, January 19, 2017, A14.

207 Brady Dennis, "Scientists Are Frantically Copying U.S. Climate Data, Fearing It Might Vanish under Trump," *Washington Post*, December 13, 2016, www.washingtonpost.com, accessed January 17, 2017; Tatiana Schlossberg, "What Should Senators Ask Scott Pruitt, Trump's EPA Nominee? Here's What Readers Said," *New York Times*, January 17, 2017, www.nytimes.com, accessed January 17, 2017.

208 Marissa Martino Golden, "Exit, Voice, Loyalty, and Neglect: Bureaucratic Responses to Presidential Control during the Reagan Administration," *Journal of Public Administration Research and Theory* 2 (January 1992): 29–62.

209 Emmarie Huetteman, "How Republicans Will Try to Roll Back Obama Regulations," *New York Times*, January 30, 2017, www.nytimes.com, accessed February 8, 2017.

210 For the impact of environmental hazards more broadly on minority and low-income communities, see, for example, Dorceta E. Taylor, *Toxic Communities: Environmental Racism, Industrial Pollution, and Residential Mobility* (New York: New York University Press, 2014); and David M. Konisky, ed., *Failed Promises: Evaluating the Federal Government's Response to Environmental Justice* (Cambridge: MIT Press, 2015). Also, although the topic is beyond the scope of this book, state and local regulatory agencies that receive federal assistance often place landfills, refineries, or other facilities in areas where the residents are mostly minorities, thereby disproportionately affecting their health, safety, and overall well-being. The EPA's Office of Civil Rights is charged with enforcing Title VI of the Civil Rights Act of 1964, which prohibits race-based discrimination by recipients of federal financial assistance. In its entire history, the office has never issued a formal finding of discrimination under Title VI. See Kristen Lombardi, Talia Buford, and Ronnie Greene, "Environmental Racism Persists, and the EPA Is One Reason Why," Center for Public Integrity, September 4, 2015, www.publicintegrity. org, accessed July 7, 2016.

211 Anthony J. McMichael, Rosalie E. Woodruff, and Simon Hales, "Climate Change and Human Health: Present and Future Risks," *Lancet* 367 (2006): 860.

212 Jonathan A. Patz, Diarmid Campbell-Lendrum, Tracey Holloway, and Jonathan A. Foley, "Impact of Regional Climate Change on Human Health," *Nature* 438 (2005): 310–17.

CHAPTER 5. CONCLUSIONS

1 *Ledbetter v. Goodyear Tire & Rubber Co.*, 550 U.S. 618 (2007).

2 "Durability" and "sustainability" are used interchangeably here. Compare, for example, the usage by Jeffery A. Jenkins and Eric M. Patashnik, "Living Legislation and American Politics," in *Living Legislation: Durability, Change, and the Politics of American Lawmaking*, ed. Jeffery A. Jenkins and Eric M. Patashnik (Chicago: University of Chicago Press, 2012), 3–19.

3 Jacqueline Chattopadhyay, "Are Press Depictions of Affordable Care Act Beneficiaries Favorable to Policy Durability?," *Politics and the Life Sciences* 34 (2015): 7–43; Maoz Rosenthal, "Policy Instability in a Comparative Perspective: The Context of Heresthetic," *Political Studies* 62 (2014): 172–96; Eric M. Patashnik and Julian E. Zelizer, "The Struggle to Remake Politics: Liberal Reform and the Limits of Policy Feedback in the Contemporary American State," *Perspectives on Politics* 11 (2013): 1071–87; Carter A. Wilson, *Public Policy: Continuity and Change*, 2nd ed. (Long Grove, IL: Waveland, 2013); Lockwood, "The Political Sustainability of Climate Policy"; Thompson, *Medicaid Politics*; Kingdon, *Agendas, Alternatives, and Public Policies*; Baumgartner and Jones, *Agendas and Instability in American Politics*; Patashnik, *Reforms at Risk*; Patashnik, "After the Public Interest Prevails"; David R. Mayhew, *Electoral Realignments: A Critique of an American Genre* (New Haven: Yale University Press, 2002); Schattschneider, *The Semi-Sovereign People*; Anne Schneider and Helen Ingram, "Social Construction of Target Populations:

Implications for Politics and Policy," *American Political Science Review* 87 (1993): 334–47.

It is important to note that this chapter does not examine strategies in implementation as a way to promote durability of policies (e.g., delegating implementation to independent commissions as compared to administrative agencies). For such treatment, see, for example, David E. Lewis, "Policy Durability and Agency Design," in Jenkins and Patashnik, *Living Legislation*, 175–96.

4   *NFIB v. Sebelius*, 567 U.S. 519, 132 S.Ct. 2566 (2012).

5   *King v. Burwell*, 576 U.S. ___, 135 S. Ct. 2480 (2015).

6   Mathew McCubbins, Roger Noll, and Barry Weingast, "Administrative Procedures as Instruments of Political Control," *Journal of Law Economics and Organization* 3 (1987): 243–77.

7   See Patashnik and Zelizer, "The Struggle to Remake Politics"; and Hacker, "Privatizing Risk."

8   Theda Skocpol, *Protecting Soldiers and Mothers: The Political Origins of Social Policy in the United States* (Cambridge, MA: Belknap, 1992), 58. Also see Jacob S. Hacker, *The Divided Welfare State: The Battle over Public and Private Social Benefits in the United States* (New York: Cambridge University Press, 2002).

9   Paul Pierson, *Dismantling the Welfare State? Reagan, Thatcher, and the Politics of Retrenchment* (New York: Cambridge University Press, 1994), 29–30.

10 Patashnik, *Reforms at Risk*.

11 *Regents of the University of California v. Bakke*, 438 U.S. 265 (1978). Subsequent U.S. Supreme Court decisions continued to uphold the use of affirmative action. See, for example, *Grutter v. Bollinger*, 539 U.S. 306 (2003); and *Fisher v. University of Texas at Austin*, No. 14–981 (2016), www.supremecourt.gov, accessed June 23, 2016.

12 Today, patriotism and fear are motivating factors.

13 See U.S. Foreign Intelligence Surveillance Court, "Report Describing the Government Assessment whether the End of Bulk Collection Has Mooted Claims of Certain Plaintiffs," January 8, 2016, www.fisc.uscourts.gov, accessed June 23, 2016, which indicates that lawsuits have not subsided after December 2015, when the government, pursuant to the USA Freedom Act of 2015, could no longer collect bulk metadata. Recall, however, that it can continue to conduct such searches via private telecommunications firms, which retain such data.

14 Richard Fabrizio, "Gun Sales Rise, Then Level Off, after 9/11," *Portsmouth Herald*, February 10, 2002, www.seacoastonline.com, accessed June 27, 2016; Stephen Gutowski, "Gun, Ammo Sales Spike after San Bernardino Terrorist Attack," *Washington Free Beacon*, December 15, 2015, www.freebeacon.com, accessed June 27, 2016.

15 Gutowski, "Gun, Ammo Sales Spike."

16 Matt Grant, "Gun Sales Soar after Orlando Mass Shooting," WESH 2 News, June 23, 2016, www.wesh.com, accessed June 27, 2016.

17 As noted in chapter 2, Manning's sentence was commuted by President Obama in January 2017, and she was released from prison in May 2017.

18 Denver Nicks, *Private: Bradley Manning, WikiLeaks, and the Biggest Exposure of Official Secrets in American History* (Chicago: Chicago Review Press, 2012).

19 However, following whistleblower channels is not necessarily effective, as we have seen in the case of Thomas Drake, a senior NSA official who formally complained about the agency's warrantless surveillance. Years later, his house was raided by the FBI and he was ultimately forced to resign; he was indicted on ten felony charges, which were eventually dropped. See Mark Hertsgaard, *Bravehearts: Whistle-Blowing in the Age of Snowden* (New York: Skyhorse, 2016).

20 *Bazemore v. Friday*, 478 U.S. 385 (1986).

21 Recall, however, as addressed in chapter 3, Senator Kay Hutchinson (R-TX) introduced the Title VII Fairness Act, which, had it passed, would have derailed the Ledbetter Act.

22 Interestingly enough, however, she did not support the Paycheck Fairness Act because of her concerns about how it would affect businesses.

23 In addition to Senators Hutchinson, Murkowski, and Snowe, Susan Collins (R-ME) also supported the bill.

24 The Ledbetter Act further amends the Age Discrimination in Employment Act of 1967, and modifies the operation of the Americans with Disabilities Act of 1990 and the Rehabilitation Act of 1973.

25 It should be noted however, that the U.S. Supreme Court's ruling in *Shelby v. Holder*, 570 U.S. 2, 133 S. Ct. 2612 (2013) struck down a key provision of the 1965 Voting Rights Act. In effect, those states with a history of deliberately seeking to block African Americans from voting can presumably resume those practices. Some states (e.g., North Carolina) have already begun making sweeping changes to their election laws. Until Congress works to fix this problem, the *Shelby* ruling can lead to the wholesale disenfranchisement of African Americans that we witnessed historically in the United States.

26 See National Women's Law Center, "The Lilly Ledbetter Fair Pay Act Five Years Later—A Law That Works," January 2016, www.nwlc.org, accessed June 27, 2016.

27 *Johnson v. Portfolio Recovery Associates*, 682 F. Supp. 2d 560 (E.D. Va. 2009).

28 See Portfolio Recovery Associates Group, "Mark Johnson and Portfolio Recovery Associates, LLC Announce Resolution of Laws," February 1, 2010, files.shareholder.com, accessed June 27, 2016.

29 Executive Order 13506, "Creating the White House Council on Women and Girls," March 11, 2009, obamawhitehouse.archives.gov, accessed June 27, 2016.

30 This executive order amends E.O. 11246.

31 Allen Young, "Why California's GOP Supports an Equal-Pay Bill," *Sacramento Business Journal*, August 27, 2015, www.bizjournals.com, accessed June 29, 2016; Allison Stevens, "DeLauro: It's Time to Close the Wage Gap," *Truthout*, January 27, 2009, www.truth-out.org, accessed June 27, 2016; Cherise Charleswell, "Decoding the Paycheck Fairness Act," Hampton Institute, May 6, 2014, www.hamptoninstitution.org, accessed June 27, 2016.

32 Young, "Why California's GOP Supports."

33 *Congressional Record*, House, July 30, 2007, H8945, emphasis added, www.congress.gov, accessed November 5, 2015.

34 Institute for Women's Policy Research, "Pay Equity and Discrimination," n.d., www.iwpr.org, accessed January 19, 2017.

35 Anne L. Schneider and Helen M. Ingram, eds., *Deserving and Entitled: Social Constructions and Public Policy* (Albany: State University of New York Press, 2005).

36 Mary E. Guy, "Three Steps Forward, Two Steps Backward: The Status of Women's Integration into Public Management," *Public Administration Review* 53 (1993): 285–92; Norma M. Riccucci, "The Pursuit of Social Equity in the Federal Government: A Road Less Traveled?," *Public Administration Review* 69 (2009): 373–82; Nicole Parcheta, Belal A. Kaifi, and Nile M. Khanfar, "Gender Inequality in the Workforce: A Human Resource Management Quandary," *Journal of Business Studies Quarterly* 4 (2013): 240–48; Cailin S. Stamarski and Leanne S. Son Hing, "Gender Inequalities in the Workplace: The Effects of Organizational Structures, Processes, Practices, and Decision Makers' Sexism," *Frontiers in Psychology* 6 (2015): 1400; Suzy Fox and Terri R. Lituchy, eds., *Gender and the Dysfunctional Workplace* (Cheltenham, UK: Edward Elgar, 2012).

37 Recall also that in June 2016 the Pentagon announced that it was lifting its ban on transgender persons from serving openly in the military.

38 But see Taylor, "A Win for Transgender Employees," who argues that the courts should defer to the EEOC's *Macy* decision under the deference principles laid out in *Chevron U.S.A. v. Natural Resources Defense Council*, 467 U.S. 837 (1984).

39 *Baldwin v. Foxx*, EEOC Appeal No. 0120133080 (July 15, 2015), www.eeoc.gov, accessed July 11, 2016; *Macy v. Holder*, EEOC Appeal No. 0120120821 (April 20, 2012), www.eeoc.gov, accessed July 7, 2016. As noted in chapter 3, the courts have not explicitly ruled that transgender status is a protected class, but they have ruled that Title VII protects persons from discrimination by their employers if they fail to act in accordance with their perceived sex or gender. Also see discussion of *Grimm v. Gloucester County School Board*, No. 15–2056 (4th Cir. 2016) in chapter 3, where the court deferred to the position of the U.S. Department of Education, which maintains that transgender students can use the bathroom that matches their gender identity.

40 See Lewis et al., "Degrees of Acceptance."

41 Celia Kitzinger, *The Social Construction of Lesbianism* (London: Sage, 1987).

42 Max Bearak and Darla Cameron, "Here Are the 10 Countries Where Homosexuality May Be Punished by Death," *Washington Post*, June 16, 2016, www.washingtonpost.com, accessed June 29, 2016.

43 "77 Countries Where Homosexuality Is Illegal," Erasing 76 Crimes, May 28, 2016, 76crimes.com, accessed June 29, 2016.

44 Haeyoun Park and Iaryna Mykhyalyshyn, "LGBT People Are More Likely to Be Targets of Hate Crimes Than Any Other Minority Group," *New York Times*, June 16, 2016, www.nytimes.com, accessed June 29, 2016.

45 Michelle A. Marzullo and Alyn J. Libman, "Research Overview: Hate Crimes and Violence against Lesbian, Gay, Bisexual and Transgender People," Human Rights Campaign Foundation, May 2009, 1, www.hrc.org, accessed June 29, 2016.

46 *Hearings before the Subcommittee on Health, Employment, Labor, and Pensions on the Employment Non-Discrimination Act of 2007*, September 5, 2007, www.gpo. gov, accessed June 30, 2016.

47 Ibid.

48 Ibid.

49 See, for example, *Couch v. Department of Energy*, EEOC Appeal No. 0120131136 (August 13, 2013); EEOC, "Fact Sheet: Recent EEOC Litigation Regarding Title VII and LGBT-Related Discrimination," March 1, 2016, www.eeoc.gov, accessed June 29, 2016; EEOC, "Processing Complaints of Discrimination by Lesbian, Gay, Bisexual, and Transgender (LGBT) Federal Employees," n.d., www.eeoc.gov, accessed June 29, 2016.

50 Centers for Disease Control and Prevention, "LGBT Youth," November 12, 2014, www.cdc.gov, accessed June 29, 2016.

51 Pew Research Center, "How LGBT Adults See Society and How the Public Sees Them," June 25, 2013, www.pewresearch.org, accessed July 7, 2016; Pew Research Center, "Growing Support for Gay Marriage: Changed Minds and Changing Demographics," March 20, 2013, www.people-press.org, accessed July 7, 2016.

52 David Remnick, "Ozone Man," *New Yorker*, April 24, 2006, www.newyorker.com, accessed July 13, 2016.

53 *Massachusetts v. EPA*, 549 U.S. 497 (2007).

54 See, for example, *Coalition for Responsible Regulation, Inc. v. EPA*, 684 F.3d 102 (D.C. Cir. 2012).

55 *West Virginia v. EPA*, 2016 USCA Case #15-1363 Document #1594951.

56 *Massachusetts v. EPA*, Oral Arguments, No. 05-1120 (November 29, 2006), www. supremecourt.gov, accessed July 14, 2016.

57 *Massachusetts v. EPA*, 2007, 503.

58 The Trump administration and the EPA under the direction of Pruitt may be attempting to alter or eviscerate the CPP, but, as discussed in chapter 4, it may be an uphill battle.

59 McDermott, Cashore, and Kanowski argue that in the area of environmental policy, durability may be a sign of ineffectiveness because pollution targets are ephemeral. Constance L. McDermott, Benjamin Cashore, and Peter Kanowski, *Global Environmental Forest Policies: An International Comparison* (London: Earthscan, 2010). Indeed, as discussed in chapter 4, the goal of the Paris Agreement is to cut greenhouse gas pollution 26 to 28 percent from 2005 levels by 2025. By the time the agreement is actually ratified, those targets may be outdated.

60 Patashnik, "After the Public Interest Prevails"; Lockwood, "The Political Sustainability of Climate Policy."

61 U.S. Energy Information Administration, "Analysis of the Impacts of the Clean Power Plan," May 22, 2015, www.eia.gov, accessed July 13, 2016.

62 Coral Davenport, "Conservative to Fund Republicans Who Back Climate Change Action," *New York Times*, June 29, 2016, A19; Stephen Koff, "Environmental Groups to Hit Rob Portman with TV Ads for His Global Warming Proposal," Cleveland.com, April 7, 2015, www.cleveland.com, accessed July 12, 2016.

63 Davenport, "Conservative to Fund Republicans."

64 Debra J. Salazar and Donald K. Alper, "Reconciling Environmentalism and the Left: Perspectives on Democracy and Social Justice in British Columbia's Environmental Movement," *Canadian Journal of Political Science* 35 (2002): 527–66.

65 John Cianchi, *Radical Environmentalism: Nature, Identity and More-Than-Human Agency* (London: Palgrave MacMillan, 2015), 1.

66 As discussed in chapter 4, U.S. Senator James Inhofe (R-OK) has called global warming a conspiracy and "the greatest hoax perpetuated on the American people." Inhofe, *The Greatest Hoax*.

67 Terry M. Moe and William G. Howell, "Unilateral Action and Presidential Power: A Theory," *Presidential Studies Quarterly* 29 (1999): 851.

INDEX

ABOUT THE AUTHOR

Norma M. Riccucci is Board of Governors Distinguished Professor at the School of Public Affairs and Administration at Rutgers University–Newark. She has published extensively in the areas of public management and policy, including the books *How Management Matters: Street-Level Bureaucrats and Welfare Reform* and *Public Administration: Traditions of Inquiry and Philosophies of Knowledge.* She is the recipient of several national awards and is a fellow of the National Academy of Public Administration.

Made in the USA
Middletown, DE
07 August 2023

36313361R00172